Leading Colleges and Universities

CHENEY

LEADING COLLEGES AND UNIVERSITIES

Lessons from Higher Education Leaders

Edited by Stephen Joel Trachtenberg, Gerald B. Kauvar, and E. Gordon Gee

JOHNS HOPKINS UNIVERSITY PRESS BALTIMORE

 Published 2018
Printed in the United States of America on acid-free paper
9 8 7 6 5 4 3 2

Johns Hopkins University Press
2715 North Charles Street
Baltimore, Maryland 21218-4363
www.press.jhu.edu

Library of Congress Cataloging-in-Publication Data

Names: Trachtenberg, Stephen Joel, 1937- editor. | Kauvar, Gerald B., editor. | Gee, E. Gordon (Elwood Gordon), 1944- editor.
Title: Leading colleges and universities : lessons from higher education leaders / edited by Stephen Joel Trachtenberg, Gerald B. Kauvar, and E. Gordon Gee.
Description: Baltimore : Johns Hopkins University Press, 2018. | Includes bibliographical references and index.
Identifiers: LCCN 2017030367 | ISBN 9781421424927 (hardcover : alk. paper) | ISBN 1421424924 (hardcover : alk. paper) | ISBN 9781421424934 (electronic) | ISBN 1421424932 (electronic)
Subjects: LCSH: College presidents—United States. | Universities and colleges—United States—Administration.
Classification: LCC LB2341 .L2687 2018 | DDC 378.1/11—dc23
LC record available at https://lccn.loc.gov/2017030367

A catalog record for this book is available from the British Library.

Frontispiece: Tom Cheney/The New Yorker Collection/The Cartoon Bank

Special discounts are available for bulk purchases of this book. For more information, please contact Special Sales at 410-516-6936 or specialsales @press.jhu.edu.

Johns Hopkins University Press uses environmentally friendly book materials, including recycled text paper that is composed of at least 30 percent post-consumer waste, whenever possible.

To Francine Zorn Trachtenberg, Mary Susan Bradshaw, and Elizabeth and Eva Patrón, and to Greg Britton, who had faith in what he had not seen but in which he believed

Contents

PART III: EXTERNAL CHALLENGES

Preface

The aim of this book is to reveal how successful presidents handle common but complex tests that try their political acumen, their judgment, their intellect, their empathy, and their ability to plan thoughtfully and improvise creatively.

Each contributor to the book has had success as a president or other significant leader in postsecondary education. Those who contributed were eager to write—or in some cases, had to be convinced that their perspectives were important—and come from a wide variety of institutions, from community colleges to liberal arts institutions and research universities. Some institutions are independent; others, state supported. The institutions are diverse geographically and in mission; the contributors represent a diversity of interests, personal characteristics, backgrounds, and positions.

The editors asked contributors to avoid advice, particularly that of the "floss daily" variety. They were asked instead to provide examples, stories, and anecdotes that were illustrative of the ways they dealt with the issues and problems they faced. For the most part, we asked two current or former presidents to write on one of 20 topics in four categories: getting started, internal challenges, external challenges, and personal challenges.

We also asked our colleagues to provide answers to five questions for presentation as a sidebar to their chapters:

What I wish I had known when I started
What I wish I had done when I finished
What I wish I had not done while in office
What I wish I didn't know when I finished
How I knew when to stop

Their answers to these questions provided the grist for the final chapter in which the editors tried to find the common threads from the essays and sidebars, not in the belief that the key(s) to successful leadership prowess would be discovered, but in the hope that the candid answers we received would prompt thinking among presidents and would-be presidents—as well as among boards, search committees, state boards, legislators, and others involved in the selection of presidents and chancellors.

This book is not a primer on how to be a successful college or university president. Were there a primer for presidents (or a one-size-fits-all curriculum), it would have been published a long time ago; whether it would have been useful as well as instructive may be in doubt. As two of your editors noted in their previous book, *Presidencies Derailed: Why University Leaders Fail and How to Prevent It,* failure to learn from the failures of others (or oneself) will end in doom. Even some who know history are doomed to fail; experience is not always the best teacher, though its tuition rate is among the highest. To recapitulate, the common causes of derailments are ethical lapses, ranging from lavish spending to limited information sharing; poor interpersonal skills, such as arrogant attitudes and volatile tempers; inability to lead key constituencies; failure to understand the institutional culture; failure to meet business objectives; and board shortcomings, ranging from flawed search processes and conflicts of interest to dysfunctional board dynamics.

It is the editors' hope that offering candid reflections and examples from successful practitioners will prove more effective and interesting than trying to codify the principles (should there be any) of senior-level leadership. While some readers might cavil that a few of our contributors lost their jobs at the institutions they served, that should not detract from their many successes while in office. Presidents must please many constituencies; failure to please all (or even those who sign your paycheck) is not equivalent to failure in office. Many took risks on behalf of the future well-being and competitiveness of their institutions rather than their personal futures. It is our belief that our contributors, to parrot the language of the commercial for the Farmers Insurance Group, "know a thing or two because they have seen a thing or two."

Your editors are grateful for the support we have received during the protracted gestation of this book from Greg Britton, editorial director of Johns Hopkins University Press; from our colleagues Jackii Wang and Joshua Alvarez at George Washington University, and Jay Cole at West Virginia University; and from Heidi Fritschel, our copy editor. Presidential aides and assistants at the institutions where our contributors labor were generous in their support for the project and their efforts to keep it on track. Our contributors were always graciously willing to take editorial advice, though many provided just what we needed right out of the box. Georgia

Nugent gave us splendid advice and constant encouragement; we are grateful for her wisdom and enthusiasm.

The weight of tradition precludes us from mentioning those to whom we are not grateful.

Stephen Joel Trachtenberg
Gerald B. Kauvar
E. Gordon Gee

When multiple authors put together a book it is highly unusual for two of them to single out a third for a job well done, but in the case of this book that is what we wish to do.

Each of us brought skills to the project; one of us exceeded the parameters of the job beyond the other two. Gerry Kauvar displayed a subtle and deep understanding of the myriad of issues confronting leaders in higher education and enriched the book by pairing viewpoints and experiences in a manner that enriches the reader's understanding and appreciation of the subject explored, the consequences of actions taken and not taken, and opportunities seized and missed.

Without his overarching direction, this book might never have seen the light of day. We are deeply appreciative of his skills, talent, patience, and, last but not least, forgiveness of our shortcomings.

Stephen Joel Trachtenberg
E. Gordon Gee

I GETTING STARTED

1 Becoming a President

William Kirwan

Given the critical importance of presidential leadership, it is ironic that projecting and selecting a successful first-time president is basically a crapshoot. This is not the case with other academic leadership positions. Seeking a dean, an institution simply needs to look at individuals who have been successful department chairs. In looking for a provost, a pool that includes effective deans will likely lead to a positive outcome. Both positions, dean and provost, are natural extensions of chairmanships and deanships, respectively. Each requires similar skills but with a larger span of control. The presidency, however, is a totally different animal, requiring capabilities not readily visible in lower-level academic positions.

For those who assume the presidency following a trajectory of administrative positions in academe, there is a rude awakening. Until that moment, an individual's focus and constituency have largely been the internal academic community. But the president is the face and voice of the institution to the external world. Make a mistake or say something impolitic in any other administrative position, and the damage usually remains within the cloistered walls of the campus and is soon forgotten. Not so for the president. A misstep reverberates throughout the larger community and can be tweeted to alumni around the world, make headlines in the newspapers, or become the focus of local newscasts. There really is no adequate preparation for the enormous responsibility that uniquely falls to the president as the embodiment for the external world of the institution he or she leads.

Higher education in general does a poor job of leadership development, perhaps worse than any other major enterprise in America. We have great scholars who think deeply about this subject and whose research is widely used by the private sector and the military. Ironically, with rare exceptions, higher education ignores what its own faculty experts on leadership preach to others. While the situation may have improved somewhat over the years, my own experience is probably not atypical. My first administrative position was chair of the Department of Mathematics, which was the largest and arguably the most complex department at my university, owing to its enormous service course load. Literally, one day I was a full professor totally immersed in teaching and research, and the next I was department chair managing an enterprise with 100 faculty, 300 graduate students, a large staff, and a multimillion-dollar budget. I assumed the position blithely ignorant of the university's complex budget processes or the intricacies of its human resource policies and management.

By the time a person from the academy reaches a presidency, however, he or she has become, mostly through trial and error, well grounded in the internal operations of the institution. But then the external world suddenly opens before them, and they become like young butterflies bursting out of their cocoons. Successful presidents must have the capacity to turn the arcane aspirations, goals, and initiatives of the institution into language the public will support. This is a different language than they have used in lower-level positions, promoting their units within the cloistered walls of the university. Presidents must have the ability to lead major capital campaigns, to look donors in the eyes and unblinkingly ask for millions of dollars in support of institutional priorities, a task that is usually not part of their previous administrative experience. Presidents must work effectively with governing boards to make certain each respects the responsibilities of the other and to ensure that, together, they present a united front to the institution and the external community. This is a highly complex challenge that has no precedent in prior administrative positions.

Higher education is replete with examples of successful provosts who were less so as presidents. While a president should have all the attributes of able provosts, they must also possess another dimension of talent, one that is essentially invisible until they land in the job. My strong advice for provosts and others with thoughts of becoming a university president is to find ways to represent the university externally before seeking a presidency. Volunteer to visit alumni clubs, speak to business organizations and groups of elected officials on behalf of the institution, and solicit gifts from potential donors. Determine whether these kinds of activities are rewarding or a burden. If the latter, I suggest that a presidency may not be the right career goal because these are the kinds of activities that will occupy an inordinate amount of a president's time and go a long way in determining his or her success.

Getting Started

I was selected to serve as president of two institutions, the University of Maryland (UM) and the Ohio State University (OSU). Launching my tenure in these positions could not have been more different.

Before being appointed president at UM, I had served on the faculty of the mathematics department for 24 years, including as chair of the department, and as the university's provost. Over the years, I had led or served on numerous university-wide committees and commissions and had been a regular member of the Campus Senate. Not only was I a well-known figure on campus, but I had a deep knowledge of the challenges and issues it faced, its strengths and weaknesses, and, most important of all, the voices I could trust and the individuals I could rely on to act in the best interest of the institution. This body of knowledge was of extraordinary value and immediate benefit to the university.

In the year of my appointment, higher education was reorganized in Maryland, bringing all but two of the state's four-year public institutions of higher education into a single system. The University of Maryland, College Park, was declared the state's flagship university in statute, with the promise of a significant increase in funding, provided that the campus came forth with a credible plan for how the funds would be spent. Formulating such a plan was possible because, as the new president, I had such a long history with the institution. Developed with remarkable consensus, the plan placed the campus on a new trajectory and elevated its public perception, which subsequent presidents have continued to advance in admirable fashion.

The far more normal circumstance is for an institution to find new leadership externally, which is what occurred when I was appointed president of OSU. I knew no one at the university other than its popular outgoing (and later incoming) president E. Gordon Gee. Quite naturally, everyone wanted my ear to voice his or her opinions on the university's challenges and opportunities. But who was I to trust? Who was acting out of self-interest, and who was speaking with the institution's best interest in mind? There was no way for me to know. A sense of isolation, of loneliness, fell down on me in a way I had never experienced at UM.

Fortunately, I had an inspired idea. I asked Frank Rhodes, the recently retired and distinguished president of Cornell University, to come to campus and conduct a series of anonymous interviews with faculty, staff, students, administrators, and alumni about the state of the university and the steps I should consider in launching my administration. Frank wrote a superb report, drawing both on his extensive interviews and on his own experience as a highly successful president. From this report and my own information-gathering efforts, I was able to put together a talented leadership team and establish my agenda for advancing the institution.

I don't know how often others have pursued the strategy I used in securing the services of someone like Frank Rhodes, but it is the best antidote I know of for overcoming the sense of isolation and uncertainty presidents inevitably feel when they begin their tenures at a new institution.

Leading

Institutional leadership comes in a wide range of styles. There is no one style that guarantees success or ensures failure. So much depends on the needs of the institution at the time a person becomes a president. There are periods in any university's evolution when it needs a change agent and times when it needs an individual to sustain its moment. These require entirely different styles of leadership. This is a point that I feel is too often overlooked by both search committees and candidates. It is certainly a factor candidates should weigh carefully in looking at the presidency of an institution. A person with strengths at painstakingly building consensus is not likely to be the right fit for an institution in crisis and need of immediate change. A person who sees himself or herself as a change agent would probably not be a good choice at an institution facing no major issues and rising in quality and public perception.

While recognizing that successful presidential styles can come in many flavors, I believe there are at least two personal qualities that can increase the chances of presidential success. The first is humility. A major trap for presidents is to begin to believe all the praise heaped upon them by those in the community and to develop inflated egos and senses of entitlement. Seeking power and influence, many individuals attempt to curry favor with people in authority. The most common approach is to shower leaders with praise. Presidents must learn to take the adulation they receive with the proverbial grain of salt. Even more important, presidents need people around them that will speak with total candor about the president's successes and failures. Such people are rare but invaluable. Presidents also need to recognize that even successful leaders are not long remembered. Indeed, ask almost any faculty member or student who the predecessor of the current president's predecessor was, and most will have no idea. And most often, current presidents' successors will want to highlight and focus on what they perceive as their predecessors' shortcomings. Presidents should take their jobs seriously, but not themselves.

The second highly beneficial quality for a president is the ability to engage in the art of listening. When I say "art" I mean not just the ability to hear, but the capacity to empathize with the speaker, to see the issue at hand from his or her perspective. Presidents too often feel they must demonstrate their leadership by dominating every conversation in an attempt to show that they are on top of every issue, which of course they are not. It takes a person skilled in the art of listening to truly capture the pulse of an institution and its full spectrum of needs.

A few years ago, along with a dozen other presidents, I was privileged to be in a room for a conversation with President Barack Obama. After a few pleasantries, he asked to hear our thoughts on the issue we were there to discuss. As we took turns speaking, he never uttered a word but looked straight into the eyes of the speaker. At the end of the session, he summarized perfectly what had been said and told us what he had learned from the conversation. Clearly, he is a leader with mastery of the art of listening, a quality that is of extraordinary value to the president of any university.

Planning

Institutional planning is a fundamental responsibility of presidents. This usually comes in the form of a so-called strategic plan. Such plans tend to come in two varieties: useless or transformative. Obviously, the goal of any president should be to create the latter, but, sadly, the norm is the former.

The problem with most strategic plans is that they are vague and try to be all things to all people. Such plans end up on a dusty shelf, if not in the round file, because they are not tied to any specific action or to the institution's budget.

Over the years, I have been involved in the development of several strategic plans, but it was not until my presidency at OSU that I learned how to do this effectively. One of the lessons learned from Frank Rhodes's interviews described earlier was the community's strongly felt need for a sharper focus and greater investment in agreed-upon priorities. This need cried out for an institutional strategic plan.

We began the planning process in a traditional way, with committees and input from a variety of sources. From this raw material, we developed and circulated drafts of a plan, which were not well received. After the third or so iteration of this process, I began to despair that we could produce a plan that would serve the needs of the campus well.

At about this time Jim Collins published his highly regarded book *Built to Last*. One of my vice presidents, Lee Tashjian, suggested that we ask Jim to come to Columbus to be a consultant for the development of our plan. Desperate to get the plan done, I said, "Sure, let's try. See if we can get him on the phone." To my amazement, we were able to do so, and I asked if he could come and help us out. He listened politely, chuckled, and said, "I can't for two reasons. One is you can't afford me, and the other is I'm in the midst of writing another book." He went on to say, though, "I'm impressed by what you are trying to do, so if you'll bring your team to Boulder, I'll work with you pro bono for two days." We leapt at this opportunity, and a dozen of us hopped on a plane for Boulder.

I'll never forget our first session with Jim. He sat in the middle of a circle surrounded by my colleagues and me. His first question to us was, "What are your institution's values?" An embarrassing pause ensued, as we glanced awkwardly from one to another hoping someone would speak up and save the day. No one did, at least not in any coherent manner. He responded, "OK, we know where to start, and we have a lot of work to do." What followed over the next two days was a remarkable set of probing questions, frank discussions, and remarkable insights driven by Jim's superb research on successful organizations.

We boarded the plane back to Columbus full of excitement and confidence. Within weeks we sent a new draft of the plan out to the community, and it got glowing reviews. The plan was enthusiastically adopted by the board and embraced by the university community. It became the roadmap, tied to budget allocations, for advancing the university toward clearly identified goals. The plan was aspirational but laced with reality. It was grounded in the university's history and traditions but forward looking. It was based on specific initiatives but tied to measurable results. Best of all, it led to positive outcomes for the university.

The lesson I learned from this experience is that the time and effort that go into strategic planning can be worth it but only if done well, drawing on the advice of experts who understand the elements of successful planning.

A few concluding thoughts for those considering or recently appointed to a presidency: First, take full advantage of the honeymoon period. Campus communities are typically ready and willing to give a new president the benefit of the doubt. Plan carefully, engage the community, but recognize that this a period when presidents have an especially good opportunity to succeed with bold initiatives or major reorganizations. Second, steel yourself for a roller-coaster ride of emotions. There will be periods when everything appears to be running smoothly and you can seemingly do no wrong. Inevitably, such periods can and will turn on a dime, and often on divisive matters over which a president has no control but which the president must address. Don't get intoxicated by the highs or discouraged by the lows. One will regularly replace the other. Finally, in my 53 years of working in higher education, I have never seen a time when this field was in greater need of enlightened, courageous, and selfless leadership. For those willing to accept the call, there is a rare opportunity to help guide higher education into a new era of even greater impact on our nation.

2 Transition to the Position

Winning the First Quarter

James P. Clements

In some ways, a presidential transition is like the start of an athletic contest. The game is rarely won in the opening minutes, but if a team isn't careful the mistakes it makes right out of the gate can spell near-certain defeat even before the team finds its stride.

When asked "What do you intend to do in your first weeks or months on the job?" it is common for a leader to respond that he or she is going to listen and learn from those around him or her to get the lay of the land before embarking on major changes or decisions. It is the right instinct, but following it can be difficult—especially when you are the person charged with leading a high-profile institution. It can feel like the entire world—faculty, staff, trustees, alumni, even students—is watching and waiting to see what magic you will produce, whether to heal a damaged campus or elevate an institution to new heights. And, truth be told, there are a great many people with deep ties to and strong affection for the institution waiting with great interest to see how the latest steward of their university is going to move it forward.

Still, if anything, the ability to pause long enough to take the pulse of the institution and gain an understanding of its unique culture before rushing headlong into action is even more important during a presidential transition than in other leadership roles because the costs of getting it wrong are higher. After all, higher education history is filled with stories of presidents who got off on the wrong foot with the faculty and never recovered, or who made their own jobs significantly more difficult by upsetting well-connected alumni by being tone deaf to an institution's time-honored traditions.

I have been fortunate to serve as president at two outstanding public land-grant research universities over the past nine years, first for nearly five years at West Virginia University and since December 2013 at Clemson University. I arrived at each institution under unique circumstances and at different places in their respective histories.

The environment at West Virginia was unsettled, with the previous president leaving after a less than a year amid some controversy. By contrast, the presidential transition at Clemson came as part of the institution's natural evolution, with my predecessor retiring and returning to the faculty after a long and outstanding 14-year run as president, during which time Clemson emerged as one of the best public universities in the country. Despite those differences, key elements of my transition process were similar at each university. The tactics and approaches that served me well as I worked to help bring together the West Virginia University community as a young, first-time president were equally useful when I came to Clemson five years later as the person charged with leading the work to build upon a solid foundation laid by my predecessor.

Perhaps most important, it's imperative to come to terms with the fact that just as no one becomes a university president without the help and support of colleagues, mentors, family, and friends, it is impossible to succeed in the role of president on an island. No university views itself as dysfunctional to the point where a knight in shining armor is needed to save the day. Rather, they are looking for a leader to elevate the good work already being done and remove obstacles that get in the way of achieving the institution's long-term goals.

At both West Virginia and Clemson, I moved swiftly to embrace the history and traditions of my new home. In fact, my first official duty as president of Clemson was to represent the university in the 2014 Orange Bowl game against Ohio State University, which provided an ideal springboard for me to make important initial connections within the Clemson family in an informal, positive setting. As an added bonus, Clemson won the game in exciting fashion, something I have always considered to be a good omen.

Embrace the Unique Nature of the Institution

Universities are enduring institutions that in many cases have been built over a century or more. That long-term success is predicated on the fact that many talented people have come before you—including many on campus who are waiting for the opportunity to help you guide the university to its next step. To me, it was essential that I quickly identify those trusted individuals on campus and in the community who could lend credibility to my work to help move the institution in the right direction. That support is especially vital in the early days of a presidential transition, which are times of stress and uncertainty for the entire university community.

At both West Virginia and Clemson, I actively sought the advice of trusted sources of institutional knowledge, especially those in leadership positions within the administration and on the faculty—and in the case of Clemson, my predecessor. At West Virginia, I was aided greatly by the well-respected interim president who preceded me, Peter Magrath, who had been president at three institutions and led the National Association of State Universities and Land-Grant Colleges (the precursor to the Association of Public and Land-Grant Universities).

Identifying and building trust with key performers, especially those who have been associated with your institution for a long time, is vital to a successful transition. The input those colleagues provide is invaluable when it comes to addressing the most pressing issues and to avoid stepping on the landmines that are inevitably strewn across institution. Perhaps more important, it sends a message to the entire university community that you will respect the good work and traditions built by those who have come before you.

At West Virginia, I was fortunate to be able to lean on a few outstanding and well-connected leaders who helped me navigate the somewhat choppy waters into which I had plunged. Perhaps no one had a greater positive impact on my transition than the late Charles Vest, a West Virginia alum who rose to become a long-serving president at the Massachusetts Institute of Technology (MIT) and who was a member of the university's governing board at the time I started. Chuck was an icon in the engineering and higher education worlds, and his appointment to the governing board in 2008 was universally applauded because of his reputation and his deep ties to the institution. Chuck quickly became a mentor to me, providing advice and counsel on a wide range of issues and helping me get involved with important organizations such as the US Department of Commerce's Innovation Advisory Board, which helped boost the university's national reputation.

There were others, such as former West Virginia University President David Hardesty who help introduce me and my wife to the Morgantown community and offered sage advice on the importance of maintaining some semblance of work-life balance, and Carolyn Long, a retired local school superintendent and chair of the university's board of governors who provided invaluable support as I learned to deal effectively with the state legislature and Board of Education. It takes a team to effectively guide an institution as complex and important to its community, and often state, as a university, so the quicker you can move to identify the sources of influence and information, including those who may not be the most visible, the quicker you can begin to move the institution forward under your own power.

Don't Be Afraid to Reach Back to Move Forward

In my view, there are three kinds of former college presidents:

1. The ones who are like bubblegum on your shoe—they stick around longer than you want, becoming something of an annoyance that's hard to shake.
2. The ghosts who are never to be seen or heard from again, even when you could use their help or advice.
3. The ones who, because of their love of the institution, are there to help when asked but otherwise are secure enough to give the new president the space to establish his or her own identity and build his or her own culture.

The first two types of former presidents add little value to a new chief executive and can actually hinder a transition either by inserting themselves where they don't belong or by being unavailable to provide basic support. If you're fortunate enough, however, to have the third type of former president at your disposal, you would be foolish not to take full advantage of his or her insights and talents.

That is the situation I inherited at Clemson, where my predecessor had led the work to steadily build the university into one of the nation's top public universities. Jim Barker is a Clemson man through and through. He graduated from the university's School of Architecture and eventually returned as dean of the school, where he served for more than a decade before becoming president. He remains on the faculty today, where he is widely admired and respected. He was a great help to me early in my tenure. As just one example, I leaned on President Barker's advice when Clemson's vice president for economic development resigned early in my tenure to accept a position as president at another university. I didn't know anyone well on the main campus, and President Barker provided valuable insight about the strengths of team members and the role that had been vacated, which guided me toward a thoughtful solution.

President Barker definitely was not bubblegum on my shoe, nor has he become a ghost since his retirement as president. Not every president is fortunate enough to have his or her predecessor willing and able to help in such ways, but those people are out there in some capacity in every university community—whether it is the longtime senior administrator, the influential alum who wants nothing more than to see his or her alma mater succeed, or the savvy executive assistant who knows how to get things done without being asked. The key is to devote the attention and energy, amid the seemingly endless demands on your time, to identify and cultivate those relationships as earnestly and quickly as possible.

Remodeling versus Tearing Down and Starting Over

Individuals ascend to university presidencies because they have strong ideas on how to improve the educational experience for students and enhance the service and scholarly missions of a given institution. Often, these ideas have been forged through past successes—and failures—and it's only natural that a new president would look to dip into a familiar playbook as a way to hit the ground running. Additionally, key members of the university community often expect that change will be coming—and coming quickly. The instinct for decisiveness, the need to put your own stamp on the institution, should be tempered, however, by the understanding that it's often better to remodel a house with good "bones" than it is to raze it and start over. It's a lesson I learned shortly after arriving at Clemson, as we started the work to create a new strategic plan for the university.

The existing plan had been, by most any measure, a success. Clemson had ascended into the upper echelon of the *U.S. News and World Report* rankings, research activity was on the rise, and the university was gradually gaining a national reputation for academic quality. There also was strong alignment on the goals and objectives within that plan. In short, although the time had come for the university to sharpen its focus and begin planning for the next decade, there was no reason to rebuild the strategic planning process. Instead, we used the existing strategic plan as the building blocks to create new, concrete aspirational targets for success and a focused set of guiding principles and actions to get us there.

For those who had been at Clemson for a long time, our new ClemsonForward plan, launched in the summer of 2016, offered continuity and validated the good work they had been doing for many years. For those newer to Clemson, including myself, the process that resulted in the ClemsonForward plan was a way to meld Clemson's past excellence with some new ideas and strategies designed to keep us moving ahead. As an added bonus, the process brought the entire campus together and in many ways signaled a seamless end to the transition from one administration to the next.

The adage "hurry up and wait" is generally used to relate feelings of frustration and inefficiency. By contrast, "wait (just a bit) and then hurry" is a good way to think of a measured, but still proactive, approach to presidential transition. Wait long enough to be sure you understand the culture and traditions of your new institution. Take the time to earn the trust of key influencers across the university community. Be willing to ask those who have been there awhile for help before committing to major decisions early in your tenure. There will be plenty of time to leave your mark on the institution and many, many hard decisions that you will be required to make. Taking the time to build a foundation of trust and inclusiveness from the start will allow you to create a good game plan and help ensure that the contest isn't lost before you have had a chance to win the game.

What I Wish I Had Known When I Started I wish I had personally known more of the power brokers related to the university—especially the ones who were highly influential but not as high profile as others such as the governor or major donors. Luckily for me, within a few weeks after I started as president at West Virginia University, former Governor Gaston Caperton hosted a dinner event for me with approximately three dozen of the most influential people connected with the institution. That gave me great access to sources of information soon after I started.

What I Wish I Had Done When I Finished I left my first presidency before several of our major building projects were finished. We undertook approximately $1 billion in construction projects during my tenure, and many facilities were well on their way to being completed. I just didn't get the joy of seeing them open and being used by the university community.

What I Wish I Had Not Done While in Office During many periods, especially during the transition, I worked so many hours that I didn't have enough balance in my life. Presidents, like all university employees, need time to refresh and recharge their batteries. It is important to make time for yourself and your family, even when the demands of the job are especially great.

What I Wish I Didn't Know When I Finished I hope I still have many years left as a university president, so check back with me when I am closer to the end of my career.

How I Knew When to Stop I knew it was time to move on from West Virginia University when Clemson called. It was the one place, through a combination of its national reputation and my wife's family ties, that I knew I really wanted to be other than West Virginia. I hope to stay at Clemson as long as I am having fun and making a positive difference.

Embarking on a Love Affair

Michael K. Young

"Don't go anywhere that you can't fall in love with." This was the first and best piece of advice I received before assuming a deanship. Frankly, it may well be the only piece of advice that any of us need. At least, it is the single piece of advice from which virtually everything else follows.

That isn't to say that the more predictable advice isn't useful: ask and listen; remember what it is like to be a faculty member; surround yourself with a good team; delegate; support; follow up; measure results (OK, maybe this is important and not entirely obvious advice); have integrity; accept responsibility; be appropriately transparent; embrace conflict; etc., etc.

At the most fundamental level, though, love seems to me to be the key. It allows us to see the institution as it really is, but also to see what it could become. It enables us to nurture and support our people and institution, but also to make the hard decisions that are in their best long-term interest. We are able to see the best in people and the institution and give them appropriate encouragement, support, and resources to realize their full potential. At the same time, we are clear-eyed enough to see weaknesses and misalignments that undermine the people and the enterprise. Perhaps most important, we can be boundless in our ambitions for our people and our school.

A sincere love of the institution also is essential to developing an appropriately ambitious agenda for the school and galvanizing everyone around that vision. And when everyone sets their sights higher and embraces a more challenging and exciting vision, many of the troubling and frequently disabling conflicts, disagreements, and controversies become less important and are no longer the roadblocks they were before. Our love for our institution, and our capacity to convey that love by recognizing what that institution is and what more it can become, invariably enables others to transcend the limitations with which they were previously concerned (or, in many cases, obsessed) and join us in expressing their passion for the institution through hard work and engagement.

This passion for the institution and the people also makes the job easier in other important ways. Most critically, it generates at least some of the goodwill we need to succeed. In every leadership position I have held, those with whom I am working want to know whether I really understand and love the institution to which they have devoted so much of their lives. If I do, they want to work with me. If I don't, they don't. I know that sounds simplistic, but it has had surprising resonance in every job I've ever held. It seems to be the first and most important thing people want to know, and everything I do thereafter is viewed through the lens of that answer, determining whether they will embrace me—and my actions—or view me and everything I do with disabling skepticism.

This approach may, of course, create other challenges we need to work through. For example, we are generally hired for a reason. Someone—the search committee, the president or chancellor, or the members of the board—thought we had a certain amount of experience, success, perspective, and ability that would be useful to the institution at that point in time. It is important to bring all that to the job. We shouldn't immediately try to become someone entirely different just because we took a different job. At the same time, we need to be careful how we explain and call on that prior experience and success. Everyone delights in telling us myriad ways in which our new institution or job is totally different from our prior experience. This is an entirely natural reaction, but it is hardly ever true. Why do they say it? In large part because they want to know that we really understand and love this institution, not where we were before. Remember, your stepchildren don't really want to know how you so successfully raised your biological children. (Neither, for that matter, does your new spouse.) So we must draw on what made us successful in the first place but do it in a way that demonstrates our understanding and respect for our new institution.

All the love in the world, moreover, will not necessarily—in fact, probably will not—make you beloved. There has always been a healthy tension between faculty and administration. You may well be surprised that close colleagues who commiserated with you in the faculty lounge about the predations of the administration now view you as the "administration," even if you assumed the job only yesterday. All your years at the barricades repelling the barbarians count for nothing—the moment you assume the job, you are the barbarian. Moreover, as our institutions become more complex and complicated to run, we are increasingly viewed as CEOs, and nobody loves CEOs these days, even if they respect and appreciate them.

But that isn't to say that the pushback and criticism aren't valuable. Listen to your critics and those with deeply opposing views. In most cases, those views come from their love of, and genuine concern for, the institution. Even when it feels personal, don't take it personally. They are frequently concerned about your ideas, far less often about you. So assume in the first instance the goodwill of your critics. There will be plenty of time to test that goodwill, and sadly in some cases it will be found wanting. But for the most part people devote their lives and their energy to our institutions because they think what we do is important. To them, it genuinely matters, and it is essential to recognize that, whether we agree on the details or direction of any initiative within the university.

Even more broadly, starting from a place of love allows you to assume the goodwill of virtually everyone with whom you work. Almost everyone at the university could be working somewhere else and probably for a lot more money. They cast their lot with our institutions because they believe in them and because they believe they can do more good in the world at our institutions than anywhere else. This goodwill is perhaps the most powerful resource we have. Use it. Exploit it ruthlessly. You will occasionally be disappointed, but for the most part you and the institution will be richly rewarded for the trust you repose in those with whom you work.

Of course, when you are disappointed in your people, because they lack the requisite goodwill or are otherwise a poor fit for the job in which they are stationed, move them on and do it with some dispatch. Among my most common mistakes—of which I have a long list—is excessive delay in moving people out of positions for which they are not well suited or in which they simply can't find ways to support what we are doing. I suppose this mistake is borne of a genuine and useful desire to allow people the dignity and respect to which I believe they are entitled by their previous service (and, frankly, to avoid offending their supporters, who, believe me, always exist!) and to make the move in a way that sustains that dignity. But when it is clear that change is necessary, do it—and if at all possible do it quickly.

With all the goodwill, trust, and love in the world, you will still confront controversy and conflict. As one of my predecessors in my current job aptly said, a ship dead in the water makes no waves. But if you start by generally assuming goodwill and if your love for the institution and its people is unshakable, you can—and should—embrace conflict. Conflict and controversy allow you to get to the very heart of issues and make decisions and take actions that actually matter. Conflicts often highlight people's very different fundamental assumptions about the direction of institutions, and resolving these issues allows you make critical decisions from which all future actions flow. Avoiding these intense but critical debates simply papers over differences and never requires people to wrestle with the most basic questions about the nature of what you are trying to accomplish and the methods for accomplishing it. This isn't to say you should court controversy or create artificial conflicts, but when they arise, a complete, open, thorough, and honest airing of differences can be enormously useful, indeed often essential. Managing conflicts effectively is of course equally important, but managing them by repressing them is perhaps the biggest mistake of all.

At the same time, love for your institution and its people leaves you room for a certain amount of caution when interacting with people. Upon taking my first major administrative job, I discovered that a number of faculty had brilliant ideas, the amazing wisdom of which my predecessor somehow had been unable to see. My first reaction was to support them all. But after making a few decisions that were simply dumb by any real calculation, I learned to listen to my senior associate dean and a few trusted faculty who had long experience at the school. They were able to give me the rest of the story, as Paul Harvey used to say, and the rest of the story was frequently amusing, sad, or just slightly looney, and even more frequently confirmed the wisdom of my predecessor in rejecting those requests. My mantra around the office became "and now for the rest of the story. . . ." On occasion, circumstances or the nature of the request had changed, and it actually was a brilliant idea. But making a practice of listening to past history gave me a much better sense of what was in the best interest of the institution, as well as in the interest of the petitioner and others who might be affected by my decision.

Love for your people also makes it easier to tell people not just what you think should be done, but why. Bring people into the decision-making process. I am always amazed at the quality of advice I receive before I make a decision if I bring others into the process and make clear to them why I am trying to do something. They frequently help me devise much better ways of accomplishing our goals. Transparency about my thinking process and the basis for my judgment generally leads to more useful and effective participation in decision making and, equally important, in the actual execution of ideas. Moreover, nothing ever plays out exactly as we plan it. If people understand why we are trying to do something, they are generally much better able to adjust to changing circumstances and unexpected barriers and to help others contribute to achieving the goals you have set.

A genuine love for the institution, its mission, and its people also helps you weather the first 18 months. Everyone related to the institution gauges how much you love them by how soon you visit their part of the school and how soon you interact with them. And you have to dive into these interactions with genuine intensity (in my case, this always adds 15 pounds to my frame and destroys any hope of staying in shape or pursuing any interest outside of my job for that initial period). In my experience, this inevitably makes for a pretty taxing 18 months or so. At the same time, if the institution has captured your heart, it is exhilarating and gives you the understanding that sets the stage for much of what you will do thereafter. It also demonstrates your passion for the institution and thereby generates much of the goodwill and support you need to succeed. And things do get easier, at least in terms of time and schedule.

A small amount of reciprocal love can also go a long way. Find a strong assistant who knows the school well, who can interact with people in a way that reflects your style of interaction, and who can—and this is very important—say "no" to you and to others. A few senior administrators who love you enough to say "no" or, when appropriate, "hell no" are also critical. I have enormously fond memories of one senior administrator in particular, from whom I learned a great deal, who would come into my office almost every evening and start the conversation like this: "Well, Mike, the idea you had earlier today is not the stupidest idea you have ever had. It's probably in the top three, but not number one." He would then explain why it wouldn't work. Equally important, he also always took the time to understand what I was trying to accomplish and why and then would devise a better way to achieve our desired end. We all need advisors like that, whether they are senior administrators, trusted faculty, or even alumni and other supporters. We must find people who are willing to be brutally honest with us and who have nothing to lose by being candid. And we can help confirm their honesty and the certainty that they indeed have nothing to lose by ensuring that their honesty is never punished, disdained, or discredited.

Finally, make sure you secure a tenured position. These jobs, of whatever stripe, are increasingly complex and difficult. Unexpected events are now the norm, and sometimes even the most appropriate and careful response isn't enough. Moreover, stakeholders abound and are increasingly emboldened. And unlike most businesses, virtually everyone with whom you interact has attended an institution like yours, sent a child to an institution like yours, or at least driven by it once. That engenders in them total confidence that they know how your institution should be run and how you should do your job—and that they know it much better than you do. No one laughed when a colleague recently said to a group of university presidents that he hoped that when he was finally fired, it was for something that he had actually done. Tenure allows you, when the final credits roll, to retire with grace to a job that you know you love and, one hopes, at an institution with which you are already having a love affair.

3 Building a Leadership Team

Designing a Team for Collective Success

Mildred Garcia

The success of a president hinges on building a strong leadership team. The lone leader making remarkable transformations at an institution is a thing of the past.* While I've studied leadership and particularly applaud *Redesigning Collegiate Leadership: Teams and Teamwork in Higher Education*,† the lessons that had the most impact on me came from combining theory and literature with my own experiences.

Before becoming a president, I served on various leadership teams around the country. While I learned a great deal about what not to do, I was also fortunate to be a part of the transformational power of the right leadership team being built at the right time by the right president. Now in my third presidency, I've had my share of successes and mistakes in building leadership teams and hope to share the cumulative knowledge I've gathered through research and practice with a new generation of academic leaders.

Teams You Inherit

Congratulations—you've been hired, and you're walking into your new position, where you inherit the previous president's leadership team. Despite all the Googling you've done on each other, this team doesn't really know you and you don't really know them. This is not the best way to start a relationship or begin your presidency.

Understanding the culture you're walking into will be important as you make the decision whether to keep the existing leadership team in place. With this in mind, make an effort to get to know them before your start date.

* G. Hernez-Broome and R. L. Hughes, "Leadership Development: Past, Present, and Future," *HR. Human Resource Planning* 27, no. 1 (2004): 24–32.

† E. M. Bensimon and A. Neumann, *Redesigning Collegiate Leadership: Teams and Teamwork in Higher Education* (Baltimore: Johns Hopkins University Press, 1994).

Call them individually shortly after the announcement of your appointment; set up meetings with them before you arrive, even if it's only over coffee; ask for an updated resume, job responsibilities, and an updated organizational chart. You'll be surprised to learn that some of the organizational charts you received as a candidate were out of date. Equally surprising, academic leaders often fail to update their resumes for months, years, or since obtaining their present position.

After reviewing the updated documents, meet with each member of the existing senior leadership team one-on-one upon your arrival. Ask about their accomplishments, what mistakes they've made and what they've learned from them, their role on the team, and how they see the team working together. Listen carefully, take notes, and be receptive. Let them ask questions about you. This is a time to get to know each other and begin building a relationship. Ask for their advice and counsel—what do they recommend to you as a new leader? Who should you meet with? What landmines do they foresee?

Finally, be clear about expectations and be honest. Remember, these individuals are thinking about their own viability on your team. Some presidents ask for everyone's resignation in writing with the understanding that they will hold the resignation for one year before making a decision. Indeed, it's not unheard-of for members of the senior leadership team to offer their resignation upon the new president's arrival. Regardless of what protocol is followed, I have always told the existing team that we have a year together to see how we gel. This lets everyone know upfront that we are on the clock and that time is of the essence as we strive to develop the kind of synergy necessary to lift an institution.

Hiring New Members to the Team

When hiring new team members, be involved from the beginning of the process until the appointment is made. Ensure that the search committee is as diverse as possible, with sufficient faculty from different colleges as well as faculty, staff, and students that mirror the ethnic and gender diversity of the campus community. It's puzzling to me that most presidents charge a hiring committee and then step out of the process until three finalists are presented. This is a good way to end up with three finalists who may not be the right match for you or your team. I participate from beginning to end, and while I share my hopes and expectations with the committee, I also sit in on every committee meeting, including the first interviews.

The job description is crucial, so it is imperative to spend time ensuring that it is clear and accurate. In addition to the typical skills and talents required by the position at hand, what else should this person be adept at? Most of my experiences have been in diverse urban areas, and I therefore look for individuals who have proven experience working with a diverse student body, faculty, and staff. It is important to ask the candidate about programs that have been led and implemented on his or her watch and, more important, about the results and successes of those programs.

Whatever successes have occurred under my leadership are a direct result of hiring individuals who see themselves as part of the team; who strive not to serve their own best interests, but rather those of the team, the institution, and most importantly the students; who understand the university's mission, values, and goals in a way that shines through in their actions and work, both on and off campus.

I first witnessed the power of such a team as the chief student affairs officer at a community college in the South Bronx. It was my inaugural experience serving a truly diverse student body, many of whom were low-income, underrepresented, and first-generation students.

Fortunately, the president I reported to knew how to build teams with talented individuals whose skills and passion not only complemented each other but also aligned with the university's mission.

Because I was only 28 years old—younger than many of the team members reporting to me—and a woman of color, I thought there would be some credibility issues. I had this in mind during a budget crisis when the team was discussing what needed to be eliminated without sacrificing our highest goals. I dug my heels in, ready to fight for my division. You can imagine my surprise when the dean of faculty offered to give up one of his faculty positions to my division, understanding that students need advisers to succeed and that cutting Student Affairs did not align with our mission and values. Even more surprising, everyone on the team, including the president, agreed. Here was a diverse team of leaders that put the institution and its students first, even if it meant cutting from their own divisions and resources. They were indeed a "dream team," and I owe my success as a president and leader to my attempts to build similar teams at every university I've served. Moreover, given the power of this kind of anecdote, it's important to share such stories in interviews so that candidates thoroughly understand the expectations you have for your team.

Be Proactive with the Search

Filling positions with the right candidates is crucial; everyone on your team should be proactive in seeking the right person for the job. Gone are the days when you place an ad in the *Chronicle of Higher Education*, either in print or online, and sit back and wait. Talented, smart, and committed individuals have choices; if your institution is the right choice, it's your job to ensure they know that. Let everyone on campus see the job description, and encourage them to share the opening throughout the world. Use your networks, share with national organizations, contact your colleagues at other institutions—you will need champions to share why great candidates should join your institution.

Some institutions use search firms during this process, and while I don't disavow the practice, it's important to remain attentive, watching carefully for the bait and switch. In one of my quests to find a vice president, I spoke to an individual at a search firm who I, along with my colleagues on the search committee, truly believed understood what we were looking for. To my surprise, this person delegated the work to someone who didn't capture our vision and thus was not a champion for the culture and mission of the institution. Learning from that experience, we hired a different search firm, ensuring that the person we dealt with not only understood our goals but also would remain directly involved throughout the search. This search firm was successful, and the person we hired was perfect for the institution at that particular time.

Hire People with Disparate Talents from Multiple Ethnic Backgrounds and Disciplines

Besides hiring smart and talented individuals, I make certain they are vastly different from me and the other members of my team. My degrees are in higher education and business, so I seek out vice presidents whose backgrounds are in engineering, the arts, humanities, or communications—any discipline that varies from mine and the other established members of the team. Further, I strive to hire people smarter than me, always with an eye on a possible successor who has a different way of viewing and experiencing the world.

If you believe in hiring smart, diverse people from all walks of life, you must model the behavior you seek. At present, I have the most diverse team

I've ever assembled, composed of individuals who not only represent a variety of disciplines—engineering, art history, finance, public relations, computer science, law, and history—but are also ethnically diverse and gender balanced. They are African American, Latino, Caucasian, Asian American, and Middle Eastern, coming from many walks of life, from lower socioeconomic backgrounds to upper-class upbringings. Most important, each is empowered to offer his or her unique perspective, ideas, and solutions, thereby strengthening the team.*

The results? In four years, six-year graduation rates for first-time freshmen have improved by more than 20 percent; the achievement gap has been eliminated for transfer students and cut in half for first-time freshmen; our total gift commitments increased by 119 percent; and the university ranks number one in California in awarding bachelor's degrees to Latinos as well as fifth in the nation in graduating students of color.

I am convinced that a less diverse team from similar backgrounds and disciplines could never have achieved these goals. Endless studies support this claim, including one from McKinsey & Company showing that companies that value and promote gender, racial, age, experience, and ethnic diversity in leadership and throughout their workforce are likely to experience greater success.† In the world of for-profit companies, this success means larger financial returns, but in the world of public higher education, it translates into greater rates of academic success for students.

Seek Candidates Who Love and Understand the Mission and Values of the Institution

Successful candidates for your team must fit in not only with you and the rest of the team but also with the institution. For example, at a comprehensive institution, while research is important, teaching and community service are also central to the mission. Hiring someone who does not understand this or believes otherwise creates dissonance. At a public institution where the teaching load is stated publicly, a team member who seeks to minimize this load by having graduate students or part-time faculty conduct most of the teaching creates problems. Make sure the search committee and

*C. Webb, "How Small Shifts in Leadership Can Transform Your Team Dynamic," *McKinsey Quarterly* (February 2016), http://www.mckinsey.com/business-functions/organization/our-insights/how-small-shifts-in-leadership-can-transform-your-team-dynamic.

†V. Hunt, D. Layton, and S. Prince, "Why Diversity Matters," McKinsey & Company (January 2015), http://www.mckinsey.com/business-functions/organization/our-insights/why-diversity-matters.

search firm know the mission and values of the institution, particularly in the area in which the candidate will be working, and appoint candidates who not only understand the institution but also are passionate about serving its specific mission and students.

Seek People with Proven Collaboration across Multiple Areas of Responsibility

While interviewing, ensure that questions capture how the individual has collaborated within teams, across divisions, and throughout the university. Ask for specific examples of how the individual collaborated in difficult situations, and have the person provide details of mistakes made and lessons learned. This exercise can be energizing for candidates, because it gives them a glimpse of a leadership culture in which they will be asked to step up, offer their opinions, and take ownership of projects with colleagues who can empower them to succeed.*

Be Prepared When Interviewing Finalists

In addition to taking obvious steps, such as carefully reviewing finalists' resumes, be clear with the candidates about the priorities for the position. What do you expect to be accomplished? Have an in-depth conversation in which you ask the tough questions, such as, "Why have you jumped around so much?" Listen carefully and allow the person to ask questions. If you know this is your preferred candidate, explain the situation he or she will be walking into. I was once hiring a vice president the campus unanimously supported, with the exception of the majority of the direct reports. Rather than let the candidate go blindly into this difficult situation, I explained it to him. I told him he would be leading a closed group that didn't collaborate, wasn't transparent, and preferred someone who would enable them to continue their behavior. Transparency allows the individual to know the environment they are entering as well as your expectations for change.

For senior positions, I usually ask people to stay for five years with the understanding that when the term is up, if they aspire to a higher-level position, I will do everything in my power to support them. Conversely, during the interview process, be wary of anyone who hasn't stayed longer than five

*M. Chopra, "Want to Be a Better Leader? Observe More and React Less," *McKinsey Quarterly* (February 2016), http://www.mckinsey.com/global-themes/leadership/want-to-be-a-better-leader-observe-more-and-react-less; Vanessa Urch Druskat and Steven Wolff, "Building the Emotional Intelligence of Groups," *Harvard Business Review* 79, no. 3 (2001): 80–90.

years in a previous senior-level position, as it is unlikely they will stay with you long enough to reach long-term goals.

Before making a final decision, personally call the candidate's references and listen to the silences. You can learn just as much from what is not said as from what is. Ask open-ended questions, and seek out examples and anecdotes. Furthermore, tell the candidate you will be going off the reference list; if he or she disapproves, be wary. I ask references questions like, "I see you have X position open at your campus. Why didn't you ask the candidate to stay?" You would be amazed by what is learned.

All of this takes time and energy, but the cost of making a wrong decision is much higher. To that end, if, after all your efforts, you don't find the right candidate, don't settle. It is much better, easier, and less costly to extend the search than to hire the wrong person for the team and institution.

Building the Team

With your team in place, you have completed one of the most important tasks a leader faces. Now it is essential to make the time to bring the team members on board by holding retreats every semester, meeting with them as a group to reiterate your own philosophy and that of the institution. At the retreat, make sure you are away from interruptions, emails, and phones. Building a team doesn't happen overnight; it takes concerted work. Find a facilitator who can help the team synergize.

If there are issues among the team members, they need to speak to each other rather than with others. I find people have a hard time doing this when they disagree, but the retreats enable you to work through it without building resentments. Make it clear that you and the team can and should engage in difficult dialogue and debates behind closed doors, but once a decision is made, the team speaks with one voice in the public sphere. Set an expectation that team members will not throw one another under the bus. During one of my presidencies, I learned that one of my vice presidents was speaking ill of a colleague. In a one-on-one meeting with this VP, I mentioned that I had heard this, that I wasn't going to ask if it was true, and that it was not up for discussion. I made it clear, however, that if I continued to hear about such behavior, I would expect a resignation on my desk in 24 hours. I never heard another word.

During your first retreat, and continually throughout your tenure, engage in collective crafting of "shared commitments" and "rules of engagement"—that is, what you will do as a team and what will not be tolerated. As an example, I share here my current team's rules of engagement (see sidebar). I hold the team accountable for these commitments and insist they do the same for one another. In a debate in an Academic Senate meeting, one of my vice presidents was absent, so her point of view, which was different from that of the majority, could not be voiced. Two other vice presidents never thought about their colleague and voted with the Senate against the vice president without knowing the full context. Harsh discussions ensued from me and the absent vice president, and those individuals saw the error of their ways.

You must also model the behavior you expect from the team. Allow individuals to disagree with you in meetings. Have open, truthful dialogues. Be the one who acknowledges the elephant in the room, and give permission for difficult discussions. Allow the team to see that you expect them to disagree with you and that you don't hold grudges.

Meet regularly with each team member. Get to know their passions, motivations, hobbies, and families. Let them get to know you. Find time for the entire team to socialize outside of work. During slower periods, I invite my team to the University House with their significant others. Their food and drink of choice are always available, and camaraderie is built. I also schedule one-on-one dinners with each of them with no agenda. Finally, I meet with each team member on a formal one-on-one basis weekly or biweekly. Each quarter we review agreed-upon goals and how they are accomplishing these goals. At the end of the year I require team members to submit a self-assessment on their progress on meeting the goals, and we work together to craft goals for the upcoming year. Further, every year at a cabinet meeting we share our approved goals for the year and discuss in detail what we need from each other to accomplish those goals. Thus, we all know what direction we are going and how we're going to get there. We also meet every week as a team, setting aside time for strategic discussions and operational issues.

It is also important to sit down with the team and dissect what may have gone wrong with a particular initiative, project, or strategy. Engaging in a blameless autopsy helps the team learn from failure and avoid future pitfalls. During our restructuring at Cal State Fullerton, I created a division of Human Resources, Diversity, and Inclusion after our accreditation team noted that, upon my arrival, we didn't have a true human resource function as a result of the budget crisis. Moreover, we realized we needed to do more to diversify our faculty and staff to mirror the student body. We thus created this new division composed of individuals from two different areas

**Rules of Engagement:
Cal State Fullerton Senior Leadership Team,
August 2016**

1. Personal conduct
   a. Be loyal
   b. Be honest
   c. Be trustworthy
   d. Show respect
   e. Be courteous
   f. Have integrity
2. Communication practices
   a. Be clear
   b. Be direct
   c. Be a good listener
   d. Be mindful of two-way communication
   e. Use discretion and confidentiality
   f. Be open to shared and/or new ideas
   g. No surprises
   h. Criticize privately
   i. Listen to the silences
3. Management practices
   a. Be accountable and hold others accountable
   b. Have respect for the chain of command

of the university. While it remains an excellent idea, through blameless autopsy we realized the mistakes we had made along the way—mistakes that must not be repeated as we continue to restructure the university in the name of greater student success.

Finally, find the time to thank team members when great work is done. Do this publicly and often: highlight them in your email messages to the campus community, call them out in your convocation addresses, write op-eds in your local paper about the successes they've led, or just take them out for a drink. You can never say thank you enough. I have a tradition: after two full days of commencement ceremonies graduating nearly 10,000 students, I take the team out for dinner and drinks and share a toast in their name.

c. Be responsible for effective administrative functions
d. Be a team player
e. Bring solutions, not just problems
f. Informed decision making
g. Ensure timely follow-through

4. University perspective
   a. Work across the university
   b. Don't work in silos
   c. Empower each other to be effective
   d. Be a university advocate
   e. Demonstrate Titan pride
   f. Be a public face for the university
   g. Collaborate
   h. Respect diversity while working toward unity
   i. Lead by shared vision

5. Esprit de corps
   a. Celebrate and recognize accomplishments (even the small ones)
   b. Have fun
   c. Have concern for each other's well-being
   d. Reconcile and heal relationships

It couldn't be done without them, and the success of the presidency is tied directly to our collective success as a leadership team.

What I Wish I Had Known When I Started President Barack Obama said in his final Democratic National Convention speech that no one really knows what it is to be a president until you are actually sitting in the seat. Indeed, as a young practicing scholar, when I imagined a university presidency, it was difficult to wrap my head around the enormous responsibility the job entailed. I remember my mentors and friends who were presidents telling me that the tremendous honor and opportunity to serve as president is matched only by the tremendous burden one carries in doing so. They said that the work is incredibly demanding 24/7/365, that you are out almost every night and must always be "on," and that you are never really away from the presidency—even when you are on vacation or with friends and family on the weekends. I remember asking myself, "How hard could it be? I work really hard now!" What I didn't understand is that you don't just work a presidency, you live one. That doesn't mean you give up yourself, but you do live and breathe the success of the students, faculty, and institution you are charged to serve. No matter where you are or what you're doing, you're thinking about what is going on at the institution, the new academic year, and goals that must be set—for in the end, you are responsible. With this in mind, my advice to future presidents is to acknowledge that, as President Obama stated, you will know what it is to be a president only when you are sitting in that seat. Allow the challenges to amaze you; enjoy the life-changing and transformative nature of your work; and embrace the fact that your impact transcends one classroom, division, or college and taps into the academic goals and life dreams of the thousands of students, faculty, staff, and alumni you serve.

What I Wish I Had Not Done While in Office Never sign a document you have not reviewed. In the first couple of months of my first presidency, a document was brought to me that needed to be sent to the State Department immediately. I asked the interim provost, who by the way wanted the presidency, if I had time to read the long document. The answer was no—it had to be sent that evening—so I signed it. Later, when speaking to officials at the State Department with whom I had good working relationships, I learned the document was incomplete and poorly prepared. My embarrassment turned to action, and from that day forward, I made the following abundantly clear to my teams: their lack of planning does not constitute a crisis for me. At any given time, a president is managing countless time-sensitive projects and should not be expected to drop any or all of them because a member of the team procrastinated or failed to deliver something in a timely manner. The onus is on those who report to the president to ensure that, whenever possible, information and materials are presented for review long before any due date or time constraint. Further, I need time to read what I'm being asked to sign, for it is my credibility and the credibility of the institution that are on the line. Therefore, I ask that any document needing my signature be presented to me at least one week before it's to be sent out.

How I Will Know When to Stop I will leave if I no longer feel the passion for the students and the mission of the institution, or if I believe that together, as a collaborative team, we are not lifting the institution we have committed to lead. Today, I wake up every morning feeling joyful and blessed for having a position I love, for serving students whose ambitions and dreams inspire me, for working for a university with a mission that aligns with my passion, and for knowing that, in some small way, I, along with everyone who works on campus, contribute to the success of a new generation of diverse leaders who will one day lead and lift our communities, the nation, and beyond. I'll know it's time to stop if I no longer feel tears in my eyes as more than 10,000 students march proudly across our commencement stage, ready to demonstrate to the world that Cal State Fullerton has not only transformed their lives and family legacies but also prepared them to succeed in and contribute to a multicultural world.

Balancing Skills and Temperaments on a Leadership Team

Marvin Krislov

Getting the right people on the bus and in the right seats, as Jim Collins would say,* is essential to running a college or university successfully. Since few presidents turn over an entire executive staff upon arrival, shaping a team involves a mix of the old and the new, and different personalities. In my various positions—in the federal government, at a public university, and at a private college—I have approached the creation of the leadership team with the understanding that maintaining the right balance of skills and temperaments is essential. For the new president or CEO on the block, I believe it is critical to respect the institutional traditions and culture while focusing on those areas ripe for growth and improvement.

We routinely replace staff (and faculty) when someone leaves. But it is always worth asking, "Is this the right position? Is it well situated within the organization? Should we consider changing or eliminating it?" These are tough questions, and existing staff typically resist dramatic changes. But on

*J. Collins, *Good to Great* (New York: HarperBusiness, 2001).

several occasions, I have changed or eliminated positions to align with current needs and best practices.

When to Look for Leadership Staff

When we determine that a position should be filled, it is often tempting to promote from within and avoid searches—the time and cost can be overwhelming. In my experience searches, even with strong internal candidates, help clarify the position requirements and bolster the eventual candidate's legitimacy. A quick example: my transition to Oberlin was facilitated by a magnificently talented associate vice president for development. Many people assumed that I would ask her to become the assistant to the president. I asked her to apply. But I also conducted a search to ensure that we were getting the best person and to establish an emphasis on due diligence and credibility. She emerged as the strongest candidate, and the search reinforced the values that I hoped to bring to the job. She is now my chief of staff and has succeeded admirably.

Internal candidates offer both advantages and disadvantages. We know (or think we know) how they will behave on the job. They know the organization. But they may or may not have the imagination to take the leap—to consider new ways of working. Most successful teams contain both internal candidates and those who come from the outside. In conducting a search where there is a viable internal candidate, it is important to consider the longer-term implications of a candidacy. Many internal candidates prefer not to apply for a job because they fear that rejection will undermine them with their colleagues or the new boss. On the other hand, it is difficult to evaluate internal candidates unless they agree to be part of the pool. This delicate dance can be challenging for internal candidates and their prospective boss. But not engaging in it can result in the loss of some very talented candidates.

The Search Process

Not every search needs to be assisted by a search consultant, have a large committee, and take months and months. While this tends to be the norm in high-level academic administration, there may be times when a shorter search without consultants or large committees can produce strong results. Factors to consider include the strength of the unit and the available internal and external pool, including whether we expect to need a more regional or national candidate pool. Competition for strong candidates can vary depending upon the season and even upon the year. A recent change in federal law or interpretation can increase or decrease demand, as can changing enrollments or economic circumstances.

Like most presidents, I have seen searches succeed or fail with or without consultants, with or without large committees. Critical to a successful process is a strong search chair who communicates frequently and thoroughly with the president (or other decision maker). At least as important is the role the president or other institutional actors play in recruiting and in persuading the best candidates that the position is desirable. In addition to the search committee, relevant senior staff members and campus constituencies should be consulted in many searches. Keep in mind that the successful candidate will need not only to do the specific job but to be part of a team. It is important to determine whether the candidate has the ability to listen and respond appropriately to a range of folks on campus. However, I would also caution that an outside candidate who is viewed as a change agent may provoke anxiety that may well be expressed as hostility by existing employees. The president or the relevant supervisor must filter such reactions and determine how much antipathy is warranted. To help determine "fit," I have encouraged including students in relevant searches. If confidentiality is an issue, any and all consulted should be asked to commit to nondisclosure to protect the candidates.

Whom to Hire

Selecting the best candidate can be challenging. Different candidates bring different strengths. Fortunately, I have found search committees to weigh pros and cons effectively and thoughtfully, and I have never encountered serious disagreement about whom to select. Qualities I prize include hard work, talent, and integrity. Although experience or technical skills are usually vital, I have found that sometimes it is right to trade off some direct experience if a candidate is incredibly talented and hardworking. One example: we were choosing between a candidate with greater technical expertise and one who could see the big picture and showed a strong desire to learn and grow. We chose the latter candidate, and he has had a wonderful career in positions of ascending authority.

A sense of humor, or the lack thereof, may presage success or failure. An example: those interviewing a candidate for a senior position sensed that he would not "roll with the punches" during the hard times, and indeed references suggested that this had been a previous concern. We decided to move on to other candidates.

Reference checks sometimes can be considered pro forma, but they should be conducted seriously and thoughtfully. I may call other presidents or friends because I suspect I may get a more candid appraisal that way. One piece of advice I've followed is to go at least two jobs back to get a more accurate picture. As one who has given and received references, at times it is more credible to hear that a candidate has strengths and weaknesses (as opposed to hearing that the candidate has no faults). When one has a sense of the weaknesses, it is easier to assess whether the person would fit the position.

When Change Is Needed

When is change needed, and what is that change? I suspect most presidents, including myself, would prefer to help improve someone's performance rather than move the person out. For many reasons, we need to make sure that expectations have been clear and that the person has been guided appropriately. Sometimes we can adjust job descriptions or even positions to play to someone's strengths, although this can be risky and can create unrealistic expectations. We don't want to move a problem from one shop to another. On the other hand, some of my fondest managerial memories are helping struggling employees find success in different positions or with different training and support.

But there are times when the moment of reckoning arrives. The person has been supported, mentored, cautioned, and warned. She or he has been given every opportunity to improve and may have even been given a "last chance" document. Occasionally there may be a precipitating crisis—an act of malfeasance or a display of poor temperament—but more often the question is figuring out when enough is enough. While polling a community is not appropriate, I recommend consulting with key, fair-minded observers who can be discreet. In addition to campus constituencies, board members or others can illuminate a situation. One example: an outside consultant helped me understand that a staff member's values and my own were not aligned and would likely never be. We needed to move on. Other questions to ponder: Has the person improved? Does the person understand what is needed? Have we done everything reasonable to communicate our expectations? If the answers suggest a change is necessary, it is best to do so in a way that maintains the person's dignity and allows everyone to move forward with a minimal amount of pain.

Consolidating the Team

Finally, to integrate a new member of an executive team, it is crucial that the president or supervisor facilitates the development of relationships within the college or university. Social gatherings or retreats often play an important role, and the president should set the tone by conveying enthusiasm and support for the new member of the team. Should glitches develop, the president should address them promptly so that a new person does not get off to a bad start. Gossip, even at the healthiest of institutions, can damage people, and often simple and direct communication can stave off this danger. How would the new member of the team know that a particular tradition or ritual is sacrosanct? How would she know that a colleague has a personal history that makes him particularly sensitive? The president might even ask someone to be a mentor to a new person so that these concerns are minimized.

Amazingly enough, with the right spirit, leadership teams at colleges and universities generally survive and thrive through changes. Recently, we hired a consultant to help us think about the way we solved problems as a group. By dividing us into smaller groups and setting clear rules on the brainstorming process, the consultant helped us break through some barriers that had emerged. Even with highly functional teams, outside perspectives can help improve group thinking and process.

Being aware of these considerations is critical to a president's success. In the 2014 fictional movie *Draft Day*, Cleveland Browns general manager Sonny Weaver Jr., played by Kevin Costner, faced with a struggling professional football team, acquired the number-one pick in the college draft. His boss, and the football world, expected him to pick the Heisman Trophy winner, the leading college quarterback. However, extensive due diligence revealed a disturbing fact: although the quarterback had been co-captain of his team, not one of his teammates had attended his twenty-first birthday party. Just before Weaver executed his pick, he called the quarterback to ask him about this. The quarterback said he couldn't remember that night.

This, along with another question related to integrity, led Weaver to go in another direction. To me, this movie suggests that even the most talented player might not be the best candidate if the person lacks the right qualities for the team. At the end of the day, at any college or university, it is, after all, a team that leads the institution. The president must make final decisions, but his or her ability to forge a strong team will ultimately make the difference in success or failure.

What I Wish I Had Known When I Started My presidency at Oberlin began a year before the economic meltdown. Had I known the future, we might have done some things differently. On the whole, however, we survived the downturn quite well, thanks to prudent management, particularly by our CFO and our board of trustees.

What I Wish I Had Done When I Finished I just finished my 10-year run at Oberlin College and am starting a new position as president of Pace University. I'm only giving myself four weeks between jobs, and I think a longer break might have been advisable. A longer period between two presidencies (or a presidency and another job) can facilitate the renewal that one needs. These jobs take a lot out of you (and your loved ones), and it is refreshing to be somewhere without the constant refrain of phone, text, or email messages.

What I Wish I Had Not Done While in Office Ignored my gut. We all need to consult and get buy-in to decisions. But there are times when we may have a perspective that others don't share, and it may well be worth listening to your instincts. It's a balancing act, but sometimes it's useful to pay attention to them even if others may not fully agree.

What I Wish I Didn't Know When I Finished The power of misinformation. Particularly in this era of social media, lies, half-truths, and partial information run rampant. At the institutional level, we are bound to respect accuracy, privacy, and certain norms of behavior. The internet has no such constraints. To address this concern, frequent and transparent communication is best.

How I Will Know When to Stop I'm still having fun. That's the most important thing. When the president does not enjoy the pleasures and rewards of campus life, it's time to think about moving on.

4 Maintaining Good Relations with the Board

Lawrence S. Bacow

For almost every new university president, board governance is a mystery. No matter how well prepared you may be for the presidency, until you sit in the president's office, you don't know what it is like to manage a board. While provosts and deans may attend board meetings, they rarely get calls from board members urging them to hire or fire someone, to admit a particular student, to support (or oppose) some cause, or to invite a particular speaker to campus (or withdraw an invitation that the board member thinks was improvidently granted.) Provosts and deans rarely have to navigate the treacherous waters of telling a trustee that he or she cannot do business with the institution or cannot influence decisions in ways that would be to their personal benefit. And provosts and deans rarely have to respond to the constant admonition that academic institutions should be run "more like a business." Furthermore, the president who pushes back against his or her board always must be aware that these same people sit in judgment of his or her performance and ultimately hold his or her professional future in their hands.

I do not mean to suggest that all trustees are problematic—far from it. Many bring years of valuable management and leadership experience to the boardroom as well as a passion for the institution. They understand what it is like to run a complex organization and appreciate both the loneliness and challenges of command. These trustees recognize what they know and what they don't, and are willing to share the former while acknowledging the latter. The successful president, working in collaboration with the board chair, will both recognize how to tap the wisdom of his or her board and help each board member learn enough about the nuances of higher education to contribute to the work of the board and the success of the institution.

One of the many things that make running a college or university challenging is that everyone who went to college seems to think they can run one. Trustees are sometimes guilty of this conceit. For many, their knowledge of the institution is likely to be frozen in time at the date of their graduation, typically as undergraduates, often 20, 30, or 40 years before. In effect, they were consumers of the institution's educational services (and for comprehensive universities, of a narrow slice of these services.) Now as trustees they are responsible for the production function of education not just at the undergraduate level but also for professional and graduate education. In addition, they are responsible for the production of knowledge in a research university and for clinical care at universities with medical schools and other health sciences professional schools. This is like putting someone on the board of Bank of America whose sole knowledge of banking is that they had a passbook savings account and belonged to a Christmas Club 30 years ago.

An aside: A few years ago I served on the presidential search committee for a small liberal arts college on whose board I sat. Early in the process, the search committee chair, a bank president, asked us to consider "nontraditional candidates" including those from the business community. At this point I asked him whether he thought I was a good university president. He said, "Larry, I think you are terrific." After thanking him I asked if he would hire me to be the CEO of his bank. At that point the light went on for him, and we went back to talking about candidates who knew something about higher education.

Trustees are rarely selected for their subject matter expertise when it comes to higher education. They often know relatively little about the nuts and bolts of running an academic institution. They typically do not understand academic culture. They don't understand or appreciate shared governance. They are mystified by the complexities of fund accounting. They often don't appreciate what it takes to improve a school's academic reputation. And perhaps most important, many do not recognize (or appreciate) the boundaries between governance and management. To paraphrase Richard Chait, one of the leading scholars of college and university governance, most college and university boards consist of part-time amateurs overseeing full-time professionals.

So what is a president to do?

A Pitfall to Avoid

Many new presidents worry that their boards will micromanage them or, worse, meddle in important academic decisions where the trustees have virtually no expertise. So their response is to chest their cards—to ration information by sharing only the bare minimum needed for the board to perform its fiduciary duties. The problem with this approach is that trustees are not stupid. To the contrary, most have been selected precisely because they have achieved great success in some other field. They know when they are being managed. So their response to the "chest your cards" strategy is to ask even more questions, which, given an uninformed and suspicious board, may lead to even greater meddling.

A far better strategy, in my opinion, is to share information with the board quite openly but to do so in a context where you are also educating the board about the real challenges facing the institution, the competitive space in which it operates, and the strategy being pursued to make the place better. In other words, rather than trying to fend off the board, try to make them true partners with you. Again, to paraphrase Richard Chait, effective boards create tailwinds for their presidents, not headwinds.

Creating a Partnership with Your Board

Educate Your Board

Most of us went into education because we like to teach. As president, your job is to teach your board about the business of higher education. For example, most trustees have little understanding of what faculty do on a day-to-day basis. Some believe that faculty teach a half a dozen hours a week and do little else. Inviting a few faculty members to describe a typical day to new board members can go a long way toward helping trustees appreciate the full range of activities that engage a faculty member. Similarly, board members rarely understand the competition for first-rate faculty. I once invited three deans to present to the board three actual faculty retention cases. The deans came armed with our offer letters and those from other schools that were trying to lure away our best faculty. The presentations drove home the point that we compete for faculty not just on salary but along other dimensions including space, teaching loads, start-up packages, research support, and graduate student assistantships. If we wanted to hire and retain the very best faculty, we needed to be competitive on each of these dimensions.

During my time as president of Tufts University, I frequently gave my board homework assignments. I routinely sent them articles and books on relevant topics in higher education. I offered to purchase each trustee a subscription to the *Chronicle of Higher Education,* explaining that it functioned as the *Wall Street Journal* of our industry. Perhaps the best thing I did to educate my board about "the business" was to persuade them that we should have a smattering of academics serving on the board. We agreed that as a matter of custom, 10 percent of the board at any point in time would consist of Tufts alumni who were faculty at other institutions. These included a Harvard dean and three other distinguished faculty from Princeton, the University of Michigan, and Boston University. In addition, we had a former university president who had previously served as a dean at Tufts. These board members elevated every conversation and provided useful context for discussions about space, student life, tenure, graduate education, academic policy, and the budget. More often than not, when an uninformed trustee made a crazy suggestion, one of the academics on the board responded, patiently explaining why the suggested idea would not work, thereby sparing me the responsibility.

I cannot emphasize enough the importance of educating your board about what it takes to make your institution better. Trustees are stewards of four pools of capital: physical capital, financial capital, human capital, and reputational capital. Well-functioning boards make decisions at the margin to move resources among physical, financial, and human capital with the goal of enhancing the institution's reputation. Transfers can be made among these pools. There are times you build the balance sheet, times you build facilities, and times you build the faculty, staff, and student body. Ultimately you need all of these resources to succeed. But if trustees don't understand how money, space, and people come together to create a great academic institution, they cannot do their job. Without guidance, they are likely to focus far too much on the balance sheet and income statement to the exclusion of everything else. Your job is to teach them.

Create a Job Description for Trustees

Just as board governance is a mystery for most new presidents, so it is for most new trustees. They often don't understand their role. If your institution does not already have it, work with your board chair to create a job description for trustees. For example, the job description should cover a few obvious topics: expectations of attendance at board meetings, preparation for meetings, confidentiality of board deliberations, philanthropic expectations, and avoidance of conflicts of interest. Even more important, the job description should communicate that board members should not act parochially, lobbying the board and the administration on behalf of their favored part of the institution. Trustees are fiduciaries for the entire school, not trustees from the law school or athletics. Similarly, a job description might describe what role, if any, trustees should play in admissions in highly selective institutions. This is a sensitive topic that should be addressed directly lest board members become lobbyists on behalf of the children of close friends and business associates.

Finally, it is good for the board to understand what your expectations are for communication with individual trustees between board meetings. Some presidents prefer that trustees communicate directly with them rather than with other members of their administration outside the boardroom. Personally, I think this is a hard policy to enforce and may place members of your team in an awkward position when approached with a specific request by a member of the board. A better approach might be to explain to the board why such requests often create difficulties for members of the administration and ask that board members give you a heads-up before reaching down into the organization. A good board secretary can be enormously helpful in screening and routing such requests.

Adopt Metrics to Guide the Board's Work

One additional way to educate a board is to create an agreed-upon set of metrics to guide the board's work. If the goal of a board is to make an institution better, what are the indices of such progress? At Tufts, this question led to an interesting and important conversation about strategy. First, we needed to agree on the competitive space in which we operated. Which institutions were we going to measure ourselves against? How aspirational should we be in choosing them? And second, what specific strategies were we going to pursue, and what metrics would we use to gauge progress? In answering the first question, we realized that we were the only institution in our competitive space that was not need blind. We concluded that that to compete effectively, we would need to raise the resources necessary to substantially enhance our financial aid offers. Thus we agreed as a board to drive our discount rate up—a counterintuitive strategy for most boards. Ultimately, through a series of such discussions we agreed upon a dashboard that included metrics covering admissions, student performance and satisfaction, faculty quality and research productivity, finances, and board performance. The latter included attendance at meetings, percentage of trustees making contributions to the annual fund, and percentage of trustees who had made a commitment to the capital campaign. (In the discussion of a trustee job description, the board had agreed that every trustee would make an annual contribution to the annual fund and a commitment to the capital campaign.) I started my president's report at each trustee meeting by going over the dashboard. Creation of this document not only helped drive strategy, but also focused board discussion and questions in useful directions.

In addition to creating the dashboard, we made an annual presentation to the board comparing Tufts with our two closest aspirational competitors: Brown and Dartmouth. This presentation consisted of a deep dive comparing our balance sheets, operating statements, endowment performance, fundraising, admissions, financial aid offers, research volume, space utilization, and other factors. Where relevant, we normalized the data to account for differences in student and faculty size. Since these data were presented annually and included prior years, the board could easily see where we were making progress and where we were losing ground. The board loved both the dashboard and the Brown-Dartmouth-Tufts annual presentation. Perhaps most important, the board owned these metrics. They were ultimately viewed as not just a measure of how the administration was doing, but a sign of the success of the board.

Make Your Problems the Board's Problems

During my first few years at Tufts, I used to get calls from trustees telling me I had a problem with mice in the dormitories, advising, housing, development—you name it. Often multiple trustees would call about the same issue, some telling me to do one thing, others telling me to do exactly the opposite. After getting tired of being caught in the middle, I decided to pursue a different strategy. Tactfully, I expressed my frustration to the board and said explicitly that I wanted my problems to be their problems. With the agreement of the board chair, we then began each board meeting with an executive session in which I met alone with the board with no staff present. I began this session by describing what was keeping me awake at night. Sometimes it was personnel problems, sometimes financial concerns, sometimes student issues. Often my board was surprised to learn what was on my mind. By taking the board into my confidence, I got the benefit of their best advice while also focusing their attention on real issues. They also really enjoyed these conversations.

Admittedly it was easier to do this after I had gained the confidence of the board and vice versa. That said, I think the overall approach is sound. If you can make your problems the board's problems, you stand a much better chance of having your board create the proverbial tailwind for you.

Make Your Board Meetings Interesting and Relevant

Most college board meetings are boring. They often consist of a series of dull presentations from the administration and dull committee reports, followed by a few questions from the board followed by a series of (hopefully) unanimous votes. Rarely are real issues put before the board, in part because presidents and others worry that if they put forward anything other than a fully baked proposal, trustees will meddle. As a result, the real business is conducted outside the boardroom. The problem with this approach is that it leaves trustees frustrated and disengaged. In my experience, frustrated and disengaged trustees are rarely generous to the institution with either their time or their resources, and may also be more inclined to make mischief.

Also, good potential trustees who have high opportunity costs will not want to serve on such boards or, if they do, will not want to attend meetings. Far better to make the meetings interesting, relevant, and meaningful. In the process, you also stand to get useful work out of your board.

One mistake is to try to do too much in a board meeting. Better to focus an entire meeting on one important strategic issue than to try to cover too much ground. The issue may be the future of a particular academic unit, the campus master plan, programmatic goals for an upcoming capital campaign, or risky student behavior, to name just a few potential topics. It is far better to dig deep on one issue than to skate lightly over many.

In many meetings, far too much time is spent taking a series of routine votes. It makes more sense to put all the noncontroversial but necessary business into a consent agenda, ask if there is any discussion, and then vote on it all at once.

A good way to engage the board is to give individual members something to do. During the height of the financial crisis in February 2009, we were contemplating whether it was necessary to cut our budget further. At that point, we had already cut $40 million out of a $650 million budget midyear. To pare further would require cutting back on many important strategic initiatives. The issue turned on how long we believed the recession would last. Rather than have a free-floating discussion, we asked three board members who ran large public companies to come to the meeting prepared to discuss what assumptions their companies were making regarding their own capital and operating budgets over the next three years. Their presentations anchored our conversation about the university budget and also gave other trustees a window into how these three companies and CEOs were thinking about the economy. It was one of the best meetings we ever had.

Give Trustees Opportunities to Provide Feedback on Meetings

One risk on any board is that some members may feel that they have less influence than others. While you can work with your board chair to address these concerns by ensuring equity in committee assignments and by engaging board members outside the meeting, it is also useful to institutionalize a process of regular feedback. A good practice is to send out an evaluation form following every board meeting. Ask not only for feedback on individual sessions, but also what topics people would like to see addressed at future meetings. Summarize and share the feedback with the board so that members know that you are taking their advice seriously.

You can also use the feedback process to help keep rogue board members in check. Often, there will be one or two trustees who like to hear themselves talk. They may even hijack a meeting. One way to deal with such individuals is to ask for open-ended comments on the evaluation form and then share these comments verbatim but without attribution with the entire board. In this way, others may call out individual board members for bad behavior. It is like sending a cruise missile from over the horizon aimed at the offending board member—very effective.

Working with Your Board Chair

All of the above advice is predicated on a good working relationship with your board chair. Few relationships are as important to a president: you will not succeed unless you develop a good relationship with your chair. My advice is to negotiate the relationship early. Discuss expectations about the frequency of communication, when the board chair expects to be involved in specific decisions, how you will be evaluated, how you expect the chair to help in dealing with difficult trustees, where your job ends and the chair's job begins, etc. This should be a candid and open conversation in which you explain what you hope to get out of the relationship. While you may not agree on everything, at least you will know what the chair's expectations are for you, and vice versa. Moreover, you stand a far better chance of forging a true partnership with your board if you first create a true partnership with the chair.

Let me conclude by quoting Richard Chait one more time: "It is difficult for any institution to be better than its board." It is worth investing your time to help your board become an asset and not a liability because you are unlikely to succeed as president without a high-functioning board.

5 Developing Relations with Faculty and Staff

Go Far Together: Creating a Healthy, Inclusive Culture for Faculty and Staff

Freeman A. Hrabowski III

The early 1990s saw a steep reduction in defense spending in the United States, and Maryland—home to large numbers of military and security personnel and defense contractors—felt the impact keenly. The cuts' impact reverberated through the state's economy and soon resulted in dramatically reduced university budgets. Our university system's board gave all of its institutions—including the University of Maryland, Baltimore County (UMBC)—an order: cut programs.

Never a desirable directive, a mandate to cut programs is particularly difficult for a new president. I was in my first year as interim president. Further complicating matters was the highly proscriptive approach the board of regents took. They had identified the programs they thought should go, including theatre, ancient studies, and social work.

Recognizing my vulnerable position and the potentially damaging impact of these cuts on our campus, I knew this was not a challenge we could tackle with just the senior leadership—or even with just the departments that stood to be most heavily affected. We had to engage as many of our faculty, staff, and students as possible in developing our response and in implementing a strategy to make cuts while protecting core programs. We would have to demonstrate to the regents that we had thought deliberately about our values and priorities. We would have to make our case to people who were not graduates of our institution and who didn't have any emotional or family ties to our campus or our students and families. We would have to be united in our advocacy.

My senior leaders and I immediately engaged shared governance leaders, including the faculty and staff senates and student leaders, to develop a set of guiding principles we could use to shape our thinking as we considered the difficult options before us. Two overarching principles emerged from those discussions. First, we were committed to protecting and maintaining the strength of our core academic programs. Second, we were committed to remaining a "people place," where faculty, staff, and students feel cared about and supported. We recognized that the pain of cost containment might not be shared equally, and we were focused on maintaining a spirit of goodwill.

With those core principles established, we fleshed out more specific guidelines for cost containment. We had to look in the mirror and be as honest as possible about who we were as an institution—our values, priorities, strengths, and challenges. We discussed our mission to be a public research university emphasizing a strong liberal arts undergraduate program and graduate programs in science, engineering, public policy, and human services. We had to ask the fundamental question: were we working to be comprehensive at the graduate level or excellent in selected programs? The best decision for this campus was to be superb in a small number of doctoral programs rather than mediocre in a broad array of disciplines. Building consensus about our identity allowed us to make the hard decisions about which graduate programs to cut, based on both fit with mission and student demand. In that process, trust was more important than ever.

The good news is that by identifying several programs that we as a campus chose to cut, we could then focus our attention and energy on fighting to keep the strong liberal arts core and the undergraduate program in social work, which was the largest such program in the state.

When the board of regents met on campus, I spoke about our students' hunger for a broad education. Our Greek and Latin courses were full at 8:00 a.m. My colleagues and I reminded the regents that our students, as middle-class people, had as much right to study the classics as people who attended wealthy institutions. The students were particularly creative in their approach. The arts students staged a mock funeral—dressed in black, carrying a coffin with "theatre" inside—as a peaceful demonstration. The regents were deeply moved. Faculty had worked with alumni to have the head of the Greek Orthodox Church write a letter to the board, imploring them to understand the significance of programs in the classics. We were all energized by the creativity and the willingness of colleagues and students to rebel when appropriate.

And our campus kept our theatre, classics, and social work programs. That success wasn't about me as president or just a small group of faculty and administrators. It was about a collective effort based on our recognition that our future was at stake and understanding that what happened would affect all of us, including those in the sciences. We wanted broadly educated students. This all transpired in my most vulnerable period as president, but we worked together to make decisions with authenticity for the good of the entire university. We were able to come out of that crisis stronger than ever. Ever since, I have believed strongly in the importance of bringing the campus community into the work.

Many universities talk about the importance of shared governance, but I continue to ask the question: what does that term really mean, and why is it important? As a long-term president, I have come to appreciate how much richer the decision making and governing of this university have been as the result of broad participation—characterized by transparency of information and collective accountability. Faculty and staff take ownership of our challenges, rather than viewing relationships as us versus them. They understand that their voice matters, but that I am responsible for making final decisions based on substantive consultation. We set priorities and deal with difficult issues together.

It may appear easier and simpler for a few people to make decisions and move ahead, but only when representative groups struggle with challenges and engage in robust and complicated dialogue are we able to develop a collective vision of the campus, a sense of clarity about the values that are most critical, and broad buy-in.

The longer I am in this position, the more I appreciate the African proverb that says: If you want to go fast, go alone, but if you want to far, go together.

An Expansive View of Leadership

As a practical matter, this means presidents need to take a more expansive view of who should literally be at the table. Our President's Council, which meets every two weeks, includes not only deans and vice presidents but also the heads of the Faculty Senate and the Academic Planning and Budget Committee. Time and again, presidents and provosts around the country have been surprised to hear that faculty sit on my leadership team. I respond that campuses are different, and the culture of each campus will determine the ways in which the faculty and staff should and can be involved most effectively in decision making. No matter the culture, though, it is critical for faculty leaders to know about the institutions' problems and to engage in substantive discussions with the president and other leaders. Faculty bring an important perspective to the table, and they are well positioned to communicate with their colleagues and to be supportive of the campus when controversial decisions must be made. Beyond the President's Council meetings, I host monthly meetings with the Faculty Senate's Executive Committee, and I attend a portion of all meetings of the full senate. As a result, over the past two decades, faculty leaders have been instrumental with such administrative matters as strategic planning, budgeting, and fundraising. Because of their involvement at the ground level, they also have been committed and vocal supporters of the process and the choices ultimately made.

Staff are also closely involved in campus decision-making processes. I have regular dinners with leaders of the Professional Staff Senate, and each semester I attend a meeting of the full professional senate. For the past few years, the professional senate has run a highly successful mentoring program for staff, which provides formal professional development activities and a framework for one-on-one mentoring. Leaders across the ranks, including many vice presidents and my chief of staff, have served as mentors to staff earlier in their careers. The professional senate, along with the senate for non-exempt staff, has been instrumental in developing our healthy campus initiative, in shaping changes to staff benefits and employment policies, and in advocating with faculty for policies and practices that promote work-life balance. Staff and faculty also worked carefully with us when we needed to decide whether to continue to have a childcare center on campus because of unexpected capital costs. They helped us develop strategies for cost cutting and revenue generation that enabled us to keep the center.

Putting Real Value on Service to the University

For shared governance to work well, the administration cannot stop at investing in the processes. An institution must place a real value on service to the university. Shared governance positions have to be attractive to the most productive and accomplished faculty and staff. In the earlier years of my presidency, there were periods when the senates had difficulty convincing some of their most respected members to serve in leadership positions. Many people believed that the work would be lacking in substance yet time consuming. Faculty, in particular, were concerned that the work would take them away from research and teaching. My approach was to pull together current and former leaders and some of the most admired faculty on campus to help explain to people the important role faculty could play in making decisions about the future of the institution. What worked best was drawing on trusted personal relationships between some of the faculty and me and among the group as we worked to convince more people to be involved. Successful leaders talked about ways to balance university service and teaching and research. We also determined that the university needed to provide additional support, in the form of administrative assistance, to persuade more people to get involved. If faculty and staff leadership positions are taken only by those who are not respected on campus—because nobody else would do it—it is hard, if not impossible, to develop mutual respect among the groups. On our campus, my colleagues and students are constantly working to attract the best thinkers to shared governance.

Likewise, having visited campuses across the country, I have found that the healthiest institutions are those that have been able to identify faculty and staff who exert influence with their peers and to support them in assuming leadership roles. They are colleges and universities that place real value—for example, through reduced teaching loads and greater opportunities for advancement—on being a good citizen of the university community. In turn, good university citizens invest in their institution and their surrounding community. They mentor students and younger colleagues, and stretch their own understanding of higher education. They engage in the surrounding community and take seriously the responsibilities of service. If an institution cultivates and invests in engagement and service, it will find that some of the most accomplished faculty and staff agree to assume roles in shared governance.

The senates, then, are not only high functioning and influential but also serve as a training ground for senior administration. At UMBC, for example, former presidents of the Faculty Senate have gone on to become deans of the College of Arts, Humanities, and Social Sciences and the College of Natural and Mathematical Sciences and even Provost.

Getting beyond Silos

Shared governance organizations also play an important role in helping faculty and staff move beyond their own units. Those groups are a starting point for building a campus-wide culture in which people assume responsibility for the entire institution. A consultant once asked my leadership team to always ask the following: Is an action in the best interest of the university, not just your unit or division? It's a question you also want your leaders on the ground—faculty and frontline staff members interacting with students, parents, and other constituents—to be asking constantly. Effective leaders foster a culture that discourages responses like "That's not my problem" or "That's not my job."

To cultivate this kind of culture, campus leaders must talk regularly with campus constituents about what's most important to the institution. And institutions have to be willing to ask tough questions about where they are: Is there general agreement about priorities and mission? Are faculty, staff, and administrators focusing on the academic performance of students, coherence of the general education program, or student preparation for graduate school and jobs? Is there broad consensus about the importance of internships, community service, and other co-curricular activities? Does what happens outside the classroom complement what happens inside the classroom? Does the campus disaggregate student data to understand the status of different racial and ethnic groups and men and women? Such conversations must be ongoing, happening both as part of formal processes such as strategic planning and as part of the day-to-day functioning of the institution.

Security and Risk Taking

Sometimes, we have to be willing to address uncomfortable issues and rethink our assumptions about ourselves. In such cases faculty and staff have to feel secure and supported in order to be honest about challenges we are facing. Shortly after I came to UMBC, we started asking tough questions about minority student achievement. There was a yawning gap between African American and white students' graduation rates that we had largely ignored. We had to take a long look in the mirror.

Even once we took a clear-eyed look, a number of people questioned whether the university should place special emphasis on influencing African American student achievement. They suggested that giving special attention to one group was unfair to the others. They felt comfortable voicing those concerns, and they were taken seriously. Yet those people could not find one African American student who had earned an A in an upper-level science course in the history of the university. Eventually, swayed by data and changes they observed, those faculty became some of the biggest supporters of our efforts to close the achievement gap. If they had not been engaged in thoughtful, robust debate and felt heard, they would have simply shut their minds.

Recognizing Groups That Need Special Attention

Even when the overall culture of an institution is inclusive and healthy, groups may need special attention. For example, about 15 years ago, my campus became increasingly focused on the underrepresentation of women faculty in the science, technology, engineering, and math (STEM) fields. We listened to the voices of women and men faculty and department chairs and began to understand differences in perception between genders about the climate for women in STEM. We learned from one another about best practices, such as the critical role mentoring plays in the development of women faculty and the importance of engaging department chairs and deans in open, robust discussions about the particular challenges women faculty members face in STEM fields.

In 2003, with funding from a National Science Foundation Institutional Transformation Award, we established the UMBC ADVANCE Program to focus on the recruitment, selection, and promotion of women faculty in STEM fields. Our goals were, and remain, ensuring that women are well represented in all departments and that they are advancing through the faculty ranks and into leadership positions. The program supports leadership development, increases networking opportunities, and provides support to all STEM faculty on issues concerning family and medical leave, the tenure and promotion process, grant writing, and other pertinent issues related to faculty life at UMBC. The data reflect how effective the model can be. Since 1999, we have more than doubled the number of women faculty in tenure-track STEM positions, while the number of men in these positions has increased by only 20 percent. In fact, women now occupy nearly a quarter of all tenure-track STEM positions, compared with only 13 percent in 1999. In addition, 39 percent of the adjunct professors in those fields are women. Women who participated in leadership development groups have moved into leadership positions, including dean of the College of Engineering and Information Technology, vice provost for faculty affairs, and dean of the Graduate School. Of course, we still have further to go.

More recently, we've focused heavily on increasing the representation of minority faculty across the disciplines. In 2010, we created the Executive Committee for the Recruitment, Retention, and Advancement of Underrepresented Minority Faculty. That group encouraged the provost, deans, and me to institute a rigorous faculty diversity hiring protocol. For example, every search for a tenure-track faculty position must now include a diversity plan. We have implemented several initiatives, including the UMBC Postdoctoral Fellows for Faculty Diversity Program, the Emerging Scholars Program, and the Strategies and Tactics for Recruiting to Improve Diversity and Excellence (STRIDE) Committee, which works closely with departments on continuing to transform their hiring practices. Today, 7 percent of our full-time, tenure-track faculty are African American (above the national average of 4 percent), and 2 percent are Hispanic. Clearly, work remains.

Our emphasis on strengthening the diversity of the faculty and staff and building strong relationships among different groups, along with regular discussions with student leaders, have been helpful during recent periods of protest on campuses and in communities across the country. Our strong relationships and consultative culture were especially helpful during the 2015 Freddie Gray protests in Baltimore. The provost and I issued special statements reflecting our values and strong support of engagement. I also found it helpful to speak at town hall meetings about the challenges in Baltimore and other cities and about the role universities play in providing thought leadership.

We were founded in 1966 as an institution that would educate people of all races and backgrounds. We are part of a great American experiment in higher education that continues today. We can talk about relationships between administrators and faculty, or administrators and staff—but we also must talk about relationships among these groups and with our students. We are home to people of all backgrounds—reflecting the diversity of thought, race, gender, religion, and sexual orientation in our country—many of whom may not be accustomed to one another. How do you get people to work effectively, not just next to each other, but in collaboration with one another? In my speeches at the opening of the academic year, I encourage students to go beyond their comfort zones and to connect to fellow students and others across boundaries.

This is one of the great challenges facing higher education institutions today. We must start by building strong relationships on campus that allow faculty, staff, students, and administrators to ask tough questions of themselves and one another, to have difficult conversations, and to embrace change. We may not always move quickly, but together, we can go far.

What I Wish I Had Known When I Started I wish I had known that everything I say is taken very seriously by all those around me. Consequently, I wish I'd known how important it is to be disciplined in thinking carefully before acting, even when simply joking. During my first years as president, I continued to be surprised when I realized people had initiated new projects based on a throwaway line or side comment from me.

What I Wish I Had Done When I Finished The campus decided to have a big celebration to commemorate my twentieth anniversary as president. Even though I am not done with my work as president, I should have asked for a short sabbatical—a few months—to take time to reflect on that period and to rejuvenate myself.

What I Wish I Had Not Done While in Office I wish I had not obsessed so often, especially in my earlier years. One of my older mentors gave me the best wisdom of my career: live life seriously, but don't take it seriously. I wish I hadn't taken the work and myself so seriously in those early years. Of course, I wanted to do my best, but it wasn't productive for me to worry so much.

What I Wish I Didn't Know What I wish I didn't know is also what I'm especially glad I do know—which is that, truly, there is nothing new under the sun. Every time my young colleagues believe we've never been challenged like this before, either as a country or as a university, I really do understand that these matters are cyclical and that we go through bad and good times. The lesson is to remain calm and use our best thinking to work through the issues. What I know is that the only way a leader can remain effective in bad times is to exude optimism and hope.

How I Will Know When to Stop A wise former president once said to me, "Freeman, you don't want to stay so long that they no longer want to put a statue up for you." That wisdom has made me laugh every day since.

Building Strong Ties with Faculty and Staff at Liberal Arts Colleges

A. Lee Fritschler

There are few jobs in modern economies more pleasurable or more rewarding than being president of one of the nation's top liberal arts colleges. The cornerstone of both the success and the pleasure (those two characteristics are bound together) of a presidential assignment is building strong relationships with both faculty and staff.

The small college is different from larger academic institutions, as well as other institutions in society, in that the faculty are central in managing the institution. The liberal arts college has two dominant constituencies: faculty and mostly undergraduate students. The large university has several faculties, and they vary greatly in terms, academic specialties, outside interests, experience, and aspirations. Further, a university typically has professional schools, sometimes including hospitals, a large number of part-time faculty and students, and a much wider distribution of human and professional attributes, goals, and interests than does the typical liberal arts college. Further the large university has thousands of alumni who relate to the institution in a variety of ways, some not closely related to academic matters. Colleges have Division III sports teams (schoolgirl/schoolboy athletics); universities have semiprofessional teams. Alumni relate to a university differently from how they interact with a small college.

In large institutions the need for several administrators is obvious. And the larger the staff and scope of the institution's mandate, the smaller the role of the faculty (and the president for that matter) in the affairs of the institution. The president of a small college can know or at least be acquainted with more than half of its staff. A large university, on the other hand, is more like a large corporation than a small college. A CEO's world is typically the headquarters C-suite. Even the most engaged president is likely to know only a small percentage of the employees even in the headquarters building.

For those recruiting a college president and for someone attempting to be appointed to the position, one of the first points to consider is that the faculty is at the center of most things important to a college. The faculty is almost solely responsible for curriculum, student evaluation, and requirements for a degree. The faculty is also central to the recruitment, advancement, evaluation, and tenuring of faculty members. They play important roles in the recruitment of students, admissions standards, alumni relations, fundraising (grants and contributions), and some budget and management issues. For many of these functions they work more closely with staff than they would in a larger university setting. Success requires that staff members understand and appreciate faculty and learn how to work successfully with them. At Dickinson College, for example, as president I was the chair of the faculty and presided over all of the monthly faculty meetings. This gave me a first-hand understanding of faculty concerns and gave faculty members a chance to speak to me formally during the meetings or informally before or after.

Presidential selection committees should look for a strong commitment to the liberal arts style or mode of education and some credentials based on working within one. Prospects should be able to demonstrate their interest and success in working with faculty- and student-based organizations. Some teaching experience and perhaps even a peer-reviewed publication or two should be required. Then there are the intangibles. Any successful president must be comfortable in an environment dominated by faculty and students. This is a unique characteristic. Does a candidate have the experience or necessary skills to work with a faculty and with students who have much to say about how these colleges operate?

There are ways of testing candidates' level of comfort with these aspects of the job, but unfortunately most of them are rather weak and quite subjective. Selection committees should look for a person who will find it enjoyable to participate in faculty seminars, congratulate faculty on their publications, and participate in scholarly events. Hosting visiting scholars, artists, poets, musicians, and playwrights for dinners in the president's home (that is what those grand quarters are for on most campus) should be a routine matter and not a special event. These sorts of events should be a part of the joy of being a president, not a chore. (This also takes a special, committed spouse—no small part of the requirements for a successful presidency.)

We found what worked best for us in recruiting for leadership positions, provosts, deans, and directors was to employ a consultant who specialized in working with small college search committees. Typically they engage in only one or two searches at a time. This seems to work because these consultants come to know the institution well and develop an easy relationship with the search committee.

If possible, and it usually is, a successful president should offer to teach a course in his or her discipline, at least occasionally. I taught a senior seminar in the political science department in all but one of the 12 years of my presidency. It was a good way to keep in touch with what seniors were thinking, to stay abreast of the discussions of the faculty, and to give me a window on campus life in real time. It was well worth the 2.5 hours per week in the classroom and an equal amount of preparation time. It is also important to be visible on campus as much as possible and to visibly enjoy it. This is easy on a college campus. There is an endless stream of special lectures, concerts, art exhibitions, and plays to attend. It is a nice life and should be savored.

Being president takes much time, more than eight hours a day. But the time commitment should be viewed as part of a total commitment to an institution. My spouse and I quickly came to see that the job of a president was not only a full-time activity but also a lifestyle changer. We had not only a new commitment to a new professional life but also a new set of friends, and many of our older friends and acquaintances faded away. We spent most weekends on college business. Most of our vacations away from campus were spent with trustees and faculty who became our new close friends. This can be viewed as a special opportunity or a burden. We chose the former and enjoyed it, but after we left the college we had to work to reestablish the friends we had before the 12 years of our presidency took precedence. We were nearly forgotten by several of them.

A presidency is a full-time, in the fullest sense of that word, position. I argue that a president should not accept corporate board appointments for this reason as well as to make certain of being in full compliance with the rules and intent of the Sarbanes-Oxley Act. This federal legislation requires that independent directors be committed to the advancement of the corporation and not simply collecting a check. Furthermore, any time spent on outside board activity reduces the time one spends on college matters. More important, the fiduciary responsibilities of a corporate board member can easily conflict with a president's fiduciary responsibility to the college. It is difficult to imagine exceptions to this. Insurance companies, banks, suppliers of everything from food service to construction materials, and textbook publishers all have fiduciary requirements that conflict with those of any college president. In the past, presidents of colleges sought board placement as a way of enhancing inadequate compensation. Those days are well behind us. Service on not-for-profit boards and with local government or volunteer organizations is a different matter. Such service can enhance a presidency.

A successful president should be oriented to the academic life of a college campus and fully support it, but there is another dimension. A president must also be a good manager and if possible should enjoy traditions and standards of being a good manager. Even the smallest institution has a large staff of professions and trades that are not directly related to academic matters. My institution 20 years ago had a faculty of about 175 and a staff of at least twice that number. That staff was diverse in function, ranging from counselors, admissions officers, and librarians to skilled carpenters, electricians, plumbers, and groundskeepers. A successful president should enjoy managing those staff and create an environment for success. One way of doing this, I found, was to learn about their skills and their concerns. It was an enjoyable challenge to find ways to enhance their skills, often based on their suggestions. I was lucky to be the president of an institution in area of the country with a workforce of highly skilled, dedicated tradespeople. Our food service was local and committed to expanding student appetites beyond fast foods.

We found that contracting out these functions required more management than working with our local staff. We built a large, modern library during my tenure, employing local contractors. One Sunday morning as the building process was approaching midway, I used my construction door key to enter the construction site and wander through. I heard a pounding noise in a distant upper floor of the building. I followed my ears to find a local tradesperson pounding away. I reminded him that it was Sunday and he had the day off. He said he awoke during the night and thought he had done something incorrectly on the previous day and he wanted to correct his error before Monday morning. Working with such people is a great pleasure.

In other areas of management, we started a consortium of three neighboring institutions for purchasing and some other back-of-the-house administrative matters. In 20-plus years that consortium has grown into a regional enterprise. We also signed a contract with three neighboring colleges to create a centralized buildings and grounds operation. In the year I left, the college was bequeathed a large nearby farm. It has become a major supplier of fresh products to the cafeteria and the promoter of sustainability on campus. The buildings and grounds departments are central to making all this work.

I would be remiss were I not to mention the work of a dedicated group of professionals charged with the daily administrative tasks of any organization. Quite normally these professionals do things no president could do without them, and they do their work with little supervision. To do their jobs successfully, they too must realize they are working in a special environment and enjoy the experience.

A successful president has four additional macro tasks: working with a board, public relations, fund raising, and coming up with or at least creating an environment in which big ideas can be created and sustained. The faculty and staff can play important roles in these tasks as well.

Almost all private colleges have large boards, often around 30 members, compared with state institutions, which have small numbers of board members. The state boards are almost always appointed by governors whereas private boards are self-perpetuating and generally composed of successful alumni of the institution. I found that members of the board had great interest in what the faculty were doing but found it difficult, given time and other constraints, to learn as much as they wanted. So we found ways to engage faculty members with the board that turned out to be successful from both points of view. Faculty made presentations to the board on their special interests. Socially, we occasionally arranged for small groups of board members to have dinner in faculty homes when the board came to town. Instead of arranging a large dinner with only a few invited faculty and staff, we had the food service cater a half dozen or so of these smaller dinners. This small idea was a big success.

We also developed an important role for faculty in alumni relations and fund raising. At nearly all of our alumni events across the country, faculty made presentations on their research interests and teaching innovations.

Recruiting students to attend the college was never easy in the competitive environment in which liberal arts colleges exist. We organized what we called road shows: several faculty members along with the president and others traveled together by bus to present "show-and-tell" sessions for prospective students in cities in which we thought we could do better.

The college had a budget committee made up of faculty, students, and staff. The committee was advisory, and its work was very useful in managing the institution. Being elected to that committee became a popular, sought-after achievement.

A president of even a small institution should have an agenda for big ideas. Of course, big ideas cannot be successfully implemented without faculty support and enthusiastic involvement. Led by faculty who had keen international interests and contacts, we expanded our study abroad opportunities for students from about three centers to a dozen. In each case a faculty member ran the overseas center and made impressive inroads into the country and culture involved. At one point about half of our students studied abroad.

I discovered early in my tenure that the large Washington-based higher education organizations had little time or interest in liberal arts college presidents. So three of us in neighboring institutions decided to form an new national organization. We invited about 100 college presidents to convene in Annapolis, Maryland, to discuss the issues we faced. About 30 presidents came to the first meeting, and the number grew significantly in subsequent years. Today the organization has about 200 members and still convenes in Annapolis every year. No surprise, it is known as the Annapolis Group.

Early in my tenure I decided to carefully select the one yearly national meeting of a higher education association I would attend. These are time-consuming and expensive gatherings, and I wanted to use my meeting time productively. I decided to focus on the Association of Governing Boards of Universities and Colleges (AGB) because I thought my college had a problem of low visibility outside of academe and I had spent most of my career in academe. I thought AGB, an organization of trustees, could help me solve my institution's visibility deficit given its members' experiences in other institutions, while putting me in touch with a world of leadership about which I knew little. I served for eight years on the AGB presidential advisory board. I also found participation in Council for Higher Education Accreditation (CHEA) activities to be a wise choice for me. We are a self-governing industry, and the accrediting work of that organization is central to our continued well-being.

Another of our big ideas came from a faculty member who was upset with the teacher training around the state and thought we should find a way to encourage some of our graduates to go into careers in elementary and secondary teaching. I was persuaded. There were many obstacles to doing this on and off campus. On campus, the prestige majors led to the professions—medicine and law. Teaching was considered a default profession when nothing else seemed to be attractive. So we established a program within the college that required students already admitted to the college to apply and be admitted to this new program. Admission was highly selective twice: once for admission to the college and once for admission to this program. Only 20 students were admitted. We developed special courses and arranged sessions with prominent education leaders in the state and in Washington, DC. Upon graduation, the students were given $10,000 in cash—half was for spending on personal needs, and the other half went with them to the schools where they were hired to be used for school supplies. It became a popular and prestigious program, making the point, we thought, that teaching is a profession of the highest calling.

My optimism about small colleges and their leadership, which is easily visible in the paragraphs above, has, alas, eroded over the past couple of decades. The task of being president was somewhat easier in the last half of the twentieth century than it is today. The regulatory demands initiated during the second Bush administration and carried forward in the Obama years (all with good intentions) have made the job less enjoyable. By law, college and university presidents have been tasked with more responsibilities, many difficult if not impossible to manage. New regulations being pushed in Washington today largely to bring the for-profit institutions under tighter control affect all of higher education. For example, taking control of standards and quality out of the hands of higher education institutions by weakening peer review and accreditation is a serious threat to quality as we in academe have come to understand it. Further, the definitions of quality proposed by government—graduation rates, loan default rates, and graduates' salaries, among others—do not measure quality in the minds of most in the academy, including college presidents.

In addition, the number of difficult social problems on campuses seems to have grown disproportionately over the past couple of decades. The environment on campuses has become confrontational over complex social and political matters, making management a more difficult task than it was even recently (not forgetting the Vietnam War years). These changes do not change my views on what a successful president should be and do, but they have unquestionably made leadership more difficult.

What I Wish I Had Known When I Started I wish I had understood the importance of building good relationships with the various groups in the college and its neighboring communities.

What I Wish I Had Done When I Finished Found a way to reduce costs while maintaining high quality.

What I Wish I Had Not Done While in Office I worried a bit too much about the future of the world and higher education in particular. The energy expended did not help much.

What I Wish I Didn't Know When I Finished How difficult it would be to adjust to a normal faculty position in another institution after leaving one I liked a great deal.

How I Knew When to Stop When the routines of new student orientation and commencement become boring, it is time to move on.

6 Delegating Authority

Chancellors and the Delegation of Authority

Holden Thorp

How chancellors should deal with delegating authority is one of the toughest topics in higher education administration. It is particularly challenging at public universities, where elected officials and the media are always looking to public university leaders to take responsibility for everything that is going on. This makes it challenging not only to delegate authority but also to stay out of things until the right time.

I was the chancellor at the University of North Carolina (UNC) for five years and after that moved to Washington University to be the provost. When I was chancellor, I had the chance to work with an experienced provost for the first year, but when she left to run the University of Kansas, I worked with a provost who was a wonderful colleague, who did a great and selfless job, but who had never been a provost before. On his first day, we had a total of one year of experience as chancellor and provost between the two of us. This is too often the case in public universities, where there is so much turnover coming from short tenures for chancellors and provosts. I left UNC for a very different situation, to work for the most experienced and accomplished chancellor in higher education, Mark Wrighton, who is now beginning his twenty-second year and also served as provost of the Massachusetts Institute of Technology (MIT) for five years. Between the two of us, we have been either chancellor or provost now for a combined 34 years.

The ideas I express here are those that I acquired at UNC, as well as in moving from a chancellor's job to a provost's job and seeing the contrast based on the drastic differences in levels of experience. I've boiled my thoughts down to five areas:

1. Let the provost be the provost.
2. Connect with the deans.
3. Save the chancellor's decisions for the right time.
4. Realize that self-preservation is in the institutional interest.
5. Cultivate an understudy.

Let the Provost Be the Provost

When I first began as chancellor, I worked with a very experienced chief administrative officer who had served at three major public research universities. After the first year, I asked him if I was doing anything well, and he said, "You're doing a great job of not being the provost." He said the most common mistake he saw was chancellors not allowing the provost to do their jobs and missing things they were actually supposed to be doing. I had an advantage in this regard, having moved from being dean of arts and sciences and skipping provost. This meant that I didn't have to unlearn being the provost.

The most important tools that administrators have to influence the institution and solve problems are interpersonal relationships. Sometimes chancellors and provosts are hired from inside the university and thus have many existing interpersonal relationships, but often one or both come from the outside. To build relationships quickly, it's best for the chancellor to focus on external relationships and the provost to focus on the deans, faculty, students, and staff on campus. There needs to be crossover, of course, and the chancellor certainly has to have a lot of internal capital. But the chancellor needs to trust the provost to work the internal stakeholders. This approach worked well for me with both provosts I worked with at UNC and works extremely well between Mark Wrighton and me at Washington University.

When Mark Wrighton talks about his most important tasks, he starts with the job of winning friends and supporters for the university around the world. After 21 years, he has plenty of support internally. My role, as I see it, is to support his ability to be on the road and in front of donors and friends and to let him know when an internal matter needs his attention. The provost needs keep a finger on the pulse of the campus. I do this by teaching classes, engaging in activities with students, and going to as many faculty talks and seminars as possible. These are the places where people will share things informally that we can't get any other way. The chancellor does a lot of these activities as well, of course, but he is on the road more. Over the years, I've developed a much better sense of when the chancellor and provost both need to be doing something or whether it should just be one or the other of us. Decisions about this division of labor are incredibly important because members of the campus community pay close attention to who is attending what, and the chancellor needs to conserve energy and spend time away from campus doing development, international relations, and government relations.

This approach works particularly well for us in hiring deans. The chancellor is highly engaged in the process, and of course, we decide on the final candidate together. But it's important for the chancellor to allow the provost to run the process for selecting deans, for two reasons. First, the provost is going to have more time to do seek references and get to know the candidates and what they want. Second, when they arrive, deans need to feel that the provost is their primary boss and the place to go to with problems. Still, having the chancellor intimately involved allows the final decision to go quickly and ensures that the candidate is comfortable with both of us. This is a challenging task, and it goes the best when the chancellor and provost are playing their correct roles. Consequently, it is important for chancellor-provost teams to outline the choreography of these searches with each other.

All of this means that—going back to the comment I got from my chief administrative officer—the chancellor has to let the provost be the chief intellectual of the university. While the chancellor must be accessible to a broad range of stakeholders that includes many non-academics, the provost's primary audience consists of faculty members and students, and the provost can thus be much more unapologetically academic. Chancellors who are lifelong academics sometimes have a hard time managing this separation of roles, and in retrospect I could have done a better job of this at UNC. I am in a very comfortable situation at Washington University, where Mark Wrighton is so passionate about winning friends for the university that he focuses on connecting with many diverse stakeholders.

Connect with the Deans

Even though the provost has the primary relationship with the deans, it is also important for the chancellor to have a close connection with them. This is easier at a smaller university with fewer schools. I certainly should have spent more time with the deans when I was a chancellor. I've learned a lot about this from Mark Wrighton. He and I both meet with the deans frequently one on one. Some of my provost colleagues ask if I find it intrusive that the deans often meet with the chancellor, but nothing could be farther from the truth.

The deans may end up talking with the chancellor about issues that are important to the external functions of the university, such as fundraising or international matters. In contrast, when they meet with me as the provost, we are more likely to talk about curriculum or faculty hiring. So the provost is not the best conduit for the information that the chancellor would most want to get from the deans.

In addition, the deans are important stakeholders. They have both internal and external functions and get a lot of information from many different people. If both the chancellor and provost communicate regularly with the deans, it maximizes the chance that the information will come through, particularly if the chancellor and provost do a good job of communicating with each other.

Finally, deans have a challenging job and need all the mentoring they can get. Having been a provost, chancellor, and dean, I believe the dean of arts and sciences is the second-hardest academic job in the university. The other schools are also challenging to run. When both the chancellor and the provost meet with the deans, it gives the central administration the most chances to provide support to the deans.

Of course, none of this works without a great flow of information flow between the chancellor and the provost and a shared understanding of roles. The chancellor and provost are a team in mentoring the deans. They have a division of perspective (internal and external) but need to be unified in making sure that the deans are successful. Almost every university refers to itself as a "deans' university"; smart chancellors and provosts make sure that is the case.

Save the Chancellor's Decisions for the Right Time

One of the hardest things to do when you're the chancellor is to wait until the right time to make a decision. Most of us got big jobs by doing things better and faster than others. When you're a few layers down in the organization, this is a surefire way to get ahead. But when you have the top job, it is a different deal: if you make a decision, it is by definition one that no one else in the organization wants to make and very, very hard to go back on. Also, when the chancellor decides, it is a ceremonial and important event that should be reserved for the right time.

The temptations for the chancellor to act sooner than required are numerous. If it is a public matter, pressure comes from elected officials and the media. If it is internal, some matters that ultimately require the chancellor to make a decision take a huge toll inside the institution. Another big temptation comes when the chancellor wants to spare the other administrators from wrestling with something and to share the burden. While this seems like a stand-up thing to do, it actually undermines the other administrators in the long run. If an administrator down in the organization can't resolve an issue and kicks it up to the chancellor, that is not particularly damaging. If the chancellor jumps in to soon with the wrong plan, they both get burned.

The right thing for a chancellor to do is to wait for the organization—the provost, the deans, the general counsel—to wrestle with a matter until it can't be wrestled with any further and then to make a pronouncement. This approach gives a sense of finality to the matter and relieves the internal team. This should be done sparingly, of course, and the theatrics that obtain are often uncomfortable for career academics who find themselves in management.

Self-Preservation Is in the Institution's Interest

One of the things new chancellors struggle with is the fact that so much of the external perception of the university rests with them. I used to cringe every time someone said, "We want to know what the university thinks about this," and when they said, "the university," they were pointing at me. Academics spend their entire careers sharing credit with their coauthors and graduate students, so having people think an institution of tens of thousands of people can be represented by one person is hard to accept.

Get over it. There's nothing you can do about the fact that many people on the outside, and a lot on the inside, think that you speak for everyone. For that reason, it's actually in your colleagues' interest for you to stay out of the controversies and tough decisions unless it's necessary. The administrative team can recover from a bad decision more easily than you can, and your injuries affect far more people. In the moment, it may seem wise to be a good colleague to your administrative team and roll up your sleeves right alongside them when there is a huge problem. In truth, however, it's far better for them for you to protect yourself and—as stated above—save your actions for the time when there is no other choice. By doing so, you're giving your team one last chance to get an issue resolved.

Cultivate an Understudy

When a colleague of ours went off to run another university, he was at a last social function with me and Mark Wrighton. Before he left, he asked us each for advice. I said, "Don't let yourself get run down." Mark said, "Show up at everything they invite you to." A lot of people would think that these two pieces of advice are in conflict. Actually, they aren't. The chancellor's presence is very meaningful, and showing up goes a long, long way. But showing up and not doing a good job is harmful.

When chancellors get together, they spend a lot of time talking about their calendars. The pace is grueling, and people's expectations are high. The way to beat this is to have someone who can show up in your place and do a good job. Look carefully for the right person. The provost is a likely choice, but it could be someone else. It's certain that no one can show up in your place and do a good job without your help. Even though I had been a chancellor for five years myself, I still needed to understand how best to fill in for Mark Wrighton. Not only do I watch him closely at events, but he also spends a lot of time making sure that I know his goals.

You won't use your understudy very often. But the process of cultivating an understudy will help you refine your own presence while at the same time giving you some peace of mind. If something happens that requires you to cancel your presence at an important event or activity, you know you have someone who can step in. That lowers the burden considerably, even if it's not invoked often.

What I Wish I Had Known When I Started The chancellor of a public university is a public figure just like any elected official. If you are the chancellor of your state's public flagship, you have what many people would say is the most desirable job in your state. Be ready for all that entails.

What I Wish I Had Done When I Finished Spent more time with the deans. Spent more time with my friends and family outside of the university to keep perspective.

What I Wish I Had Not Done While in Office I wish I hadn't worried so much about the calendar.

What I Wish I Didn't Know When I Finished A lot of external stakeholders don't care as much about the academic side of the university as we think.

How I Knew When to Stop I knew it was time to stop when I realized I'd done all I could in Chapel Hill and could contribute more to higher education in a different environment, like the one I'm in now.

Delegation of Presidential Authority and the Unwritten University Constitution

Mark G. Yudof

The best administrative job I ever held was being dean of the University of Texas Law School. Better than being president or chancellor of three universities? You bet (or you betcha in Minnesota). The faculty was smaller than the average public university English department, the colleagues were brilliant and engaged, the students were a blessing, the legislature rarely bothered me, and the media more or less left me alone. I cannot remember a single request at that time for my travel records. Best of all, I got to write my own letters and speeches. No myrmidons to do my thinking. Indeed, not only did I write my own talks (in addition to classroom lectures and law review articles), but I remember writing an occasional speech for the campus president and chairman of the law foundation.

These halcyon days ended when I assumed the top administrative job. People frequently told me it is lonely at the top. That was not my experience. The faculty, alumni, student leaders, editorial writers, and a host of others all wanted to tell me how to do my job. Sportswriters, never accountable for their earlier prognostications, were the most egregious. But it turned out my job now involved a dozen or so direct reports and hundreds of others who worked under the vice presidents. The volume of mail, and later email, was so massive that I could personally respond to relatively few missives. And I gave hundreds of speeches each year.

There literally was no time in the day for me to research the dilemmas of wheat farmers or the complexities of study abroad programs; I had to rely on the staff for the research and for chunks of my prose. Not easy for a guy who wrote for a living for 25 years before the Peter Principle kicked in.

As a preliminary observation, it is easy for those external to the university to surmise that the president makes all of the decisions. I would receive letters asking me to intervene when a ticket collector at a sports event was rude to an alumnus. I once wanted a small coffee shop in the Main Building at Texas; the process took months and the coffee shop was placed out of doors. I met with students in my law and education seminar at Minnesota and began the class by asking how I might make student life better on campus. One student pointed out that the public policy school had scented soap. Why couldn't all the restrooms be similarly outfitted? Drawing on my magisterial presidential authority, I told the student I would get right on it. I wrote to the facilities manager. He passed my email along to the general counsel. The GC wrote that scented soap violated guidance under the Americans with Disabilities Act. The result of my intervention was that the scented soap was removed from the public policy school.

The truth is that universities work only because authority is delegated to others. The unwritten constitution says that a president should not exercise all of the authority he or she legally possesses, nor should the board of regents. Admissions and faculty appointments are good examples. Under the rules regents may have the final say on tenure, but it is generally a bad idea for them to decide whether an anthropology or physics professor merits the granting of tenure. The expertise lies elsewhere—even if mistakes sometimes are made. The curriculum is the province of the faculty, and administrators and regents should rarely if ever intervene. The university engine runs on collaboration, consultation, and persuasion, not the volatile fumes of coercion. Leadership in such flat organizations may be challenging and decisions may be delayed, but that is the nature of the organizational beast.

But what of the decisions of vice presidents and those lower in the central administration pecking order? Much depends on the context. What is the nature of the decision? How trusted is the subordinate? What expertise is involved? What is the reaction of legislators, students, faculty, staff, and the media to the decision? And what are the systemic implications if the president reverses a decision? Will all such matters end up in the president's office? Can the president efficiently and knowledgeably deal with such matters, among all of the other stuff in her day? Will she be perceived as fair or only responding to the squeaky wheel, the persistent and not necessarily the righteous? What of staff morale and goodwill? There will be other days when their cooperation is vital. Though right and wrong are always important, they are only a part of the calculus.

I recall a controversy over a new logo at the University of California. The communications folks showed it to me, explaining that it would be used only on some communications and not displace all other logos. I didn't like it. My immediate staff didn't like it. I could not make out the UC in the drawings, but I was told that we needed to modernize our image. I reluctantly gave the go-ahead. I felt out of my depth opining on an artistic matter, and I certainly was not a communications guru. I relied on the "branding" experts. Then all hell broke loose. Some media and alumni said the new logo looked like a flushing toilet (I missed that). I received a call from a statewide elected leader who expressed his outrage. I fielded calls from regents. I decided to wait, anxious not to be perceived as a troglodyte in the information age. Eventually the anti-logo tidal wave overwhelmed, and the communications vice president abandoned ship. I still possess one of the rare shirts with the discredited logo to remind me of the misadventure.

Similarly, I had a couple of encounters with architecture at the University of Minnesota. The school of architecture was building an addition, and I thought the proposed new building was incompatible with the old one. The faculty told me that was what they wanted. Apparently many faculty detested their existing facility. I demurred. But after pondering the wisdom of getting involved, I finally acted. I ordered a change to copper siding for the new building (it would be copper brown for a few years and green thereafter). The donor told me he did not like presidential interference in design matters, but he thought the building much improved. Later I received an architecture award from the school. (I also pushed hard to save and restore historic buildings.) Similarly, I was deeply troubled by the design for a new green space and residence hall for a steep grade on the Mississippi River. In that case I simply brought the architects to my office to show them the original Cass Gilbert design for the area (never built, but he did design the Woolworth Building and the US Supreme Court building). I told them to try again. They did, and the final work was quite successful.

The campus police response to student and other demonstrations is a particularly nettlesome issue. I estimate that a quarter of the regents meetings during my five years as president of the University of California were completely shut down by demonstrators. After demonstrators were given ample warnings, police had to clear the room so the board could do its business. In this process there were unfortunate but rare injuries to police and demonstrators. Students occupied buildings on some campuses, There were allegations of police overreaction to protests on some campuses, particularly when there were large crowds dismayed by planned tuition increases. On a number of occasions I remember being trapped in a car or building—along with regents and staff.

My response to such events was to investigate thoroughly and impartially before speaking out. In one case, I relied on a special committee chaired by a distinguished former justice of the California Supreme Court. In another case, the general counsel and the dean of law met with the different groups, received expert testimony, and issued a comprehensive document outlining rules on police conduct. The safety of the protesting students is critical. The right to protest and demonstrate is sacrosanct. The safety of those not protesting is also crucial—including the faculty and staff. The university's ability to function is a priority. Given the importance and salience of the issues, a president ultimately cannot delegate all of these decisions to others. Any review generally occurs after the fact, but a review may result in needed changes to police and administrative procedures.

In the police cases, I delegated the reviews to bodies outside of the normal structures and staunchly defended their impartial reports. I felt it important for me not to make the decisions based only on my own authority and perceptions. But sometimes a president may have reservations after having asked a committee to make recommendations. It is difficult when a committee has worked hard over many months and the president in his heart of hearts believes the resulting recommendations are misguided. Much thought should therefore go into whether to appoint a committee. A president should not view the formation of a committee as a safety valve; she needs to think about what the committee might decide down the road.

The best example of this problem occurred when a committee of top-level administrators developed a plan for a new tier for the UC Retirement Plan, a fund that had to be refashioned to protect its long-term ability to meet its commitments to present and future retirees. The faculty members on the committee dissented. A number of labor unions were very upset by the plan. I pondered the matter for weeks and finally decided on a modified version of the faculty plan, which I thought was fairer, particularly to lower-paid employees. I suspect my decision greatly upset my trusted colleagues. Perhaps I lost some respect. In that case I reluctantly concluded that the unhappiness of my direct reports was outweighed by the need for an equitable retirement system.

Another knotty area involves the relationship of the president to the general counsel. This is particularly treacherous in my case; I remain a dedicated law professor, occasionally demanding that briefs be rewritten. I know more about law than architecture or actuarial science. But there is a lot of law out there! The expertise of the law office and outside counsel is foundational; higher education is a regulated industry, subject to everything from environmental and safety regulations to civil rights and collective bargaining laws. A president who ignores the lawyers acts at her peril. But sometimes the lawyers do not see the broader picture; they deal with legal risk and not the overall context. I almost always respected their judgment (ditto for the audit staff), but one always needs to be careful. I recall one GC informing me that a proposed settlement of a patent suit looked advantageous, but there was one small matter he wanted clarified. I feared that the settlement opportunity would be lost if we hesitated, and I signed off on the original settlement agreement.

One last complexity is the role of the president in a university system. As Texas chancellor, I oversaw 15 campuses; UC had 10 campuses. With varying features, university systems are really federations (or in some cases confederations), and appropriately most decisions are made by the campus leadership, faculty, staff, and students. When should a chancellor or president overrule a campus decision? One instance is when the board intervenes or when legal requirements have been transgressed. What if a proposed measure has differential effects on the campuses? What is good for Berkeley may not work well at Davis or San Diego. Sometimes it seemed to me that my choices were like those of Sophie in the William Styron novel.

The bottom line is that nothing important gets implemented without the cooperation, or at least the tacit consent, of the campuses. System officers are no smarter or more insightful than campus leaders—and they certainly are less knowledgeable about local conditions. Most system employees have never held an academic appointment. My reaction was to jawbone major decisions and seek to persuade.

I can think of only one major decision where I deviated from this course. I wanted to adopt the UC Blue and Gold financial aid program, automatically entitling students to free tuition and fees if their families made less than $65,000 a year (students first had to apply for Pell and state grants to qualify for funding of any shortfall). Nearly all of the chancellors supported the idea, but a couple of them found the proposal problematic (as did some of the financial aid staff). But I thought the program critical to recruiting and retaining low- and middle-income students. I liked the bright-line income cutoff rather than the complexities of traditional financial aid forms. I adopted the plan. It was unanimously approved by the regents, greeted with enthusiasm by the public, and proved invaluable in providing access to a UC education.

I fear that my experiences with delegating authority do not provide much concrete guidance. Higher education administration is an art and not a science. Context and facts are decisive. It is not conducive to simple heuristics, which often are wrong. And surely the answer is not to avoid the delegation of authority. A major component of getting this right is to have trusted and capable individuals serving in the key roles.

But even then the problem of delegated authority does not evaporate. I have a few suggestions:

Trust but verify. As Mark Twain said in *Pudd'nhead Wilson*, it is fine to put "all your eggs in the one basket [if you] WATCH THAT BASKET." A president needs to be vigilant and to listen to others. There is a lot of whining in universities, but it pays to listen carefully to students, faculty, and staff. They always bear the brunt of decisions.

Pressing officers to consult with you prior to major decisions can prevent many crises.

A president needs to impress upon her officers that there is a broader political framework that needs to be taken into account. It is not enough that the CFO, the athletic director, the general counsel, or the risk manager have reached a conclusion based on their expertise; there are always implications beyond the particular area of expertise.

Managers (like the president himself) may oversee broad portfolios of responsibilities (e.g., budgets and facilities, university press, energy conservation, police force), and they are rarely experts in all of their assigned areas. Consult key deputies who report to the vice presidents; they often are the ones who really understand the problems. They are the permanent undersecretaries as higher-echelon appointees come and go. I did this openly, telling the managers what I was doing and inviting them to join the discussion.

Resist the temptation to appoint a committee to gain time in a crisis unless you have solid reasons to believe that the committee will act responsibly.

Pay attention to your media people. They often have a keen sense of what is likely to reach crisis proportions.

The cardinal rule of the unwritten constitution, Article I if you will, is that just because you have the authority to do something does not mean you should do it. The unfortunate reality is that neither blind devotion to subordinates and their decisions nor an arrogant belief in one's decision-making prowess is likely to win the day. It's harder than that.

II INTERNAL CHALLENGES

7 Internationalizing the Curriculum and Student Experience

Linking Internationalization to Mission

Jane McAuliffe

Just a few weeks after arriving at Bryn Mawr, I flew across country to begin conversations with some of the college's key supporters. On the first day of this trip I met one of our older alums and was quickly engaged in a fascinating discussion with her. She had graduated more than 50 years before, yet her memories of college life were vivid and striking. She laughed about successfully evading curfews and showed me photos of her busy social life that belied any notion of this women's college as a cloistered environment. She pulled out a scrapbook of Bryn Mawr memorabilia with playbills of college productions and dance cards with every slot filled. Flipping to the page that preserved one semester's "report card," she pointed with still-lingering regret at the C that marred an otherwise excellent record. As we leafed through that scrapbook together, the photos and mementos prompted a flood of stories and statements. One comment in particular caught me by surprise: reminiscing about her classmates and dorm-mates, this alumna remarked, "We were such an international school!"

What did being international mean to her then, and could it properly describe the Bryn Mawr College of today? The search committee that selected me and the board of trustees that confirmed my appointment had already made it very clear that they wanted Bryn Mawr to be much more international. They saw aspects of my background as assets that would facilitate that goal. My academic field is Islamic studies, and lecturing and research have taken me to Muslim countries in the Middle East, Africa, and Southeast Asia, as well as to many other spots across the globe. I had spent years at the University of Toronto, a major urban university in arguably the most multicultural city on the globe. My time in Toronto was followed by almost a decade as dean of arts and sciences at Georgetown University. With its schools of foreign service and of languages and linguistics, Georgetown had attracted a globally engaged faculty and administration and had graduated alumni who could be found in every part of the world. As a Jesuit university, Georgetown owed its existence to a religious order founded more than 500 years ago, an organization with its own a deep history of global engagement.

With this background and experience, I welcomed the opportunity to foster more international opportunity and visibility for Bryn Mawr. But where to start? That alumna's remark actually gave me a valuable clue and alerted me to the assets for internationalization that the college could already access. Chief among them was a keen sense, shared by every constituency, that all our students, not just those with a foreign language or international affairs interest, must be educated for a global future. Many of our faculty were already embedded in global research networks and needed no convincing about the importance of such opportunities for their students. So the will to build upon an existing foundation was already there. I never experienced, as did many of my presidential colleagues at other institutions, the need to justify efforts at internationalization. The advantages were obvious to Bryn Mawr faculty, students, staff, trustees, and alumnae/i.

That consensus was constructed on a widely known institutional history. The first foreign student arrived at Bryn Mawr in 1889, four years after the college's founding. She was a young Japanese woman who spent two and a half years in residence and then returned to her native land. Inspired by her experience, she opened a women's college in Japan, Tsuda College, and the two institutions remain closely connected through student exchanges and faculty visits. The immediate past president of Tsuda College, Dr. Masako Iino, spent a semester's sabbatical at Bryn Mawr in 2013.

The East Asian connection continued as Bryn Mawr alumnae groups in the 1920s and 1930s funded scholarships to support Japanese and Chinese students. These students and those from Europe, Latin America, the Middle East, and elsewhere who came to Bryn Mawr in the following decades, formed the basis for alumnae comments that "we've always been international." Clearly, students from far distant places, though few in number, had an outsized impact on their classmates. Many remained active alumnae, opening their homes and providing local connections for visiting classmates through the years.

Languages were another asset to which we could immediately point. Although among the smallest of the elite liberal arts colleges, Bryn Mawr taught a wider range of languages than most: Arabic, Chinese, Japanese, Spanish, French, Italian, German, Russian, Greek, Latin, and Hebrew. One of the dorms had been built to host "language houses," settings in which students and faculty could create language-immersive environments. Not unexpectedly, the faculty of these languages departments and programs urged—and even required—that their students study abroad, so, again, the percentage of undergraduates who undertook a year or a semester of study at a foreign university was much higher than the national norm.

Add to these advantages a worldwide alumnae/i presence and significant trustee enthusiasm for a more internationally oriented Bryn Mawr, and I could be certain that our globalization efforts were not starting from scratch. But while all these assets were in play, they were diffused and underappreciated, clearly in need of coordination and amplification. Consequently, as a first step, I undertook an auditing and mapping exercise, and I began to speak about globalization at every opportunity, both on campus and off. On the front page of the college website, we mounted an interactive world map that charted where our faculty had active research connections, where our students were currently studying abroad, and where our graduates were living and working on almost every continent.

The mapping exercise attracted student, faculty, and alumnae attention; it also expanded interests and raised expectations. Faculty began to suggest further forms of connection and activated their own networks for the college's benefit. Soon there were enough suggestions and possibilities worthy of exploration to warrant a full-time position. As I began the search to fill that position, I got lucky. An alumna who had been directing the international programs and initiatives of a major university—and who was a national leader among international education administrators—expressed an interest in helping her alma mater with its ambitious agenda.

With such a fortunate senior-level appointment, Bryn Mawr could begin to move forward in several directions simultaneously. On the curricular front, faculty were beginning to experiment with an innovative multidisciplinary program that offered students the option of a semester's coursework focused on a specific theme. The courses were in different departments, but the faculty collaborated on both their creation and execution so that the intellectual connections were explicitly developed. Since the same students were taking the same set of offerings, these courses could incorporate off-campus experiences. One of the first to be initiated took students and faculty to Vienna for a week. In the following semester, another of these "360°

courses" included a week in Kyoto, Japan, and its many Zen monasteries. Yet another involved fieldwork at an elementary school in Titagya, Ghana.

As the 360° courses expanded faculty and student horizons, interest in international studies as a potential new major began to percolate. Earlier efforts to develop such a program were revisited with renewed enthusiasm and, eventually, the faculty voted to institute a major concentration in international studies within which students could choose an emphasis on gender, development, or global social justice.

These forms of curricular enhancement benefited from alumnae interest, particularly among those whose own personal and professional lives had convinced them that today's Bryn Mawr graduates needed global literacy and awareness. Many of those alumnae who lived and worked abroad were eager for more than occasional and episodic contact with the college. They were also ready to open doors for current students through internships and other connections that they could broker. The time was ripe for the creation of an International Alumnae/i Council, and I hosted the first gathering of this fledging group in Singapore. The degree of enthusiasm and willingness to assist took me by surprise. Quite quickly, I found our international alumnae working to support admissions to the college from their respective regions and to advance fundraising initiatives. We immediately adopted a pattern of meeting twice a year, once in Asia and once in Western Europe, with a teleconference session for each meeting that beamed in our alumnae from the other location. As the gatherings grew and as this expanding group became more informed about today's Bryn Mawr, I began to see the emergence of a corps of ambassadors and advocates strategically placed across the globe.

In several cases, these international alumnae provided introductions to universities and university leaders in their own cities and regions. I pursued these openings while also activating my own networks of international connections and colleagues. All of these introductions and exchanges increased Bryn Mawr's visibility in the world of international higher education, with some proving even more productive. For example, a fledgling relationship with Nanyang Technological University in Singapore expanded from introductory visits to our respective campuses by delegations of faculty and administrators, to more extensive faculty visits, and eventually to an innovative summer program for students that NTU and Bryn Mawr cohosted in Tianjin, China.

Given our position as a women's college, I was especially intent upon cultivating relationships with other prominent women's colleges around the world. My vision in doing so was both short and long term. Vibrant connections with established institutions like Lady Shri Ram College for Women in New Delhi, Effat University in Jeddah, Tsuda College in Tokyo, and Ewha Womans University in Seoul benefit current students and faculty but also build the foundation for a more networked web of the world's best women's colleges. As technological advancements make telepresence more ubiquitous and more affordable, I can imagine linked classrooms in the future and even joint academic programs. As an experiment in this direction, I created a "Skype seminar" during one spring semester. This was a president-to-president program in which I hosted consecutive teleconference sessions with each of the above four institutions in a common format. The college president would gather a group of students in her office, just as I did in mine, and we'd begin a conversation about life and learning at our respective institutions. Not unexpectedly, the students soon seized the dialogue and demonstrated how ready they are to collapse cultural and geographic barriers.

The focus on women's colleges formed part of a larger effort to align our internationalization with our mission as a women's college. I came to the presidency of Bryn Mawr as the product of a women's college (Trinity College, now Trinity University, in Washington, DC) and as a person dedicated to the promotion and enhancement of this special form of higher education. But I was troubled by the usual justifications offered for the existence of women's colleges at a time when female undergraduates are in the majority at all the best colleges and universities in the nation. These narratives seemed unnecessarily defensive and compensatory, suggesting that women's colleges served students who could not thrive in competitive coed environments. The founding missions of the best women's colleges were actually much more compelling in their emphasis on righting the injustices of sex discrimination and opening opportunities for women.

Has that agenda been successfully achieved? Of course not! While great progress has been made since the period in which these colleges were founded, no one is proclaiming victory and declaring that we can now usher in the era of gender equity. Rather, there is a growing awareness that the paramount moral problem of the twenty-first century is the unavoidable reality that women across the globe continue to suffer systemic oppression and brutalization. Almost every major problem in the world—poverty, environmental degradation, trafficking, sexual abuse, and forced labor—falls disproportionately on women.

I believe that women's colleges can be a potent force for change. Their very identities and reputations give them the platform from which to launch constant challenges to these continuing injustices. Their faculties are full of scholars who can bring the perspectives of multiple disciplines to urgent research questions and whose presence at a women's college testifies to their interest in these issues. Their convening power can draw together scholars and activists in symposia and conferences that span borders and that energize smart, informed, and effective engagement.

Their alumnae often occupy prominent positions in government and the private sector, placing them in roles where they can make a difference. An innovative partnership begun by the US Department of State, in collaboration with the five remaining single-sex institutions of the "Seven Sisters," to create leadership training for women in public service around the world immediately drew a deluge of alumnae enthusiasm and support. Launched by Secretary Hillary Clinton at the State Department in December 2012, the Women in Public Service Program continues to flourish under the auspices of the Wilson Center in Washington, DC.

Women's colleges, in sum, can exercise a special kind of institutional agency. Through their curricular and cocurricular programs they can assure that each of their students will graduate with a sophisticated and nuanced understanding of the continuing injustices that women suffer around the world. These graduates, in turn, through whatever professions they enter—professors, entrepreneurs, research scientists, visual and performing artists—can be voices for change, can create opportunities for others, and can raise children who believe a more just and equitable world is their birthright.

The partnerships with other women's colleges, the scholar/activist conferences, the Women in Public Service Program—all align Bryn Mawr's internationalization with mission renewal. There is enormous potential, particularly among the best women's colleges, to graduate cadres of the brightest young women who refuse to accept structures of gender inequity in their own societies or in others across the globe. Even as undergraduates, they can create alliances and build networks for a transformed future. Students were quick to see the potential here and to initiate their own events and programming in support of these goals.

Such synergies began to multiply among Bryn Mawr's increasing international student body. Like many American colleges and universities, in recent years Bryn Mawr has seen a sharp increase in international students, particularly those from East Asia. A generous financial aid policy that treats both domestic and international students equally has accelerated this trend at the college. As international students become a much more substantial portion of the undergraduate population, they are changing the campus demography and the campus culture. A young woman from Boston whose roommate comes from Beijing is the new normal. The relationships formed in dorm rooms, relationships that often endure for a lifetime, have suddenly gone global, and the positive repercussions of this for future friendships, professional opportunities, and social justice activism can only be imagined. I would dearly love to return for an alumnae reunion at Bryn Mawr 25 years from now. I have no doubt that the significant advances in internationalization that were a focus of my presidency will have played out in exciting and unforeseen ways.

What I Wish I Had Known When I Started I wish that I had known how hard it is to persuade today's young women of the benefits of a women's college. Only a tiny fraction of this demographic will even look at this group of institutions. Once enrolled, they are immediate converts to the advantaged academic situation in which they find themselves, but getting them to consider the possibility of single-sex education is a tough task.

What I Wish I Had Done When I Finished I wish that I had written more thank-you notes and letters. Although during my final weeks in office I spoke to many people, both on campus and off, who had made my years at Bryn Mawr such productive and fulfilling ones, I wish that I had sent written expressions of gratitude as a further acknowledgment of my appreciation and abiding gratitude.

What I Wish I Had Not Done While in Office I wish that I had not sacrificed so much family time to the demands of the job. Even realizing that the sacrifices were unavoidable, the regrets about forgone family gatherings and so many missed moments with children and grandchildren still linger.

What I Wish I Didn't Know When I Finished In the last months that I was at Bryn Mawr what was supposed to be a routine summer project to upgrade the bathrooms in one of the dorms turned into a massive asbestos abatement problem. Estimates of the required remediation were so high that it forced the decision to rebuild the dorm. While it will be nice to have a new dorm, there were more urgent capital projects that had to be postponed because of this emergency.

How I Knew When to Stop When the vision that I put forth in my inaugural address had been realized or clearly embedded in the board-approved strategic plan, when several principal gifts for the next campaign had been secured, and when a successor who could build upon that foundation was easily identifiable, it seemed the perfect moment to pass the baton. The prospect of then being able to spend much more time with my family and to complete the book promised to my ever-patient publisher pushed me over the decision line.

Selling the Idea of Universal Study Abroad

Sanford J. Ungar

I'm the study-abroad guy.

When I was first selected to be president of Goucher College in Baltimore in the spring of 2001, I turned immediately to a well-placed friend for advice—the successful leader of one of America's best-endowed and most-respected liberal arts colleges, where my daughter happened to be enrolled at the time. An economist of higher education, he was prescient in foreseeing the crisis that loomed. He offered succinct and rather frightening words: "You know," he said, "not all of these little liberal arts colleges are going to survive. If you want Goucher to be one that does, you'd better find a way to make it distinctive, to be sure that it stands out from the pack." That, in retrospect, was exactly what I needed to hear. It was an excuse and a provocation to rock the boat in a particular direction once I got on board.

During the search and interview process, I had pitched myself as an international person whose attitudes and perspectives had been dramatically transformed by his own experiences overseas. Born and raised in a small town in northeastern Pennsylvania that had a rather narrow view of the universe, as the son of immigrant parents who probably believed in American exceptionalism more devoutly than anyone else I could ever meet (though they surely never knew or used that term), I had my mind expanded first by concentrating in government at Harvard and then by studying for a master's degree in history at the London School of Economics, with a fellowship from the Rotary Foundation.

But mind expansion did not, initially, include becoming worldly wise. Harvard, in my day, did not believe in granting undergraduate course credit for overseas study; most students who insisted on going abroad for anything but the summer generally took a leave of absence. At the LSE, there was every possibility to make up for lost time. Then as now, one literally encountered people there from all over the world every day; and thanks to the extraordinary, if occasionally awkward, experience of speaking at lunch or dinner meetings to more than 25 Rotary clubs in the United Kingdom during the course of the academic year, and being invited into their members' homes, I certainly took my first steps toward an understanding that the American way was not the only way of life.

That got me started. Before long, I gave up my plan to come home and go to law school, and stayed abroad for more than three years altogether. During that time I lived and worked as a journalist in Paris, Nairobi, Johannesburg, Durban, and Cape Town—and traveled to many other places, including Greece, Spain, Hungary, and the Soviet Union, not to mention Eritrea, Zanzibar, and Mozambique. I saw how fragile life and politics could be, covering, among other things, the 1968 worker-student revolt in France and the assassination of the heir apparent to the presidency of Kenya a year later. I observed the worst of apartheid, and I got caught in a military coup in Athens. You name it.

So it is that I came to believe an international awareness could make a great difference in life. Once established in Washington, I took every opportunity, as a writer and editor, a broadcaster, a commentator on foreign policy issues, and a journalism school dean, to go back overseas. Eventually, toward the end of the Clinton administration, I served two years as director of the Voice of America, supervising broadcasts in some 50 languages via radio, television, and the internet. That assignment took me to many more places—Vietnam, Cambodia, Pakistan, Bangladesh, Morocco, and the two Congos, to name a few.

Fortunately, the trustees of Goucher understood where I was coming from and where I wanted to take the college, if given the opportunity to lead it. I was playing to its strengths and traditions: Founded as the Woman's College of Baltimore City in 1885 by a group of Methodist ministers and missionaries, from its earliest days it had welcomed international students from around the world. Its second president, John Franklin Goucher, for whom the college was later named, was a legendary traveler and explorer. Before, during, and after his presidency, he would take off for months at a time on ambitious journeys of discovery and send home detailed notes on what he had seen and whom he had met. Sometimes his travels were written about and pictured in *National Geographic*. (Several years ago, during a visit to the ruins at Petra, in Jordan, my wife and I were guided by copies of handwritten journal entries from Dr. Goucher, who had made the identical trip 100 years earlier, riding through the desert on horseback to get there.) Underwritten by the wealthy father of his wife, Mary Fisher Goucher, he and she bought and donated the land for what would become a prestigious pre-K-through-Ph.D. institution in central Tokyo and also established schools at various levels in China, India, and Korea, many of them still thriving today.

A later president of Goucher, David Allan Robertson, came to the job in 1930 after establishing a national junior-year-abroad program during the mid-1920s as an official of the American Council on Education. Goucher students themselves began studying abroad in 1938. Famously, starting in 1949, they would go out and raise money to help cover the room and board expenses for a new wave of international students who were coming to study on the Baltimore campus for a year and could not afford to pay all the fees. Thus, the institution became self- consciously connected to the larger world earlier than most.

I arrived at Goucher in July 2001, just 72 days before 9/11, without a doctorate, and with only a few original ideas about how to move the college forward. One, inspired by the advice of my friend and mentor and calling upon Goucher's unique history, was to float the concept of achieving distinctiveness in the marketplace by requiring study abroad for every undergraduate. I introduced the concept rhetorically in my inaugural address in October of that year, and I took it straight to the strategic planning group I had convened for an overdue look at Goucher's future. My strong conviction was that we wanted young people to apply to Goucher for a specific, substantive reason, not just because they had an empty line available on the Common Application.

Everyone noticed. On the one hand, the notion was not as radical as it sounded, because quite a few Goucher students—just over 30 percent—were already studying overseas, in various formats, including three-week intensive courses abroad (ICAs) in places as familiar as London and Rome and as far-flung as Honduras and Ghana. On the other hand, it would turn out to be an advantage to present it as a new beginning, a sharp break from the recent past—taking a good and already popular phenomenon and making it a universal experience among our students. Coed since 1986, the college had an inspired and devoted faculty and staff and an ambitious curriculum, and it was happily situated among the 40 institutions featured in the iconic guidebook *Colleges That Change Lives*; but in truth it was difficult to distinguish Goucher from many of its peers, and applications and enrollment had recently become flat from year to year.

From the start, those of us behind the change made it clear there could be multiple ways of fulfilling the requirement: a semester or a full year abroad, a short faculty-supervised ICA offered by Goucher or a similar institution, or some other substantive program, perhaps for the summer, that our Office of International Studies or students themselves might find to satisfy their interests (always screened by the appropriate academic department). Very few of the options, other than the ICAs, would be staffed by Goucher personnel; most involved directly enrolling in foreign universities, buying spots in other institutions' study-abroad programs, or, eventually, participating in exchange consortia.

The trustees were, for the most part, highly enthusiastic about the idea—although a few were understandably worried about sending all of our students out into a dangerous world. (There was a temptation to note, of course, that the terrorist acts of 9/11, while organized and directed from overseas, had actually taken their victims on American soil.) The strategic planners endorsed the concept in the report they issued at the end of my first year. Admissions and other staff members saw that it would give them a new selling point. Most of the alumnae and alumni (as this former woman's college required itself to describe them separately) seemed to like it, too.

It was only in certain corners of the faculty that some concerted opposition to mandatory study abroad emerged. Despite my previous years as a dean, I was still a journalist at heart and impatient with academic shared governance, where, as far as I could tell, the goal was to talk all new ideas to death. But it did not take long for even this non-academic to realize that, like it or not, no such major new curricular requirement could meaningfully take effect without the cooperation of the faculty. So, naturally, we named a committee—the curriculum transformation group, or CTG—to meet over the next summer and weigh the pros and cons of taking what was now being described in some circles as a bold and risky step. Actually, as it turned out, we established four consecutive, annual summertime CTGs, between 2002 and 2006, to think things through. No point being hasty. What were the substantive objections? It is embarrassingly difficult to reconstruct them.

In retrospect, what they probably boiled down to was a suspicion, especially on the part of certain faculty members in the hard sciences, that this was all a sinister plan to reallocate resources. A compulsory study-abroad program, they felt, would be expensive (that part was accurate) and inevitably draw money away from labs and research (not necessarily so, particularly if enrollments grew along the way). Also, these were the days before the mischievous concept of disruptive innovation had really taken hold, and so those who supervised specialized tracks like premed or elementary education worried that chaos might result for their students. And a few, whether American exceptionalists or de facto isolationists, saw no particular advantage to our students' becoming internationally aware—perhaps because they had never traveled abroad themselves and felt no inclination to do so anytime soon.

I still have little knowledge of what was said during faculty discussions of the issue behind closed doors, but I do have some favorite vignettes from the protracted debate that occasionally broke out in public: On one occasion, a well-regarded faculty member who had been teaching mathematics for decades, blurted out, "What's international about math?" (One of her prized students had recently returned from studying higher math in Budapest.) On another, a senior professor of biology declared in a faculty meeting, "Biology is biology," and said he saw nothing to be learned from the way people in other countries teach it or study it; American methods are just fine—indeed, the best. A junior member of the psychology department, in a moment of boldness and bravery, commented that she thought this was a narrow, ignorant point of view, and the conversation went downhill from there. It was a good thing I had a few other initiatives, such as the construction of a new 103,000-square-foot library and central gathering spot on campus, to keep me busy.

Finally a daring chair of the faculty, sensing the pressure growing within the college community to get on with the matter, took an open vote, and the motion to require study abroad, as part of reformulated liberal education requirements, passed by a large margin. The opposition was startled to discover that we intended to put it into immediate effect; other dilatory tactics would not work. Study abroad would become a feature of every Goucher undergraduate experience, beginning with all students who entered in the fall of 2006.

My objectivity may be open to question, but by every standard measure, universal study abroad appears to be a major success at Goucher. Prospective students and their families have responded positively to the change. Perhaps it was a coincidence, but the college had its largest-ever first-year class in 2006, and in several surveys in the years that followed, upwards of 75 percent said the requirement was one of the primary reasons they had chosen to attend. Indeed, for this and other reasons, applications and enrollments increased steadily over time; when I stepped down as president in June 2014, Goucher had about 25 percent more undergraduate students than it had in 2001, when I arrived. By the usual indices of test scores and high school GPAs, the students generally came with better credentials—and often with prior international interests and experiences.

Students from all demographic groups, majors, and academic profiles reported great satisfaction with their studies and other experiences abroad. Not surprisingly, they often cited "life-changing" experiences that had opened them to a broader worldview and supplemented what they had previously learned in the classroom, no matter the discipline. And they typically said that they had come to know and understand their own country—and perhaps themselves—better from a distance. Many were particularly adept at integrating their new overseas knowledge into their community-service activities in Baltimore or their home communities. At least 25 percent of those back from their first such opportunity began immediately to plan to go abroad again, either while still in college or upon graduation—hence our goofy statistic that 114 or 118 or 125 percent (depending upon the year) of Goucher students study abroad.

Conventional wisdom has it that short overseas experiences, like Goucher's ICAs, are not particularly meaningful. But having participated in three of them myself—in Cuba, Honduras, and India—I found that to be demonstrably untrue. To be sure, a semester in Copenhagen or Prague, Chengdu or Rio, could be more significant and profound, but a first international exposure, especially for students from suburban or inner-city backgrounds, could have a powerful, eye-opening impact. Many parents, at first reluctant to permit their children to go overseas for an extended period, changed their minds after seeing the results of a short-term program.

Why should it make a positive difference to require an overseas experience of undergraduates? Anecdotally, our students said that while they realized they could probably arrange to study abroad at almost any college or university these days, they felt more supported in their planning to do so at

Goucher; there was no risk that they would feel like oddballs for wanting to go far away, as some of their friends reported feeling at other places. At receptions I hosted in my home on campus every semester for returning students, and in other venues like the dining halls, the students eagerly exchanged stories and impressions and educated each other about where they had been. Even when some of their professors seemed reluctant to broach international issues in the classroom, they tended to force the matter themselves and bring the lessons of their experience into the discussion. One can only assume this sophistication will have a lasting impact on their job choices and their careers, not to mention their personal lives and, by extension, those of their families and their friends. And who can say what the long-term effect might be on the image and reputation of the United States around the world, as more and more American college-age students go abroad?

In addition, the requirement produced constructive pressure on some faculty members to become more international in their own outlook. A few who were initially skeptical, or at least quizzical, took the plunge to lead ICAs and became immediate converts. They too spoke of "life-changing" experiences overseas.

Obviously, there was still plenty to work on at the time that I stepped down as president in June 2014. Money remains a problem, for individual students and for the college. From the outset, we offered a stipend to every student for her or his first overseas experience, and students on need- or merit-based scholarships were permitted to take their aid with them overseas for a semester; by now, special-purpose supplementary scholarship funds are also available to subsidize costs for those in need. Not surprisingly, the overall cost to Goucher of study abroad remains a modest drain on net tuition revenue. (Considerably more than it would be if the experience were recommended, but not required? Hard to say, but unlikely.)

Some students returning from abroad, especially in potentially stressful settings like crisis-ridden Rwanda and Thailand, reported experiencing a severe reverse culture shock. They had trouble dealing with mundane everyday issues back on campus after being swept up in societies that had suffered extreme trauma and dealt with life-and-death matters in recent years. At their suggestion, Goucher briefly established a new theme-housing option, called "the globe," for students who wanted to think and talk about how study abroad had affected them psychologically, and for others who were feeling anxiety about an impending foray abroad. Last I knew, no clear and convincing assessment tool had yet been found or created to measure quantitatively the outcomes of study abroad, but a new software program called the "pocket anthropologist," developed by a long-time adjunct faculty member at Goucher, showed promise on the qualitative side.

Has universal study abroad achieved its original goal of making Goucher clearly distinctive among liberal arts colleges? That *Princeton Review*, for example, says that Goucher has the "most popular" study-abroad program in the country, among other kudos, would seem to support the notion. Nonetheless, a small faction of faculty members tried annually, or even semiannually, for a time to rescind the requirement—on the theory that faculty salaries could be increased significantly if less money were spent on the program—but they seemed to attract fewer votes every time. (In fact, now that universal study abroad is such an important part of Goucher's identity, to take the requirement away could have the opposite effect: reducing enrollments and hence threatening salaries and even faculty positions.) They will surely try again, and perhaps again, but no one seems to take the threat seriously. There is no mistaking Goucher for someplace else, and in today's hectic and confused college marketplace, that is an important advantage.

Since stepping down from the presidency, I have thought hard about whether I would have proceeded differently on the study-abroad requirement if I had it to do over again. These are my conclusions:

I would show less patience with the faculty's delays in approving the requirement. The skepticism was frankly suspect, and the arguments were constantly shifting and of little substance. Goucher's position would be even stronger if universal study abroad had been put in place two or three years earlier than it was.

I would seek advance funding, presumably from a higher-education-oriented foundation, for the early stages of the initiative, perhaps to cover several years' worth of the student stipends and to send faculty members abroad to prepare them to lead ICAs. (We did the latter, to a lesser extent than desirable, with private donations.) This might have neutralized some of the faculty opposition, especially on financial grounds, and would have built a larger corps of natural supporters.

I would worry less over whether Goucher's initiative was the "first" or the "only" such study-abroad requirement in the country—and avoid making boasts that could not be fully or cleanly supported. We wasted a bit of energy tilting at windmills over this point. An even smaller, religiously based institution in the Midwest claimed to have had such a program ahead of Goucher (although its website listed several ways that students could be excused from the obligation to go abroad). Some specialized units within large universities—e.g., business schools—pointed out that they also required study abroad or overseas internships, and a small Buddhist university in California (with only a single major) asserted that it had the idea first. We would have been better off had we arrived sooner at the simple formulation that we were the first traditional liberal arts college to adopt universal study abroad.

I would move more intentionally to tie the requirement to the recruitment of a large group of international students. The fact that all Goucher students study abroad makes them uniquely well prepared to welcome peers from other cultures and societies.

As overbearing as we at Goucher might have seemed to be in talking about this, I would do even more to promote the college's decision and its resulting distinctiveness. Because many of us tired of talking about it, perhaps fearing that we were boring our higher-education colleagues, we did not spread the word as far and as fast as we might have. It's not easy to get the appropriate constituencies to pay attention in an era of electronic information overload.

What I Wish I Had Known When I Started Even though I had previously been a dean of a professionally oriented school, I had no idea how long it could take to bring about substantive change in a small college. I obviously should not have been, but I was surprised by the willingness of some faculty members to use any tactic they could devise to delay decisions that seemed to me so simple and obvious. I also wish I had been given a much more formal and thorough advance briefing on the details of faculty governance at my institution; I was left to guess at the scope of responsibility of various committees, and hence may have seemed less respectful of shared governance than I really was.

What I Wish I Had Done When I Finished Not much, really, except perhaps to have cracked down sooner on tenure-track faculty members who took pre-tenure sabbaticals but never returned to teach, as they had agreed to do. And in general, I wish I had found a way to raise the standards for faculty sabbaticals; some of the presentations reporting on "research" done while away were rather light. I also wish I had found a way to persuade more faculty and staff members (whose contracts obviously did not require it) to be present on campus for evening and weekend activities when they could have mixed informally with students.

What I Wish I Had Not Done While in Office I wish I had been less of an easy touch for some people who campaigned to become members of the board of trustees—as much for their own purposes, it seemed, as for the good of the institution. This is a more widespread phenomenon, I believe, than is recognized. I wish I had recalled sooner the great dictum of Ronald Reagan: that he wanted an administration composed not of people for whom government service would be their highest accomplishment, but rather of people who had already accomplished much and were now going to bring that experience to bear for the good of the public.

How I Knew When to Stop When the small annoyances began to seem bigger, and I found myself biting my tongue more often than was healthy.

8 Complexity and Chicanery in Collegiate Athletics

Presidential Success and Intercollegiate Athletics

Robert H. Donaldson

A school's competitiveness in intercollegiate athletics is widely (and not very accurately) believed to contribute to increases in university fund-raising, alumni support, and applications. These factors, together with the enormous publicity surrounding the most competitive programs, often redound to the benefit of the presidents of these institutions.

Presidents whose athletics programs are prominent are lionized, and not only by their alumni. Presidents of universities that enjoy success in "big-time" athletics are more likely to rise to leadership in NCAA (and even in the reform-minded Knight Commission). But when athletics scandals arise, only rarely do they diminish a president's reputation, even in the institutions that set and enforce the rules and promote higher standards. The president usually stays in place, presiding as the investigation proceeds, letting others take the blame. Sometimes, the president will even move to an even more prestigious post.

On the whole, it appears to be much easier for presidents to look the other way when infractions arise than to rein in an erring athletics program. Those who do seek to impose controls, including attempting to curb out-of-control coaches, sometimes pay the price with their support eroded and their own jobs threatened.

The Challenges Presidents Face

The proposition that presidents should take control of intercollegiate athletics—and particularly of its governing body, the NCAA—has been strongly advocated for the last quarter century by the Knight Commission on Intercollegiate Athletics. Formed by the John S. and James L. Knight Foundation in October 1989 following a series of highly visible scandals in college sports, it sought to recommend a reform agenda that would stress academic values in the face of increasing commercialization. In the intervening years, presidents have indeed played the leading role in various "reform" movements in the NCAA. But whether "balance" between academics and athletics has been achieved is highly debatable, in light of reports that show that increases in per-student spending on athletics has far outpaced increases in spending for academic purposes.

Presidents face enormous pressures to maintain competitiveness, and this usually leads them to loosen constraints on athletics budgets. In 2005–2012 spending on football alone rose 70 percent, as did coaches' salaries in the five Bowl Championship Series (BCS) conferences. A kind of "arms race" in facilities and coaches' salaries impels athletics spending, even though several studies have shown that increased spending is not correlated with improved win-loss records. Not all schools can afford these budgetary binges, however, and the result is a growing gap between richer and poorer athletic conferences.

The inflation in coaches' salaries is especially worrisome. Rare are the major university presidents, including the most successful, who are paid more than their football or men's basketball coaches. Among the five conferences with the largest athletics budgets, median coaching salaries increased 54 percent in inflation-adjusted terms from 2005 to 2011. In 2014 the 25 highest-paid football coaches at public universities averaged $3.85 million in guaranteed money.

A Knight Foundation study of 25 Football Bowl Subdivision (FBS) schools found an inflation-adjusted 43 percent increase in spending on athletics in the period 2005–2012, while the same schools were spending only 6 percent more in median academic spending. In 2014, when football coach Bob Stoops received a new long-term contract guaranteeing $5.25 million a year, University of Oklahoma President David Boren hastened to assure the public that nearly all of Stoops's pay came from private sources and ticket revenues. At the same time, however, Boren stated, "I am deeply concerned for our national priorities when I see so much invested in athletics instead of in the education and training of the next generation."*

*Jim Baumbach, "Special Report: College Football Coaches' Salaries and Perks Are Soaring," *Newsday*, October 4, 2014.

Presidents can incur significant losses in alumni and community support if they fail to attract and retain a successful coach in a revenue sport, and successful seasons are often followed by renegotiated rich long-term contracts, full of bonus provisions. These have had little effect, however, on the virtual "free agency" market for college coaches. Aware of their market value and prominence, and tempted to cut corners to remain competitive, successful coaches occasionally appear almost to dare presidents to challenge their prerogatives in their respective programs.

The occasional president will take up the challenge. University of Cincinnati president Nancy Zimpher forced basketball coach Bob Huggins to resign in 2005 after the popular coach, long dogged by cases of academic failure by members of his teams, was arrested for driving under the influence. Zimpher was harshly criticized by many fans, but she survived the controversy and later became chancellor of the State University of New York. In neighboring Indiana, Indiana University president Myles Brand fired long-time coach Bobby Knight—a demigod on the IU campus—after first giving him a "zero tolerance" warning, for rough treatment of his players. Brand's highly publicized willingness to fire Knight in 2000 was thought to be a factor in his selection two years later as NCAA president.

Ironically, the man who holds the record for occupying the most university presidencies, E. Gordon Gee, tripped up and was forced to retire from his second stint as president of Ohio State University after joking about his failure to fire his very popular football coach, Jim Tressel, who was under investigation for lying to the NCAA about knowing that his players accepted various perks from grateful alumni. Asked at a press conference if he would fire Tressel, Gee replied, "No. Are you kidding? I'm just hopeful the coach doesn't fire me." Several months later, after the university had received a harsh punishment for the team's infractions and Coach Tressel had resigned, Gee himself was ushered out of his office. (In a rare case of "double-Teflon," Gee later became interim president of West Virginia University and Tressel was named president of Youngstown State University!)

"College football proved to be Gordon Gee's undoing," David Frohnmayer, president emeritus of the University of Oregon, was quoted as saying. He went on to observe that that college sports, "and particularly football, can get a president's administration into trouble faster than almost anything except having their hand in the till."*

*George Schroeder, "College Football Proved to Be Gordon Gee's Undoing," *USA Today*, June 4, 2013.

Presidents and trustees eager to move up in the athletics pecking order may attempt to move to a stronger conference, as Boise State, Texas Christian, Rutgers, and Temple have done in recent years. This "upward mobility" has contributed to unprecedented instability in conference memberships. Schools in major media markets are coveted, as revenues from television contracts have become vital to the fiscal health of conferences. Some schools that did not formerly play "big-time" (FBS) football have sought to build their reputations by building up their athletics programs, greatly increasing their spending on facilities and coaches. Recent examples include the University of Buffalo (formerly SUNY-Buffalo), the University of South Florida, and the University of Texas-San Antonio.

The arms race extends to the frenzied recruitment of the most competitive "student athletes"—even to the extent that presidents are willing to allow coaches to overlook the lack of academic qualifications of some top high school or junior college prospects. Although the NCAA has ostensibly toughened requirements for both initial and continuing eligibility, there are numerous press accounts of universities that cut corners in order to admit and retain players. Some have focused on the "basketball academies" that specialize in presenting admissible credentials for players, many of whom intend to join the ranks of the "one and done." Even in 33 academically selective colleges studied by William Bowen and Sarah Levin in their book *Reclaiming the Game*, recruited athletes are as much as four times more likely to gain admission than are other applicants with similar academic credentials, and the typical recruit is more likely to rank in the bottom third of the class than are non-athletes.

More numerous are the accounts of special academic programs that colleges have devised, presumably with the knowledge of their presidents, in which athletes can be protected from the normal grading standards that might cost them their continuing eligibility. The University of North Carolina is only the latest example—if a particularly egregious one because it featured a willing faculty collaborator who awarded passing grades for "no-show" students. Also all too familiar are cases of academic support staffs in the athletics program who steer students away from challenging courses and even write the papers for athletes who cannot avoid them. For years the media have exposed cases of athletes who attend college until their eligibility is exhausted—or even graduate—without attaining functional literacy.

Other than UNC, such top-ranked academic institutions as Stanford, the University of Southern California, and Michigan have been exposed for allowing these corner-cutting practices. Especially for presidents of public universities with large research budgets and high academic esteem, the temptation to be competitive in big-time college sports has been irresistible. Only six of the institutions ranked among the top 33 public universities by *U.S. News and World Report* do not belong to one of the top athletic conferences. Four of the six are in California, which poses an especially interesting case. It is clear that the two University of California schools with big-time programs (UCLA and Berkeley) are much better known to the public beyond California and to out-of-state applicants than UC campuses with smaller athletics programs but equivalent academic quality (such as the campuses in San Diego and Irvine).

The NCAA has prided itself on reforms that it says are intended to promote the welfare of student-athletes, but it has recently found itself under attack by some of those same students. Presidents have not put a stop to rampant commercialization of their athletic programs, but they have staunchly resisted letting athletes share in the revenues from product endorsements or from the use of star athletes' names and images. The early stirrings of a movement to declare that student-athletes are employees of universities, eligible to form a trade union and bargain for increased benefits, have evoked strong resistance from the NCAA and the presidents who lead it.

Particularly in football, which usually brings in the largest revenues, there is growing concern about the risks of life-altering injuries that students may suffer. In both football and men's basketball, universities have allowed themselves to be relegated to the position of developmental "minor" leagues for the National Football League (NFL) and National Basketball Association (NBA), often sharing in perpetuating the illusion that a lucrative professional career is a realistic ambition (even while failing to enlist students in legitimate academic majors that could lead to a more likely alternative career).

Athletics Scandals Involving Presidents Who Led the NCAA

Several of the very presidents who have held prominent leadership positions in the NCAA (and on its "reformist" Presidents Commission or on the Knight Commission) have presided over athletics programs that have been found guilty of committing major violations. I am aware of three former chairs of the NCAA Executive Committee, two members of the Knight Commission, and a chair of the Division I Board of Directors whose institutions were sanctioned for various infractions that occurred during their presidencies. Indeed, three of these individuals were mentioned in the media as likely candidates for the NCAA presidency itself (and another once headed one of the organization's presidential search committees)

In two of these cases, the presidents involved were selected for presidencies at more prestigious universities—one, while the investigation at his current school was still underway, and the other just one day before the four-person NCAA investigating team arrived at his campus. (In this latter case, the NCAA severely punished the university in question for violations in nine sports, declaring that the culture at the institution failed to place a high enough priority on compliance with NCAA rules and concluding that there was insufficient evidence of oversight or control by the institution of its athletics department.) Clearly, a clean record of institutional control of athletics is not a prerequisite for presidential success, and athletics scandals preclude neither a new presidency nor a high leadership post in the NCAA.

Indeed, the current NCAA president, Mark Emmert, oversaw an investigation of a cheating scandal involving the football team during the time he was chancellor of Louisiana State University. Only minor violations were found at the time, but subsequently (after Emmert had left LSU) further evidence came to light that seemed to indicate that a wider problem had in fact existed. Nor were Emmert's hands clean when it came to the issue of escalating costs of big-time football. During his time at LSU, coach Nick Saban's Tigers won the BCS national title, and Saban was awarded a contract that made him the highest-paid football coach in the US. At the same time, Emmert's compensation was increased, making him the highest-paid public university president. Chancellor Emmert voiced the view that success in athletics is vital to the school because sports can be a "window into the institution" for the public. "The image so many people carry from their exposure to athletics, especially football in a place like LSU, in many ways is the definition of the institution," he said.*

Personal Testimony: A President's Effort to Promote Reform

In my own presidencies at Fairleigh Dickinson University (1984–1990) and the University of Tulsa (1990–1996), I was an enthusiastic and active supporter of the movement to establish presidential control of the NCAA and to advance reforms that would restore integrity to intercollegiate athletics. FDU was unique among NCAA member schools in that its three New Jersey

*Brent Schrotenboer, "Digging into the Past of NCAA President Mark Emmert," *USA Today*, April 3, 2013.

campuses competed in two different divisions: the Rutherford and Teaneck-Hackensack campus teams were nonfootball members of Division I, and the Florham-Madison campus teams competed in Division III.

At a time of growing professionalism in college football, I considered myself—thanks to an unusual circumstance—a president who could unabashedly embrace professionalism. FDU's campuses were close to Giants Stadium, and we were approached by members of the Giants staff who sought our cooperation in dealing with a problem that plagued the NFL: the fact that a large proportion of its players had left their respective colleges without completing their bachelor's degrees. Professional careers were precarious, subject to sudden termination due to injury or waiver. Admirably, the Giants organization wanted its players to have meaningful career options when their playing days ended.

FDU and the Giants established a degree completion program that allowed Giants players to earn transfer credits in FDU classes, enabling them to graduate from their former institutions. Eventually, approximately one-third of the Giants players were enrolled at FDU, and some even continued their studies at the master's level. I could thus say that the Giants were the FDU football team. The relationship between the university and the Giants was amplified when the Giants established their training camp for a few years at the FDU Florham-Madison campus.

In coming to Tulsa, I became president of the smallest school that played Division I football. A private institution with high academic standards and just over 3,000 undergraduate students, Tulsa had struggled with the challenge of maintaining its eligibility for Division I competition. I inherited an NCAA investigation caused by attempts made by the prior administration to keep its D-I status by padding the rosters of some of its teams. The investigation resulted in a probation penalty that banned Tulsa from postseason competition for a year.

Tulsa was also searching for a new conference home. It was a longtime (and highly competitive) member of the Missouri Valley Conference, but it was the only MVC school that continued to play Division I football. Scheduling a football season as an independent was a daunting task, and so the university sought and found a new conference home in the newly expanded Western Athletic Conference. A 16-team league in 1994, the WAC was the largest Division I conference in the country. Tulsa was placed, much to its liking, in a "quadrant" that included three other selective private Southwestern schools (Rice, Southern Methodist, and Texas Christian). But the enlarged conference family did not long endure, as the presidents of eight of the schools secretly met and agreed in 1999 to form a new, professedly more prestigious conference (the Mountain West). Since that time, 24 more schools have entered or left the WAC. The most obvious victim of rampant conference realignment, the WAC announced in 2012 that it would no longer be able to sponsor football. As he departed, longtime commissioner Karl Benson observed of the oft-departing members, "The club that they're currently in doesn't have the social status that perhaps another club has. As a result, they want to be part of this other club."*

Later Tulsa became a member of Conference USA, and despite its size and its limited athletics budget, it won more conference championships during its tenure there than any other conference member. The university's success in athletics came at a time when its academic reputation was growing, and it was climbing steadily in the *U.S. News* rankings. Maintaining Division I status was expensive, and in the early 1990s the board of trustees studied the option of becoming a Division III member, where it would join many other selective smaller private colleges.

But—especially in Oklahoma—a university's visibility and reputation may depend on the visibility of its athletics program. At the time I was president, the local newspaper had 16 sportswriters and 1 part-time education writer. Despite several efforts to gain national publicity for academic programs, the one occasion during my six years as president when Tulsa garnered a headline in the *New York Times* was in March 1994, when—during its centennial year—it made its first appearance in the NCAA men's basketball "sweet 16." The headline read, "Tiny Tulsa Prepares for First Sweet 16," and the story quoted my (rather exasperated) remark: "We've been trying all year to highlight things within the university to be proud of. The team is just another way of developing pride in the institution within the larger Tulsa community."

I had made it clear when I arrived as president that the university would not tolerate variable standards for student athletes. I informed the coaches that no student would be admitted as a member of an athletics team who was not capable of graduating from the university. The men's basketball coach tested me on this vow in my first months in office. Despite a winning record, he was dismissed as coach a few months later. And I introduced a new

*Jake Bullinger, "How Conference Realignment Wiped WAC Football Off the Map," SI.com, August 21, 2012, https://www.si.com/college-football/2012/08/21/wac-football-demise.

strategic plan to strengthen academic standards that included, among other things, the elimination of the physical education major. The PE major featured, among similar offerings, a course on "theory of basketball." The upgraded academic standards paid off; freshman athletes admitted in the last year of my presidency graduated at a rate that ranked the school in the top 10 of Division I-A institutions.

The basketball coaching vacancy was filled by Orlando "Tubby" Smith, then an assistant coach at the University of Kentucky, who would later become that school's head coach and win a national championship. Recognizing that the "arms race" in coaching contracts had gotten out of hand, I arranged that Tubby's contract (and that of our other coaches) would contain only one provision for paying a bonus beyond base salary: coaches would earn a bonus if two-thirds of eligible players on their teams graduated on time.

I regret to say that these reforms did not last beyond my presidency. The physical education major was reintroduced as "exercise and sports science" (though the text for the introductory course was entitled "Introduction to Physical Education"). The coaches' contracts reverted to the usual pattern, with salaries higher than ever and with abundant bonuses for athletics (not academic) success. And Tulsa has moved up in the hierarchy of big-time conferences, joining the former "Big East"—now the American Athletic Conference—in the company of the then-reigning national champion in men's and women's basketball, among other luminaries.

What I Wish I Had Known When I Started I had not had any direct exposure to boards of trustees before the first of my two private university presidencies. Consequently, I was rather naïve about how much of my time needed to be spent in the "care and feeding" of members of the board. By the time I began my second presidency, I was well aware of the excellent workshops available through the Association of Governing Boards of Universities and Colleges, and I asked then-president Tom Ingram to conduct one for our board during the first few months of my presidency. Through no fault of Tom or the AGB, however, I learned that the members of this large board—almost all of whom were local and lacking experience with private universities—required much more orientation and nurturing than I was aware. Held at arm's length by my long-serving predecessor, the board was not able to readily distinguish between supportive counsel and micromanagement.

What I Wish I Had Done When I Finished I announced my resignation from my first presidency upon my acceptance of my appointment to the second one, and the board soon appointed an interim president (later made permanent) who was able to assume the duties immediately. Consequently, my actual departure from my post came more quickly than I had expected, and I was not able to spend the time with my top staff or with my successor that might have helped them all to ease the transition. Neither in this instance nor in the case of my departure from my second presidency did circumstances allow an opportunity for me to impart to my successor information and advice that might have benefited both him and the institution. While I recognize that presidential successions may be inherently awkward, and that my image of the passing of the baton may have been naïve, I nevertheless wish I had had the opportunity to try to make it smoother.

What I Wish I Had Not Done While in Office I began both of my presidencies when my universities were in a distressed condition, and I was confronted almost immediately with the need to find the best people to fill key vice presidencies. By the time I began my second presidency, I had learned how important it was to make these choices wisely and deliberately. In fact, I had already identified people who I thought would be excellent in the roles of chief academic officer and chief student support officer. Rather than move to engineer a "search" that would bring them in quickly, I succumbed to the temptation to allow a committee of faculty, trustees, and students to engage in a full-blown search process. In neither case did the committee advance the candidate I preferred. Worse still, the candidates they did advance either bombed on their campus visits or chose not to accept the offer—and the searches extended into a second year. Desperate to fill the vacancies, I wound up settling for individuals who were not ideal for the jobs. If I had it to do again, I would have insisted on forming my own team from the outset.

What I Wish I Didn't Know When I Finished I came to my presidencies from a background of teaching and research. As I had when I was a dean and a provost, I continued as president to teach at least one class a year. I consider myself first and foremost a teacher and a scholar—as evidenced by the fact that I returned to full-time faculty status after my 20-year stretch ("sentence"?) as an administrator. During my time in administration, however, I encountered far too many talented members of the faculty who considered committee service or participation in governance to be a wasteful distraction from their real passions.

Consequently, it happened far too often that some of the most persistent faculty participants in governance were individuals who no longer found satisfaction or reward in teaching and scholarships. Commonly, these were individuals whose initial bright hopes and promise had been extinguished by one or another disappointment or failure. (They were brilliantly described by E. J. Jensen's 1995 article in *Change* magazine entitled "The Bitter Groves of Academe.") I have enormous regret—not just personal but professional—that the best and the brightest of our university faculty too rarely take a leading role in faculty self-governance.

How I Knew When to Stop When the allure of returning to full-time teaching and research was too strong to resist.

"That's My Budget Running Up and Down the Field"

Gerald B. Kauvar, Stephen Joel Trachtenberg, and E. Gordon Gee

A university in the South is building a "lazy river" to enhance its ability to recruit star high school athletes, according to its athletics director. Athletics at the institution needed $22.4 million from student fees to cover its $59.6 million spending in 2016. Each undergraduate taking a full course load pays a $344-a-year athletic fee. The university has had no remarkable athletic success in major sports. To bolster its athletic prowess the university has plans for $25 million in athletic upgrades, including the lazy river, which will cost at least $1 million.

The institution's president discussed the importance athletics play in building a great university. "If you're a state university in the South and you want to be taken seriously, there are several things you do. You do a fair amount of research. You award a fair number of PhDs. And you play Division 1 football." Alas, he's probably neither wrong nor alone.

We're not picking on this particular institution except as an example; the subordination of academic excellence to athletic success is all too typical of higher education in the US.

Here are some facts about the university—it is the number 5-ranked public university in its state. (We know rankings aren't a gold standard, but they are what we have.) The institution is number 172 among national universities. Its programs rank as follows: biology, 188th; chemistry, 117th; computer science, 90th; mathematics, 134th; physics, 83rd; business, 150th; engineering doctorates: 91st. Among top public schools, it is 93rd. High school counselors rank it 220th.

Faculty salaries are mostly average or below; it ranks 99th in total research and development for 2015; 127th in 2014 (the most recent data available) in federal obligations. After graduating, its students earn lower salaries than average for its institutional type in its state and lower than average for students at four-year public colleges.

What else, we wonder, might the annual $24 million subsidy to athletics be used for at the university? For starters, how about raising faculty salaries, reducing the 30:1 ratio of students to faculty, reducing the vast number of courses that enroll more than 40 students? Or endowing chairs to attract top-tier faculty, boosting financial aid, devoting more seed money to research that might lead to grants, creating centers of excellence?

What if the money were spent on, just to pick a letter, academic interests starting with "p"—poetry, philosophy, political science, physics, psychology, piccolo playing, painting—rather than players or star high school athletes. Instead of athletics, how about accounting, advertising, aerospace engineering, anthropology, archeology, architecture, applied mathematics, art, audiology, and Asian studies? Rather than football, why not film, finance, fine arts, foreign languages and literature, forensic science, French?

If those or other investments were made in the primary academic mission of the institution, board members might then be able to invoke the former president of the University of Oklahoma, George Lynn Cross, who argued before a budget committee, "I would like to build a university of which the football team could be proud."

The institution we describe is not alone; it is all too typical. But it does seem to have escaped the sort of scandals that have darkened the reputations of otherwise outstanding institutions. Did the president and board at Baylor learn nothing from the Penn State debacle? Did Penn State learn nothing from Southern Methodist University? Have colleges learned nothing from Florida State, the Naval Academy, the Universities of Southern California, Miami, and North Carolina?

Failures of academic oversight led to several of the scandals listed; they are some of the most damaging to institutional integrity. Faculty governance mechanisms were extremely weak or nonexistent. Gut courses were designed for athletes and taught by faculty, many of whom probably should not have been hired in the first place. Why were they hired? Why was there so little oversight of tutors? Were the faculty looking the other way or shut out of the process?

Boards and presidents must lead institutions to greater control over athletic programs. Some of the measures they will have to take to refocus the primacy of academic excellence and to ensure integrity in academic and athletic programs will alienate some alumni and donors unless they too are invested in its outcomes from the beginning.

A much stronger voice for faculty in overseeing intercollegiate athletics is imperative for restoring the creation, preservation, and transmission of knowledge that are the duties of institutions of higher education. Faculty must be involved in developing the practices that will restore confidence in intercollegiate athletics and its subordinate role in higher education.

If boards and presidents and faculty bodies do not undertake the effort to reform the governance of intercollegiate athletics, it is likely that Congress will meddle—which would probably diminish the healthy diversity of our colleges and universities by attempting to force us to focus on training rather than education.

9 Dealing with Claims and Counterclaims of Unwanted Sexual Contact

Allen L. Sessoms

Issues related to unwanted sexual contact are redefining life on college campuses all over the United States and, in fact, the much of the Western world. The issue has become fraught and often cannot be discussed or addressed dispassionately. In fact, it is probably the most "hot-button" issue on college campuses today. This wasn't always the case. In the past, incidences of unwanted sexual contact were often downplayed or in many cases simply ignored by senior administrators. Many suggested that it was something that was "part of life on campus, and in America" and could not be separated from the culture of society in general. In other words, "it wasn't our problem."*

This attitude has complex origins. In many ways it was based on the view that women are "less equal" and in some cases "less valuable" than their male counterparts. One only needs to note that, in the US, women did not have the right to vote on a national scale until 1920. To this day women still struggle to control their reproductive rights in the face of a paternalistic, and in my view totally wrong, assumption that they need to be protected from themselves. These attitudes are finally being recognized as undermining any credible academic community. It is also increasingly clear that such attitudes jeopardize the safety and well-being of everyone on a college campus, independent of gender. A few institutions, mostly women's colleges, took significant steps to confront this problem years ago. One of those places was Antioch College.

Antioch College, 1991

In 1991 Antioch College introduced an "Ask First" policy for affirmative consent for any sexual encounters, including kissing an acknowledged boyfriend or girlfriend. The policy was immediately parodied on shows like

*Associated Press, "German Lawmakers Approve 'No Means No' Rape Law," July 7, 2016.

Saturday Night Live as unworkable and generally unenforceable. A *New York Times* opinion piece written during this period pointed out the difficulty of this approach: "But adolescence, particularly the college years, is a time of experimentation, and experimentation means making mistakes." The piece further opines, "Adolescents will always make mistakes—sometimes serious ones. Telling them what's unacceptable, in no uncertain terms, is fine. But legislating kisses won't save them from themselves."*

In some sense the opinion writers were correct. You can't legislate morality. But in the ensuing years it has come to be recognized that setting boundaries and providing guidelines for sexual contact are absolutely essential to promoting a safe environment for all on our campuses. Such guidelines also try to clearly define what unwanted sexual contact is. This has proven to be not only controversial, but also, in the minds of many, arbitrary. Adjudicating between parties in a dispute can be wrenching and seen as unfair, and it can lead to public debate and lawsuits. The role of leaders is to make any determination as fair and as transparent to the parties, and to the community at large, as possible. Unfortunately, fairness to each party sometimes conflicts with the desire for transparency. In any case, it is important to never exhibit neglect or, worse, a disregard for the importance of the individuals involved in any dispute. Neglect is unacceptable under any circumstances and can lead to exceptional damage to individuals and institutions.

Deal with All Complaints

Many college and university leaders argue that they are responsible for investigating complaints only if they occur on campus. This is a misconception. If a complaint involves a student and it occurs anywhere within the college's jurisdiction, you must deal with it. A recent case at Kansas State University clearly illustrates this point. As reported on July 5, 2016, in *The New York Times*, two students informed the university that they had been raped in separate instances in 2014 and 2015 at off-campus fraternity houses. The students, in a federal lawsuit filed in April 2016, said their complaints were ignored. Kansas State responded, in part, that it was not legally responsible for reports of student-on-student rape at off-campus fraternity houses or events, even though the fraternities were sanctioned by the university.

*"'Ask First' at Antioch," *New York Times*, October 11, 1993; Robert Shibley, "Antioch's Infamous Sexual Assault Policy," Foundation for Individual Rights in Education, June 15, 2007; Nicholas Mills, "How Antioch College Got Rape Right 20 Years Ago," *Daily Beast*, December 10, 2014.

The federal government, in a letter in support of the students, said that the university's policy was "incorrect" and that Kansas State must investigate off-campus assaults.

Everyone at a college or university should understand that it is the obligation of the institution to protect its students no matter where they are within the college setting. There can be no safe havens for sexual assault. The problem with fraternities is that alcohol abuse is often rampant. In the case of the two women discussed here, both had drunk excessively and were incapacitated at the time of the alleged assaults.*

Consensual Sex without Parental Guidance

When I was serving as the president of a certain university, a situation arose in which a female student athlete got pregnant with her boyfriend—not an uncommon phenomenon. Our student affairs staff and our counselors ensured that the student received the health information she needed, but of course we could not inform her parents—that was a decision the student would have to make. Fortunately, the young woman did notify her parents, who apparently insisted that she get an abortion. They then scolded me, and the institution, for not providing "proper information" about safe sex to their daughter. The young woman returned to school the next semester and promptly got pregnant a second time with the same young man. As far as I could tell, her parents never discussed the young woman's motives with her. However, her family threatened to sue the institution and me personally for being "negligent," again, for not "educating" their daughter appropriately! The legal case did not progress, but one wonders from where the expectations derive in situations like this. In any case, leaders must be aware that those expectations are there. This fact should inform the type, and intensity, of required educational programs on sexual health that should be a part of the orientation of all students, male and female, when first entering college.

In many instances neither young women nor young men are prepared for the social environment that is central to the college experience. This is particularly true of sexual encounters. For many reasons, families are unwilling or unable to discuss these issues before sending their children off and simply assume that they "would never do something like that" or that

*Stephanie Saul, "U.S. Urges Kansas State to Heed Reports of Off-Campus Rape," *New York Times*, July 5, 2016; Jake New, "U.S.: Kansas State Must Investigate Off-Campus Assaults," *Inside Higher Ed*, July 6, 2016.

"someone else will take care of educating them appropriately." This clearly presents a dilemma for leaders. In any case, that "someone else" is expected to be the institution. You do not want your students to learn this type of information through trial and error or through tragic circumstances.

Alcohol and Substance Abuse

Lack of knowledge among students is also apparently the norm for substance abuse, including abuse of alcohol and drugs. There is now ample evidence of a correlation between substance abuse and unwanted sexual encounters on college campuses. A recent study by Georgetown University of the sexual climate on campus documented that about 50 percent of unwanted sexual penetrations at Georgetown occurred when the victim (almost always, but not always, female) was incapacitated. This is about the average for American Association of Universities (AAU) institutions nationally. Many young people come to campus unaware of the dangers of alcohol and substance abuse and of the reality that not everyone who attends college is honest or honorable or has any idea about responsible social or sexual behavior.*

All leaders of colleges and universities must accept the fact that students on their campuses (and almost certainly some faculty and staff) are abusing alcohol and drugs. According to a report by the US Substance Abuse and Mental Health Services Administration (SAMHSA), 1.2 million college students drink alcohol on a typical day and more than 703,000 use marijuana. This is an issue that also must be "owned" by college leadership; it cannot be swept under the rug by devices such as honor codes or codes of behavior. This, to some extent, leads to blaming the victim. No one should draw a causal relationship between substance abuse and unwanted sexual contact. There is never an excuse for forcing someone to have sex or taking advantage of someone who cannot defend him- or herself.†

* Georgetown University, "Report of the Georgetown University Sexual Assault and Misconduct Climate Survey," June 16, 2016; Association of American Universities, "AAU Climate Survey on Sexual Assault and Sexual Misconduct (2015)" (Washington, DC: AAU, 2015); Massachusetts Executive Office of Public Safety and Security, *Analysis of College Campus Rape and Sexual Assault Reports, 2000–2011* (Boston: Executive Office of Public Safety and Security, 2012).

† Center for Behavioral Health Statistics and Quality, *Behavioral Health Trends in the United States: Results from the 2014 National Survey on Drug Use and Health* (Rockville, MD: Substance Abuse and Mental Health Services Administration, 2015); Rosanna Xia, "1.2 Million College Students Drink Alcohol on a Typical Day, and More Than 703,000 Use Weed," *Los Angeles Times*, May 26, 2016; Robin Wilson, "Why Campuses Can't Talk about Alcohol When It Comes to Sexual Assault," *Chronicle of Higher Education*, September 4, 2014.

Blaming the Victim

Leaders must begin with the assumption the victim is never to blame. Colleges sometimes get this wrong. The example of the Worcester Polytechnic Institute (WPI) is instructive. "WPI says victim is partly responsible for assault"—this was a headline in *The Boston Globe* on June 7, 2016. The case revolves around a female student who reported that she was raped while on a study abroad trip to Puerto Rico in 2012. She asserted that a security guard who had been hired by WPI to protect her and her fellow students raped her. In response to a civil suit filed by the victim, lawyers for WPI argued in court documents that the victim engaged in risky behavior, including excessive drinking, on the night that a security guard at her university-leased apartment lured her to the roof and attacked her. The school also said that the woman disregarded instructions and training about how to protect herself from harm. The blowback was dramatic.

WPI students were up in arms after reading the *Globe* report. Almost immediately, WPI President Laurie Leshin sent an email to the campus community saying that the university's former insurance company was responsible for the line of reasoning. She stated, "WPI strongly believes that the person responsible for this rape is the rapist. And he is in prison."

In the June 24, 2016, *New York Times Sunday Review,* Laura Niemi and Liane Young note, "In a recent series of studies, we found that the critical factor lies in a particular set of moral values. Our findings, published on Thursday in the *Personality and Social Psychology Bulletin,* show that the more strongly you privilege loyalty, obedience, and purity—as opposed to values such as care and fairness—the more likely you are to blame the victim."

This is, in my view, one of the problems with honor codes or other codes of conduct. They assume that certain types of behaviors are forbidden and that everyone who attends their institutions accepts those strictures. For example, at Baylor University the sexual conduct policy reads, "Baylor will be guided by the biblical understanding that human sexuality is a gift from God and that physical intimacy is to be expressed in the context of marital fidelity. Thus, it is expected that Baylor students, faculty, and staff will engage in behaviors consistent with this understanding of human sexuality." Thus, if a student is raped after engaging in such activities, the student must be at least partly at fault. This, in my view, simply denies human nature and wrongly transfers responsibility to the victim. Also, what about the culpability of the rapist? I believe that Baylor hid behind this code for years while ignoring the complaints of rape filed by students against varsity football players. In fact, Ken Starr, the since-removed chancellor and president of Baylor, claimed that rapes did not happen on the Baylor campus, denying evidence that at least half of the reported rapes occurred in Baylor-owned facilities. Laura E. Seay, a Baylor graduate and an assistant professor at Colby College, is quoted in *The Chronicle of Higher Education* saying, "There's a sense that Baylor is a good place with good students and that this kind of thing doesn't happen here. The tendency has been to engage in victim blaming, suggesting that sexual-assault survivors must have done something to cause their assault. But it's evident that assaults have been happening on the Baylor campus just as they have happened on most other campuses, and we can't bury our heads in the sand any longer."

Another example is the Brigham Young University Honor Code, which states, in part, "As a matter of personal commitment, the faculty, administration, staff, and students . . . will:

> Live a chaste and virtuous life
> Abstain from alcoholic beverages, tobacco, tea, coffee, and substance abuse."

As a statement of principle, this honor code may be great but, as we have seen, given the realities of college life, it appears unreasonable to expect this to even be the norm. It also does not help the students.

As recounted by Sarah Brown in *The Chronicle of Higher Education*, "Mindy Weston, a graduate student at Brigham Young U., was raped just before she enrolled there as an undergraduate two decades ago: 'I didn't tell anybody for years. I knew that I would be judged. I knew that I would be blamed. And I knew the story would be twisted.'" Brown goes on to report that "when it came to light two months ago (in April 2016) that BYU officials routinely investigated students (her emphasis) who reported sexual assaults for potential violations of the Honor Code, Ms. Weston understood how betrayed the students felt; she saw it as another example of how Mormon culture—and a university whose mission is inextricable from that culture—could unintentionally blame and silence victims."

One of the keys to addressing these situations is to educate everyone, upon entry to the institution and continually thereafter, about the need to exercise moderation, to look after one another, and to embrace the problem as one that must be discussed and studied and acted upon for everyone's safety. The institution is also responsible for putting in place response mechanisms that work to protect students and are responsive to the needs of victims and their associates.*

When Is Rape Rape?

The definitions of unwanted sexual encounters are rapidly evolving. The expectation that colleges and universities will educate their students, faculty, and staff on these definitions, and will have in place appropriate consequences when "norms" are violated, is being written into statute at the federal and state levels. This goes well beyond Title IX.†

In some outrageous cases, such as the Stanford University swimmer who raped an unconscious young woman behind a dumpster on campus and was stopped in the act by passersby, the facts are clear. What is not clear is whether Stanford administrators "did enough" to protect young women on its campus, even though, in this case, the victim was not a student. Was information about sexual assault widely disseminated and discussed? Were students, faculty, and staff trained to assess situations of potential hazard and to respond appropriately? How should responsibility be defined in cases where the victim is a nonstudent and the perpetrator is a student, or vice versa?‡

A different type of situation occurred at Columbia University in 2013. A student, Emma Sulkowicz, alleged that she was raped by a fellow student, Paul Nungesser. To bring attention to her case, Sulkowicz carried a mattress around with her to class her entire senior year and became a rallying point, nationally and internationally, for campus assault victims. Nungesser was cleared of the charges by Columbia's internal process and by the New York

*Laura Krantz, "WPI Says Rape Victim Partly Responsible for Assault," *Boston Globe*, June 7, 2016; Scott Jaschik, "WPI, Facing Suit, Accused of Blaming Rape Victim," *Inside Higher Ed*, June 7, 2016; Scott Jaschik, "WPI Denies Blaming Student for Being Raped," *Inside Higher Ed*, June 8, 2016; Scott Jaschik, "Colleges Sued by Students for Negligence Turn to 'Victim Blaming' in Defense," *Inside Higher Ed*, June 17, 2016; Laura Niemi and Liane Young, "Who Blames the Victim?" *New York Times*, June 24, 2016; Sarah Brown, "A University's Struggle With Honor," *Chronicle of Higher Education*, June 17, 2016; Baylor University, "Sexual Conduct Policy," May 15, 2015; Katherine Mangan, "A Wave of Sexual-Assault Cases Kindles Anger on Baylor's Campus," *Chronicle of Higher Education*, March 27, 2016; Brigham Young Univeristy, "Honor Code Statement," November 9, 2015.

†Juliet Eilperin, "Biden and Obama Rewrite the Rulebook on College Sexual Assaults," *Washington Post*, July 3, 2016.

‡Nick DeSantis, "Stanford Says It Did 'Everything Within Its Power' in High-Profile Rape Case," *Chronicle of Higher Education*, June 6, 2016; Fernanda Zamudio-Suaréz, "Outrage over a Stanford Rape Case Might Change How Some Colleges Respond to Sexual Violence," *Chronicle of Higher Education*, June 8, 2016.

Police Department. Nevertheless, Sulkowicz persisted in her protest, even carrying a mattress across the stage during her graduation ceremony. In this case Nungesser claims that he is the victim of false claims and has garnered a number of supporters to his cause. Nungesser sued Columbia, its board of trustees, President Lee Bollinger, and one of its professors, claiming that the school failed to protect him from Sulkowicz's "harassment campaign" even after he had been cleared.*

The victim always defines unwanted sexual contact. No matter what the circumstances, if she or he does not assent to the contact, it is unwanted. How "assent" is defined, however, has become a topic of much debate, especially among students. When is "yes" clear? Is it defined only by verbal affirmation or are voluntary actions enough to be definitive? Does acquiescence constitute "yes" when there is every indication, at the time, that the contact is welcomed? Can acquiescence be "removed" retroactively, say the next morning when, perhaps, second thoughts creep in? How does one fold in the "fog" of alcohol and or drugs into consent?†

Yale

An example of this situation is that of the Yale basketball player, Jack Montague, who was expelled on February 10, 2016, near the end of his senior year, for having nonconsensual sex with his sometime girlfriend. The couple had consensual sex on one occasion, but on a subsequent one she said that did not give her consent to have sexual intercourse. He claimed she did. His accuser stated that she tried to communicate this verbally and, according to an impartial fact-finder, "pushed him, but not very forcefully." Montague, who had several drinks that night, was not aware that the woman did not consent, according to the complaint that he and his family filed against Yale, charging breach of contract and defamation. How much did alcohol consumption contribute to Montague's inability to process the not very forceful verbal and nonverbal "no"? How much did the previous encounter

*Cathy Young, "Did 'Mattress Girl' Tell the Truth? Not Very Likely," Minding the Campus, June 4, 2015; Alexandra Svokos, "Students Bring Out Mattresses In Huge 'Carry That Weight' Protest Against Sexual Assault," *Huffington Post*, October 29, 2014; Michael E. Miller, "Rape Hoax Posters Plastered around Columbia University in Backlash against Alleged Rape Victim," *Washington Post*, May 22, 2015; Sarah Kaplan, "Columbia University Sued by Male Student in 'Carry That Weight' Rape Case," *Washington Post*, April 24, 2015.

†Robin Wilson, "'Yes' to Sex? Students Consider What That Looks and Sounds Like," *Chronicle of Higher Education*, May 18, 2016; Katherine Mangan, "As Consent Rules Change, Big Questions Come to the Surface, *Chronicle of Higher Education*, May 18, 2016.

color the views of both the accused and the accuser? How much did Yale influence the accuser in order to burnish its image of not tolerating non-consensual sexual activity on its campus? Opinions vary. The outcome of Montague's lawsuit is pending as of this writing.*

Athletes and Sexual Assault

This brings us to the issue of athletes and sexual assault. Recently, we have been inundated with stories of star varsity athletes being found guilty of rape and other forms of unwanted sexual contact. The recent cases of Baylor and Vanderbilt football players immediately come to mind. However, the problem is not just with varsity athletes at NCAA Division I schools. A recent study by researchers at the University of South Florida, North Carolina State University, Northern Arizona University, and Emory University found that "54.3 percent of the intercollegiate and recreational athletes and 37.9 percent of non-athletes had engaged in sexually coercive behaviors—almost all of which met the legal definition of rape." Sexual coercion is defined as "any unwanted oral, vaginal or anal penetration as a result of verbal or physical pressure, including rape." Further, they go on to say, "As high as these numbers are, they may actually underrepresent the rates of sexual coercion, since the study relied on self-reported behavior." This suggests that leaders of all kinds of institutions, whether they have big-time athletic programs or just recreational sports teams, must be attuned to a problem that may be epidemic on their campuses.

Are there ways to begin addressing this problem? Almost certainly yes. The study suggests that the behavior is driven largely by negative attitudes towards women and misperceptions about rape and consent. What is required is an educational effort for all students, both male and female, to eliminate stereotypes about women and men, efforts to change behaviors that might be suggestive of an openness to sexual encounters when there may be none, and an effort to change campus culture to one that values all of its members and insists on absolute respect in any and all circumstances. This can only happen if the efforts are driven from the top.†

*Marc Tracy, "Expelled Basketball Player Sues Yale," *New York Times*, June 9, 2016; Susan Svrluga, "Expelled Yale Basketball Captain: Alleged Sexual Assault Was Consensual," *Washington Post*, March 14, 2016; Dan Wetzel, "Complete System Failure: Everyone Loses in Yale's Mishandling of Alleged Sexual Assault Case," Yahoo Sports, March 16, 2016.

†Belinda-Rose Young, Sarah L. Desmarais, Julie A. Baldwin, and Rasheeta Chandler, "Sexual Coercion Practices among Undergraduate Male Recreational Athletes, Undergraduate Athletes, and Non-Athletes," *Violence Against Women* 23, no. 7 (May 30, 2016): 795–812; Jake New,

What I Wish I Had Known When I Started I wish I had known the scope of the presidency. As President Barack Obama has often said of a much loftier presidency, it's something you have to experience. It really can't be described. You have to grow into it.

What I Wish I Had Done When I Finished I wish I had taken at least a year to decompress and reassess what is important in life.

What I Wish I Had Not Done While in Office I wish I had not moved as quickly as the trustees asked me to. They said they wanted a "change agent," but if they really wanted rapid change, it would have already occurred. What they meant was "change without backlash." They wanted "change my way, not yours."

What I Wish I Didn't Know When I Finished I wish I didn't know that institutions cannot care about individuals, including presidents. Once you are gone, in most cases it's as if you hardly ever existed.

How I Knew When to Stop I knew when to stop when I realized that I was being defined by the institution rather than by myself. People knew me for what I did rather than who I was.

"More Than Half of Athletes in Study Say They Engaged in Sexual Coercion," *Inside Higher Ed*, June 3, 2016; North Carolina State University, "Study: Attitudes toward Women Key in Higher Rates of Sexual Assault by Athletes," press release, June 2, 2016; Jennifer McGovern and Patrick Murray, "Consent Communication: What Does It Mean for Student Athletes?" Monmouth University, January 5, 2016.

10 The Complexities of Shared Governance and Freedom of Speech

Ben Trachtenberg

Think back to your first love. No, not your sweetheart from summer camp. I mean the first love of all academic administrators—the classroom. Back when you were a professor, when you worried more about lectures and publications than budgets and meetings, chances are you had a few smart colleagues. They knew a lot about biology, psychology, geology, archaeology. Chaucer, Cleopatra, Heidegger, Confucius, Curie. Always scribbling, cranking out scholarship. You may even still see some of them around campus.

Let me suggest that those bookish folk still know a lot of stuff, at least some of which may be useful to you in the president's office. They may not understand much about the care and feeding of trustees, but they know a great deal about their areas of expertise. And at a college or university of any size, the faculty collectively cover a wide expanse of human knowledge. Applied correctly, this knowledge can save you time, improve your decision making, and win faculty buy-in.

If you are adopting a new course registration system, an operations research expert at the business school can offer suggestions based on her study of queuing theory. Law professors can help craft student discipline policies that protect due process while also placating the Department of Education. Education faculty can report on whether scheduling additional Friday classes is more likely to reduce Thursday-night drunkenness or boost Friday-morning absenteeism.

Beyond their scholarly foci, faculty can offer insights based on their institutional service and outside activities. A physics professor might serve on a National Science Foundation committee promoting the advancement of women in science. Medical faculty might review proposals concerning research on human subjects. Others might pursue projects related to academic freedom, entrepreneurship, online instruction, intellectual property, and countless other topics that demand the president's attention from time to time. At least occasionally, these faculty—if you can identify them and convince them to serve—can help administrators make smart decisions. When administrative decisions will affect faculty directly, this sort of faculty involvement is especially valuable—and even more so for decisions that affect the faculty's core identity as a group of scholars empowered to pursue research of their own choosing and to run their classrooms as they see fit.

As it happens, regulation of campus speech—particularly instruction—is of tremendous interest to the faculty. Administrators should approach the topic with great caution. Too much regulation risks accusations of censorship, not to mention First Amendment litigation at public institutions. Too little regulation risks Title IX proceedings, in addition to more general complaints of indifference to those oppressed by harassing speech.

At the University of Missouri, free speech has been a hot topic lately. In November 2015, the UM system president and the Columbia campus ("Mizzou") chancellor resigned on the same day, in the wake of student protests concerning the university's racial climate. (The events were vastly more complicated and involved several other issues unrelated to race, but this summary will do for now.) Some observers denounced the student protestors for dragging the university's name through the mud, flinging broad-brush accusations of racism, and making unreasonable demands. Others applauded the students for their idealism, their strength of conviction, and their perseverance in the face of intimidation—as well their tangible successes. (One student launched a hunger strike to increase the pressure on the president to resign, others camped out on the quad for days in solidarity, and then much of the football team promised to boycott games until the demand was met. The president quit before the next game.) Reporters from New York and Los Angeles flew to Columbia to cover the spectacle. In one particularly unfortunate moment, a professor shouted at a student and then pushed his camera in an effort to stop him from approaching and filming student protestors, and the confrontation became national news. She would ultimately be fired as a result.

Whatever one's opinion of the tactics and message of the protestors, one cannot deny the sudden national interest in how speech is regulated at Mizzou.

Appointed interim chancellor in the aftermath of the resignations, Hank Foley knew he had free speech problems. Journalists worldwide were questioning how the home of the world's first (and best!) school of journalism could allow students to create a "no-media" zone on the quad, as well as how a communications professor ended up in an argument that got so out of hand. Meanwhile, black students—among others—continued to face hateful speech, including criminal threats. Events on the quad had made at least one thing clear: many on campus had no idea just what the rules were.

As a policy matter, it is not especially tricky to respond to someone who posts on the now-defunct social media app Yik Yak, "I'm going to stand my ground tomorrow and shoot every black person I see." The university police found him and arrested him. But when white students utter racial slurs near black students, the question is more complicated. In addition to drawing the line between unlawful harassment and criminal threats (which the university may regulate) and garden-variety racist stupidity (which is mostly protected speech), the university would need to decide all sorts of other speech-related questions presented by the protests and likely to recur. For example, are students allowed to camp on the quad? The former chancellor allowed it, but perhaps that was bad policy. Can the media be excluded from part of the quad by students seeking refuge from cameras and interviews, and is the answer to that question affected by the chancellor's implicit permission for the students to erect a tent village? What are the rules concerning electronic amplification of voices and music? Can we—and should we—somehow ban certain social media services from campus networks? And putting aside questions about legal rules, how can we build a campus at which everyone feels welcome, free inquiry is encouraged, and the best ideals of higher education may flourish as a result?

Foley, who had seen his predecessor take heat for inadequate consultation with faculty on matters ranging from governance of the medical school to graduate student tuition waivers, was smart enough to request that I (in my capacity as chair of the MU Faculty Council) appoint a faculty committee to recommend how Mizzou should deal with all the thorny free speech questions that would inevitably arise. I was smart enough to say no to Foley's first offer. The last thing I wanted was for a group of diligent faculty to devote substantial time to drafting complex regulations and guidance that the chief of police would deem impractical and toss in the garbage. Instead of my appointing a faculty committee alone, in January 2016 Foley and I together appointed the Ad Hoc Joint Committee on Protests, Public Spaces, Free Speech, and the Press. The faculty contingent boasted two free speech experts, one from the law school and one from journalism. The administrator members included the vice chancellor for student affairs, the chief of police, and the vice chancellor for inclusion, diversity, and equity. We also appointed two student members and invited someone from the general counsel's office to attend as an advisor.

Despite the committee's broad representation of campus constituencies, there were immediate complaints. One journalism student noted the lack of any students from his school on the committee roster. Others wondered whether the six faculty appointees had too little—or perhaps too much—connection to recent protests. Rather than attempting to please everyone by adding more and more committee members, we reassured interested parties that the committee's report would be purely advisory. It would not enact regulations but would instead make recommendations to the chancellor and the Faculty Council, who would then work together to craft a final version the campus could enact. Further, we promised to publish the committee's suggestions and to hold public fora, as well as smaller meetings with student groups especially interested in the committee's work. These procedural promises built trust that the substance would eventually prove acceptable to a wide cross-section of constituencies.

Further trust was earned in March 2016 when the committee produced a recommended statement reaffirming the university's "commitment to free expression," modeled on a similar statement released by the University of Chicago and adopted either verbatim or in materially identical form at Purdue University and Princeton University. The Faculty Council voted to approve the statement, and the chancellor endorsed it too.

Throughout the spring semester, the committee met to discuss draft regulations. I provided a back channel so the committee chair could anticipate how Faculty Council members—among other interested parties with whom I kept in regular touch—would react to one proposal or another. The student committee members, chosen after consultation with leaders in the undergraduate and the graduate/professional student governments, informed the committee about which proposed rules might incite student discontent. The advisor from the general counsel's office provided background on how a Missouri statute could complicate the First Amendment analysis concerning regulations of university property.

Observers on and off campus expressed occasional interest in the committee's work, and the absence of draft regulations did not stop media outlets from speculating about just what the group might eventually recommend. The *Kansas City Star* reported that the committee intended to recommend that the university enforce an existing rule that prohibits students (and others) from sleeping overnight in tents on campus.* The *Columbia Daily Tribune* managed to find a lawyer willing to opine that the theoretical proposed rules (not yet released, much less examined by the person offering his opinion) might violate the Constitution.† When reporters called I counseled patience, urging everyone to read the proposals before denouncing them, and I reiterated the plan to hold public meetings in the fall, lest anyone fear that the university would sneakily enact comprehensive speech regulations while the students were away for summer break.

Finally, in late May (after most students had indeed left town) the committee chair transmitted the committee's elaborate, thoughtful, and detailed recommendations to the chancellor and me.‡ I shared the report with the Faculty Council, and the chancellor subsequently emailed all faculty, staff, and students a link to the committee webpage at which the draft rules had been posted. It did not take long for suggested improvements to appear in my inbox. The first concerned when and where students should be allowed to "chalk." And because the draft rules prohibited the construction of "structures . . . requiring penetration in concrete or grass" without permission from the vice chancellor for operations—a person I expect is unlikely grant such permits because of his concern for the safety of students sleeping outdoors on campus, not to mention potential damage tent stakes could cause to underground cables—we anticipated that a robust debate on tents would surely arise upon the return of our students that fall.

That vigorous discussion was what we faculty council types call "a good thing." Fair arguments can be—and were—made that the university should allow student protestors to camp out. After all, last fall the camping students brought attention to important issues, and their message would likely have been less widely heard absent a continuous presence in the middle of campus.

My son, then in first grade, accompanied me one November evening to visit the tents. Akiva had brought some of his Halloween candy to share with the students. Once there he promptly made himself at home and began

*Mará Rose Williams, "Update: A Decades-Old Rule Could Stop Future Campout Protests at University of Missouri," *Kansas City Star*, May 16, 2016.

†Alan Burdziak, "Attorneys Question Constitutionality of Camping Ban Enforcement," *Columbia Daily Tribune*, May 18, 2016.

‡University of Missouri, Ad Hoc Joint Committee on Protests, Public Spaces, Free Speech, and the Press, "[Recommended] Policy on Use of University Facilities and Grounds," May 23, 2016.

enjoying a slice of the pizza that other well wishers had delivered. On our way home, he asked me why the students were protesting. I tried to explain in a straightforward way, saying, "They are upset that people treat them badly because of the color of their skin."

Akiva's response was sweet and also sad. In complete astonishment, he shouted, "Again?!" He had learned about Rosa Parks and Martin Luther King Jr. in school, and he had come to believe that racial discrimination was a problem America had solved. His disappointment at learning otherwise grew him up a little bit. If the students had not been sleeping outside—if the chancellor at the time had not provided heat lamps and extension cords but had instead prohibited overnight camping—Akiva likely would have remained blissfully ignorant somewhat longer. Eradicating such ignorance and bliss is an important project, particularly when one encounters adults exhibiting naiveté more appropriate for first graders, who can say, with a completely earnest face lacking any guile, "I thought we took care of that."

On the other hand, the vice chancellor for operations is a sensible person, and his concerns about student safety and potential property damage are real, not pretexts for quelling dissent. The time, place, and manner restrictions on expression proposed by the committee, including bans on overnight camping and on tents secured with stakes, are almost certainly within the range of regulations that the university may enforce without offending the First Amendment.* But if we are to prohibit a mode of expression so closely identified with the student movement that captured national attention this fall, at a minimum we owe students the courtesy of looking them in the eye and discussing their objections face to face. And the administration owes at least the same courtesy to the faculty who teach and advise our students. Reasonable presidents and chancellors can disagree about what sorts of speech regulation will best further the missions of their institutions. It is hard to imagine, however, how a savvy president could decide that the smart move is to enact her favored regulatory scheme without robust consultation with faculty.

Once a president is convinced of the value of faculty input, the question becomes how best to obtain it. The answer will naturally depend on the

*The longstanding UM System rule, CRR 110.010.B.4.b, states, "No University building, or part thereof, or grounds may be occupied as living rooms or bedroom except those duly set aside for such purposes" (University of Missouri System, Collected Rules and Regulations, Chapter 110: Use of Facilities and Equipment, https://www.umsystem.edu/ums/rules/collected_rules/facilities/ch110/110.010_regulations).

circumstances—the campus environment, the importance of the issue to be discussed, time pressure, and the like. Allow me to offer some broad principles that may prove helpful in various contexts.

First, if you wish to achieve something complicated and important, involve faculty as soon as possible. By including faculty early in the process, you allow them to play a more constructive role. This could well improve your ultimate results and, if nothing else, should help avoid certain missteps. In addition, the cliché that "people support what they help to create" applies as much to university governance as to anything else. If you make a decision and then seek faculty blessing, you may win approval, depending on some combination of the proposal's merits and the strength of your relationships with the relevant faculty. If you and your faculty colleagues reach a decision together, then the approval is baked into the cake.

Second, when possible, choose faculty partners who reflect the values of your institution, albeit not all in the same way. (In some cases the composition of faculty committees will be beyond your control, and you must make the best of it. Try to think ahead about procedures for selecting sensible, representative faculty.) If you need to regulate speech, be sure to include faculty with a deep commitment to academic freedom and free expression more generally. If you are considering whether faculty should use "trigger warnings," be sure to include faculty who take rigorous education seriously—lest you propose a policy that allows students to avoid academic work on the basis of negative reactions to assigned materials. And also include faculty known for their empathy for marginalized students—lest you miss an opportunity to provide reasonable accommodations that do not detract from academic rigor.

Keep in mind that one can encourage positive behavior without mandating it. Many faculty will bristle if ordered to warn students about potentially triggering course materials, and any mandate will require the university to define the sort of material that counts as triggering, which is its own minefield. A good portion of those same faculty, however, might well appreciate some advice about the sort of academic material that is genuinely likely to cause distress (as opposed to mere offense) to students. If research shows that rape survivors find it traumatic to read detailed descriptions of rape, and that a "heads up" about such material decreases the harm, I would want to know. When I teach evidence to law students, I assign part of an article in which a professor describes her own rape, along with her subsequent interaction with police and her thoughts on what evidence ought to be admissible at rape trials. Telling my students in advance about the nature of the reading assignment costs me nothing, indicates to students that I care about their welfare, and may well help a student to slog through material made especially difficult by prior assault. So I make a brief announcement in class. It would never have occurred to me to give such notice if I had not read about trigger warnings.

If a respected group of faculty can advise colleagues on when trigger warnings and similar accommodations might promote student learning, I suspect many instructors would gladly adopt best practices. And if some curmudgeons refuse, the university nonetheless enjoys the benefits of good deeds performed by others. Sometimes academic freedom and the somewhat non-hierarchical nature of university decision making necessitate that we tolerate a certain amount of stubbornness and foolishness among the professoriate. That tolerance protects us against groupthink and the uniform adoption of trendy but dangerous ideas.

Many barrels of ink—and even more bushels of pixels—have been devoted to critiques of political correctness on campus. Conservative commentators revel in exposing silly demands issued by students and bizarre diktats promulgated by assistant deans. And liberals join the chorus as well, establishing their bona fides as reasonable people not infected with out-of-touch ivory tower values. Administrators should be careful, however, lest they get so caught up in rejecting extremism that they ignore the simple message that underlies so much of what becomes known as "p.c." Put simply, universities are often not welcoming to members of marginalized groups. For decades—actually, centuries—universities were explicitly unwelcoming and banned members of such groups altogether. (The admission of women to Yale College is a recent event in the long history of that school, and Mizzou has been racially integrated for less time than it was segregated.) Then the universities admitted them and treated them badly. For example, the chilly reception of Jewish students at elite colleges is well documented, and today's occasional Title IX excesses are a reaction to years of indifference to the welfare of college women. A truly inclusive environment will not arise from the mere removal of de jure discrimination, a milestone we of course have yet to reach. When a proposal designed to promote inclusion strikes you as laughable, as some inevitably will, pause for a moment to recall how past decisions—alas, all too serious—have made the idea attractive to others. With empathy and respect, you can communicate your willingness to find another path to a worthy goal, rather than disdain for the project.

One last note about curmudgeons: Working to accommodate students from all walks of life will occasionally require the use of tactics that annoy the curmudgeons among us. So be it. Include the reformers and the curmudgeons alike in a genuine debate that stays true to the core ideals of your institution. Academic policy debates can be noisy, even unpleasant. Smart people sometimes forget that other participants are smart too, and that different beliefs may not indicate malice or stupidity. Yet with a commitment to patience, goodwill, and the development and diffusion of useful knowledge, a university will get things right most of the time. By including the faculty in the development of university policy—as early in the process as is practical—administrators increase the odds that their institutions will stay true to their old values as they encounter new problems.

And now, the thrilling conclusion: In April 2017, Hank Foley announced the enactment of new policies based on the report of the Ad Hoc Joint Committee, effective June 1, 2017. The process took time, tried the patience of many, and yielded a product that does not satisfy everyone in every respect. But we did it the right way, the final rules were improved by authentic consultation, and we performed a real service that improved the university.

11 Managing Emergencies

"Everyone Is a Risk Manager": Lessons from Hurricane Katrina

Scott Cowen

I hold that it could be true that fortune is the arbiter of half of actions, but that she still leaves the other half, or close to it, to be governed by us.

—Niccolò Machiavelli, *The Prince*

I'll begin with Hurricane Katrina, a blow of fortune we'd never imagined. I had been president of Tulane University for seven years when the storm hit and, according to our emergency plan, I had remained at Tulane, bunking in at the recreation center with a few key staff members.* On the day the levees broke, I waded out onto a campus that lacked power—no electricity, no running water, no communications—and that was slowly filling up with water. Four days after that, I finally made it to Houston, with the help of a motorboat, a golf cart, a dump truck, a helicopter, and a private plane, and saw on television what the whole country had been witnessing for a week—images of suffering and loss that to this day are indelibly etched in my mind.

The extent of the destruction wrought by Katrina on August 29, 2005, was truly colossal: more than 1,500 people died in the greater New Orleans area; more than 200,000 homes were destroyed; more than 1 million people were displaced in the Gulf Coast region, some for at least six weeks and many for months; more than 80 percent of New Orleans Parish was flooded; and 22 million tons of debris—12 times the amount of the 9/11 tragedy—were left behind by the storm. Tulane was not immune to this devastation:

* Whether the president should remain on campus in a disaster became a point of future debate: we lost five days of recovery time because I was trapped there, but at the same time my presence had symbolic value, conveying hope and purpose. The requirement that the president stay "aboard ship" is no longer in the plan, but I myself stayed for subsequent hurricanes, simply because I couldn't find it in myself to leave.

70 percent of the main campus and all of the health sciences campus were flooded, and the university experienced losses of more than $650 million.

I learned three valuable lessons from Katrina. One, develop very detailed and tested protocols for handling all types of emergencies and risks. Two, plan for the unthinkable, including a catastrophic event that could shutter your institution for a semester or more. Third, in the event of any significant emergency, make sure your institution not only survives but becomes stronger and better because of tragedy. I also developed, on the fly, a set of practical guidelines for coping with disaster: set clear goals, make safety the highest priority, communicate continuously, convey specific roles and responsibilities to everyone in the community, and preserve institutional mission, core values, and culture, no matter what the cost. I've also given thought to aspects of personality and character that are critical in an unforeseen calamity: if the best-laid plans go awry or the playbook proves insufficient, resilience, realism, and resolve make it possible to improvise the best possible solutions, however grim the circumstances.

Events forced us to act swiftly and decisively, but rather than galvanizing and improvising in the face of an emergency, I would much have preferred an established set of protocols to curtail and master contingent events up to and including hard-to-imagine disasters. Most of my "I wish I had"s are regrets about not thoroughly considering the type and magnitude of all the emergencies/risks our university could face. Tulane did not have a plan that would accommodate an emergency of Katrina's magnitude; we had a hurricane strategy—this was New Orleans, after all—but it principally involved busing and housing students out of town for hours or at most days, with no arrangement for such severe and long-term consequences as communications blackouts, lost databases, mass exodus of students and personnel for an entire semester, huge financial losses, severely damaged facilities, and an entire city under water. My learning curve was steep, matching the outsized event I dealt with.

But risk management doesn't pertain only to mega-hurricanes; it pertains to the many unknowns that threaten our safety, from viral epidemics and environmental hazards to reputational blows and financial crises. A chief consideration in emergency planning is the development of an overall strategy of risk management. At Tulane, two years before I left the presidency, we instituted an enterprise risk management (ERM) plan based on the model routinely used by corporations and governmental organizations. ERM identifies risks that could significantly affect the organization's mission and

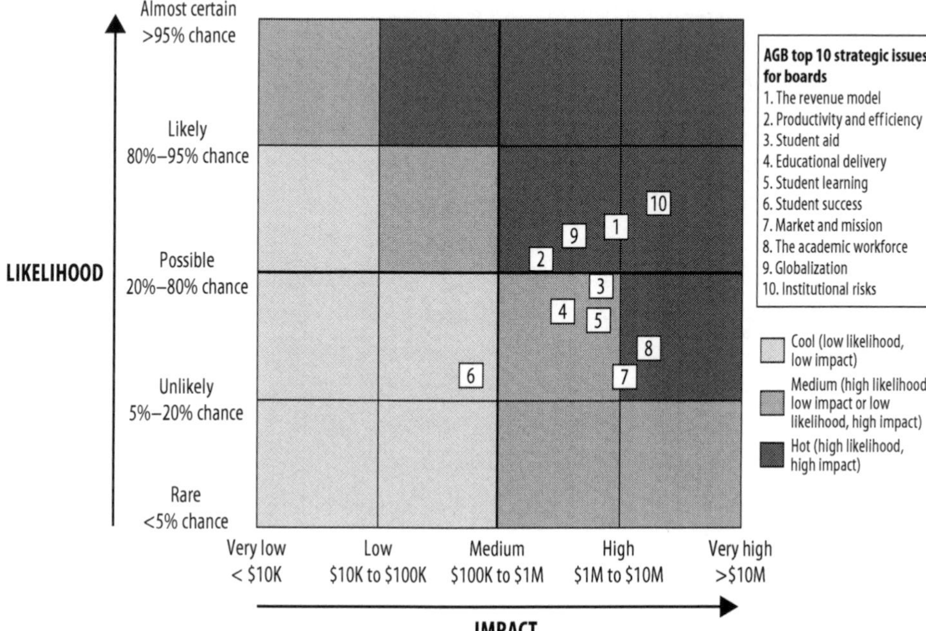

Figure 11.1. Sample heat map for "XYZ University": AGB top 10 strategic issues for boards. *Note:* A university's risk rate = impact (weighted × 2) × likelihood. *Source:* Author, based on Association of Governing Boards, *Top 10 Strategic Issues for Boards, 2013-2014* (Washington, DC: AGB Press, 2013), p. 1, and a generic heat map widely used in the corporate and nonprofit worlds. Examples of such maps can be found at Chartered Global Management Accountant, http://www.cgma.org/.

operations, evaluates the frequency and severity of each risk through a risk-ranking tool tailored to the culture and risk appetite of the organization, and maps the likelihood of a particular event on the Y axis and the degree of magnitude on the X axis to produce a "heat map." To be successful, this process of analysis must occur at all levels of the organization, with individuals aware of and outspoken about perceived risks. As a result of this concept, the ERM acronym is often referred to as "Everyone is a Risk Manager." Figure 11.1 is an example of a heat map developed by a university using the risks identified in the top 10 strategic issues for boards issued by the Association of Governing Boards (AGB), based upon that institution's risk appetite for these particular risks.

In addition to the risks identified by AGB, a university's senior leadership team should plot its own list of top risks on a heat map. (Figure 11.2 illustrates five generic risks that most universities can relate to.) By identi-

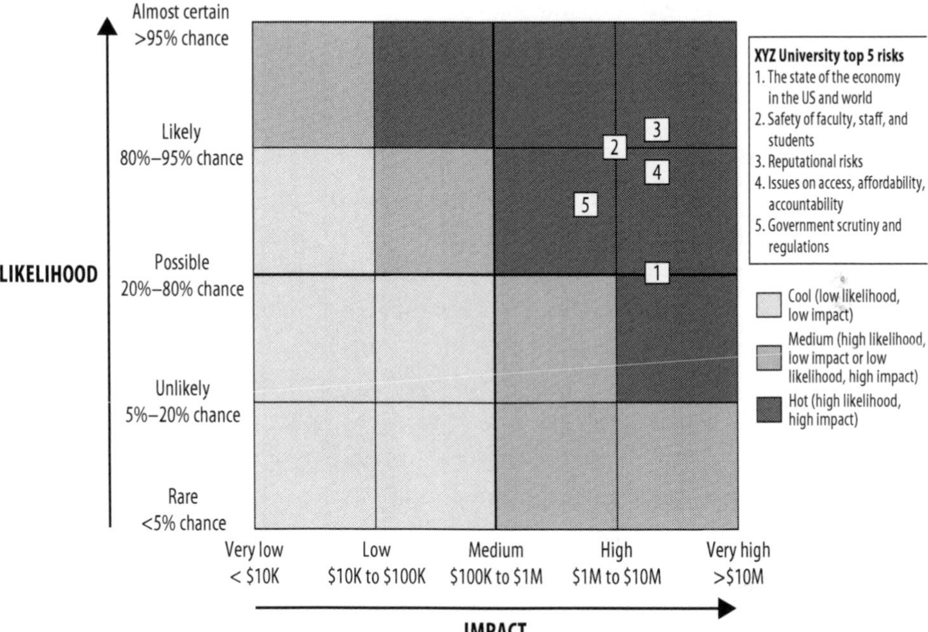

Figure 11.2. Sample heat map for "XYZ University": Five generic risks. *Note:* A university's risk rate=impact (weighted × 2) × likelihood. *Source:* Author.

fying likely trouble spots, the map focuses attention on potential emergencies that score high on both impact and probability.

Once senior leaders identify their top risks, these can be shared with all levels of the organization in various venues and formats. For example, Tulane hosted its first annual Risk and Safety Summit in 2013, which provided a platform for communicating those risks important to senior leaders. On that occasion, I noted that of the 30 to 40 top risks for large organizations, 5 were always on my mind. Of those five, four fell in the medium- to high-probability/high-impact quadrant of our heat map: the public safety of Tulane's faculty, staff, and students, always a top priority; emergency management and disasters, because of the increasing probability of severe hurricanes in the Gulf; the state of the economy in the US and the world, as slow economic growth has continued to challenge the revenue model of higher education; and proper operational and functional controls, involving everything from travel policies to the use of grant funds, given that policy lapses could lead to significant auditing problems. My fifth major concern consisted of reputational risks in relation to athletics, brought to mind by recent events at Penn State, Rutgers, Ohio State, and elsewhere. Reputational risks rated lowest in likelihood on the Tulane heat map, but highest in terms of potential impact on the institution.

It's important to note that simply identifying and prioritizing risks is insufficient; the next step is to invest in the necessary structures and resources to maintain a constant year-round focus both on mitigating risk and on responding to any emergency that might occur. For example, before 2005 at Tulane, the senior vice president for operations and CFO had primary responsibility for emergency planning. With the exception of one person, the SVP did not have a dedicated staff with responsibility for this function; instead, roles and responsibilities were spread over several people, and as a result there was a lack of clarity about who was responsible for what. Around 2011, we created several new positions to lead the charge on the ERM initiative as well as emergency response and management. Both the ERM and Emergency Management departments now report to the newly appointed chief operating officer (COO).

The reporting of possible threats is not confined to these departments; as noted earlier, "Everyone is a Risk Manager." In practice, it is often someone without official credentials who is the first to report a repair or facilities issue, a database security flaw, suspicious behavior, or anything that might be an ethical or safety violation.* Basically, emergency management and risk mitigation are top-down and bottom-up processes occurring within the ERM structure. To facilitate these processes, you need to put in place departmental risk and safety liaisons who are empowered to educate and engage the community, raising consciousness and strengthening preparation. At Tulane, the annual Risk and Safety Summit was implemented not only to acknowledge hardworking Tulane departmental liaisons, but also to educate the campus communities on common risks and generate wide awareness of the roles that faculty, staff, and students play in identifying, mitigating, and managing such risks.

Testing an emergency strategy is mandatory—an untested plan is really no plan—but tests of all-hazard plans are often imperfect, because of underlying complacency (remember half-hearted fire drills in elementary school,

*"Many serious risks are first spotted by employees without fancy titles. Who at an institution would first know that campus buildings are developing mold problems, a donor database has security flaws, or a student is becoming dangerous to others?" (Association of Governing Boards and United Educators, *The State of Enterprise Risk Management at Colleges and Universities Today* [Washington, DC, and Chevy Chase, MD, 2009], p. 3).

when no one ever thought it was a real fire?) or, at the opposite extreme, contagious panic that can overtake an entire campus. At Tulane, the university's police department once ran a simulated exercise, using the "live" mode rather than the "test" mode, that sent the message "SHOOTER" to students, faculty, and parents and a second erroneous alert, 10 minutes later, about gunshots fired on campus; significant stress and anxiety ensued until a correction was issued. The key is to create a simulation of a potential threat that gets everyone's attention, but with proactive communications informing the university community about the planned event. This type of planning offers a training opportunity to practice response skills but doesn't unnerve the entire campus. For example, during an active shooter exercise at Tulane, a campus-wide message preceded the event alerting students and faculty to an increased police presence, simulated gunshots, and warning sirens at the specific site of the exercise. Once you run these exercises, you should be able to identify weaknesses or flaws and correct them. It's important to generate such drills with some regularity and to maintain year-round vigilance.

It's also critical to record past events and codify future practices, at your institution as well as others—to pass on whatever you have learned on your watch. Much has been written about Hurricane Katrina, our ultimate test, but I still don't know for certain whether the emergency management plan we created remains part of institutional memory, given that many senior staff with personal experience of the storm have since departed. I also don't know whether the plan has been tested thoroughly enough to make the university safe from future catastrophes. Recent oversized storms such as Hurricane Sandy in 2013 have raised awareness of weather-related risks, but despite the accumulating evidence, arguments about risk assessment continue. In New Orleans, some 10 years after Katrina, more than half of the city's properties were recently removed from so-called Special Flood Hazard Areas because the Federal Emergency Management Agency (FEMA), under pressure from city officials and citing the Army Corps of Engineers' post-Katrina upgrades to the area's storm protection system, revised an earlier, more cautious risk assessment. The result has been more affordable flood insurance for home and business owners, but the question remains: how safe are we? New arguments arise that cloud our crystal balls, but it would be foolish to jettison past experience as we try to prepare for future events.

Other risks besides natural disasters also cause significant damage: guns on campus can wreak havoc; the recession of 2008 represented a financial emergency no one saw coming, one that schools across the country are still struggling to manage; athletics and lab safety pose the risk of reputational scandals—the list goes on. No institution is immune to such threats. For example, a biosafety hazard occurred in 2015 at the Tulane National Primate Research Center, with three rhesus monkeys testing positive for *Burkholderia pseudomallei* bacteria, a "select agent" originating in contaminated soil in Southeast Asia and northern Australia. This event made national news and resulted in a yearlong cessation of select agent research as the Primate Center complied with regulations from the Centers for Disease Control and Prevention and the US Department of Agriculture, including the hiring of a new biosafety director to spearhead Tulane's effort to have the research permit reinstated.*

Though lab exposures are relatively rare events, other emergencies are becoming all too common, putting them high on the likelihood scale. A review of events on US campuses during the week of June 10, 2016, the time of this writing, includes the murder of a University of California at Los Angeles professor by a former graduate student that resulted in a university-wide lockdown; several rape scandals, one at Stanford and another at Baylor, with the Baylor incident leading to the demotion of Kenneth Starr from president to chancellor and the firing of the football coach; and the closings of three small liberal arts colleges due to bankruptcy.†

All of these events are symptomatic of what seems to be a rising tide of emergencies affecting college campuses. The sexual assault crisis on US campuses is widespread and serious, with prestigious schools like Brown, Harvard, and Stanford reporting the highest numbers of rapes (ranging from 26 to 43 in 2014) and Reed College and Wesleyan topping the list of highest rate per 1,000 students at 12.9 and 11.5, respectively.‡ The vice president of government relations at the American Association of University Women, Lisa Maatz, pointed out that this isn't purely a reputational risk: "Universities need to stop trying to treat this as a PR problem, and treat it as the civil rights and public safety issue that it is."§

*Faimon Roberts, "Tulane Primate Research Center Regains Permit to Work with Dangerous Biological Agents," *New Orleans Advocate*, April 26, 2016.

†"The Week: What You Need to Know about the Past Seven Days," *Chronicle of Higher Education*, June 10, 2016, p. 3. Kenneth Starr stepped down as chancellor later in June 2016 and left his faculty position at Baylor's law school in August 2016.

‡It is possible that these high rates at small colleges reflect more responsive administrations, so that victims feel encouraged to report assaults with a much higher frequency than at large universities with large enrollments.

§Nick Anderson, "These Colleges Have the Most Reports of Rape," *Washington Post*, June 7, 2016.

An important way to protect against rape or other violent assaults on campus is through community engagement. In the case of the Stanford rape, two passersby on campus saw the event occurring and chased the offender, leading to his arrest and prosecution. Administrative policies also matter in creating safety for students: the new provost at Baylor, L. Gregory Jones, charged with meeting mandates from a consulting law firm regarding gender equity, speaks not only of regulations and guidelines but of cultivating a broadly ethical culture on campus through discussions in and out of the classroom.* Tulane's OneWave training program, an initiative launched to address a rising number of complaints concerning sexual violence, offers bystander intervention and assault prevention training.†

In response to an athletics department scandal at Rutgers University in 2013, a legal consulting firm recommended institution of an enterprise risk management initiative. A 30-minute compilation video made by the former director of player development showing verbal and physical abuse of players by the basketball coach during practices went unseen by the president of the university for more than four months, until the moment ESPN started airing portions of the video; only then was the coach summarily fired. The legal consultants urged an institution-wide risk assessment strategy, including organizational restructuring and dotted-line reporting, that would prevent any such incidents in the future.‡

I would be remiss if I left out the fiscal crisis putting many schools at existential risk, with small and mid-range liberal arts schools with narrow demographics and small endowments in most danger of extinction. A precise and detailed financial strategy with a 10-year horizon is a crucial element of ERM and emergency planning; otherwise it's all brinksmanship, with any unforeseen costs being the proverbial straw that could break the camel's back.

The good news is that many schools are finally facing up to the need for new models of financial stability and pursuing inventive strategies to not only cut costs but enhance revenue without sacrificing academic quality. Schools across the country (many of them ones you rarely hear of, from Trinity Washington University in DC to Paul Quinn College in Dallas) are

*Eric Kelderman, "Baylor's New Provost Seeks to Foster a 'Morally Significant' Culture," *Chronicle of Higher Education*, June 8, 2016.

†Sexual Violence Resources: A Guide, Howard-Tilton Memorial Library, Tulane University, http://libguides.tulane.edu/svresource/onewave.

‡"Rutgers Case Study and Recommendations," prepared by Skadden, Arps, Slate, Meagher, and Flom, LLP, for the Board of Governors of Rutgers, July 22, 2013.

embracing low-income and underrepresented students in order to increase their enrollments. Some flagship universities—Arizona State University is a leading example—are vastly enlarging their scale by increasing acceptance rates, expanding online offerings, consolidating academic programs, and creating private-public partnerships.* The financial emergency is widespread across the entire sector and unlikely to resolve in the same way for everyone, but two essential tools for surviving the crisis are innovation and planning.

All the risks mentioned here—public safety, reputational, financial—can be addressed in a coherent and effective way through enterprise risk management. ERM answers the question put by Peter Drucker in his classic 1974 book, *Management: Tasks, Responsibilities, Practices*: "What do we have to do today to be ready for an uncertain tomorrow?" The ERM process proactively prepares for that uncertainty. The single most critical component for a successful ERM program is a president who champions the ERM initiative and makes it an institutional priority. It's the job of leadership to put safety and security squarely in the forefront and provide the structure and resources necessary for implementation in order to preserve core activities and values.

What we call an emergency may be an accumulation of events or a once-in-a-lifetime catastrophe, but whatever the specific circumstances, we have a responsibility to protect, to mitigate, and to respond. No one can fully control all the vagaries of chance; nonetheless, we can attempt to curb the unpredictable and destructive forces that may arise—in fact are almost sure to arise—as time unfolds. "I hold that it could be true that fortune is the arbiter of half of actions, but that she still leaves the other half, or close to it, to be governed by us." Though the future is uncertain, we can and must take precautions—prepare our resources, run our drills, strengthen our communities, build our levees—and make ourselves ready to tame fortune.

What I Wish I Had Known When I Started I didn't know whether Tulane had an all-hazards plan—not just for hurricanes, but shooters, bombs, viruses—and whether it had been tested.

What I Wish I Had Done When I Finished I wish I had fully developed and tested all aspects of the Enterprise Risk Management (ERM) system I'd introduced in the last few years of my presidency. I also wish I had formulated a

*At ASU, Starbucks offers full four-year tuition to all its employees, with no requirement to stay with the company post-graduation.

contingency plan for the education of students if we again had to close the main campus for a full semester.

What I Wish I Had Not Done While in Office I wish I hadn't sited our backup information technology (IT) system on the fourteenth floor of a downtown office building in New Orleans, which meant we had no access to our database and communication systems when the city flooded.

What I Wish I Didn't Know When I Finished I wish I didn't know we were still vulnerable to so many risks, both for lack of a fully completed and tested ERM system and because of an increasingly volatile environment.

How I Knew When to Stop I breathed a sigh of relief at the recovery phase, but the truth is you can never stop planning for emergencies and risk. Institutions need an annual review process to assess and mitigate risks.

Acknowledgment

I gratefully acknowledge my colleagues Betsy Seifter, Heide Winston, and Joyce Fred for their contributions to this essay.

Planning for Emergency: Lessons from Virginia Tech

Charles Steger

Major comprehensive research universities are complex organizations that are exposed to a range of risks and uncertainty. Indeed, it is impossible to anticipate all of the events that may occur in these uncertain times. Any unanticipated event can constitute an emergency, but not all emergencies are of the same magnitude, and the decision-making process that is appropriate for a particular emergency is not a one-size-fits-all formula. As a consequence, it is important to think about the phases of activity involved in managing an emergency as well as the types of emergencies that can occur. And it is critical to consider these management strategies in advance—once an emergency has occurred, the speed of decision making is rapid. You are making decisions in real time, virtually always without complete information, and there is no time to build organizational capacity to cope with the situation at hand.

In outlining successful approaches, it is useful to group emergency management strategies into three phases: prevention and preparation, management during the crisis, and resilience and recovery.

Prevention and Preparation

How do you know what type of emergency will occur? There are hundreds, ranging from floods and fires to homicides and demonstrations that turn violent. Regardless of the scale of the emergency, a number of critical elements must be in place to establish a viable level of preparation:

1. Formulate usable policies and procedures
2. Set up a decision-making structure and identify key personnel
3. Create a communications plan
   a. Internal
   b. External
4. Test implementation procedures
5. Organizational culture
6. Positive community relations and sustaining cooperative agreements
7. Prepare for litigation

Each of these elements is a major undertaking in its own right. Each requires investing considerable time and resources, and maintaining readiness requires continued investment. Given all of the immediate pressures on university budgets, it is a challenge to make these investments, but do not be dissuaded—they are essential. It is easy to rationalize not making the necessary investments if you fall into a sense of complacency, believing that "nothing like that could ever happen here." And unless an emergency does occur there is little to show for the expenditure. But if you believe it cannot happen on your campus . . . you are wrong.

Beyond the emergency event itself, the aftershock can be significant. In the aftermath of the killing of 32 students on the Virginia Tech campus on April 16, 2007, more than $40 million was spent to upgrade safety and security on what was already considered a safe campus. The state provided only $1 million of assistance, with the remainder coming from the university's operating budget—a challenge in its own right. Each of these items is worthy of some comment.

Formulate Usable Policies and Procedures

Virtually all major universities are required to have in place policies and procedures for emergency management. That is not the problem. The challenge is to have a set of procedures that are actually usable during a crisis. Our legal staff works hard to write language governing policies and procedures that complies with all laws and protects the institution. Often the result is unreadable, particularly when one is confronted with making decisions in real time during a crisis. CEOs and other key personnel must be familiar with these documents, and they must be adopted by the governing board and be clearly communicated throughout the entire organization.

Set Up a Decision-Making Structure and Identify Key Personnel

At the risk of stating the obvious, it is crucial to know in advance who is in charge. This takes the form of identifying individual responsibilities as well as the responsibilities of various committees or task forces that are in place for emergency management situations. During a major emergency, external groups such as federal and state agencies will also intervene and often try to take command of managing the event. Sometimes this is appropriate, but not always. Working through these arrangements in advance of an emergency is key to successful operations during the event.

Another key to success is to build a command center. It is expensive and some would suggest unnecessary. Don't listen to them. Having a location, in close proximity to the president, where all key personnel will go and where centralized communications functions will take place is a tremendous advantage. Secure and robust communication channels are often required, given that traditional communication channels often fail during an emergency. Cell-phone capacity can be saturated rapidly, and even today many different first responders do not share radio channels.

Create a Communications Plan

When an emergency occurs, the demand for information will be instant. A chief university spokesman must be designated in advance. While easier said than done, all communication should be managed through this person, usually a vice president for university relations. Not doing so can result in serious misstatements; experience has taught us that 50 percent of the immediate information provided at the beginning of a crisis is usually wrong. It is also essential that this individual has had training or experience in crisis communications and be skilled in dealing with the media. To provide some sense of the intensity that can exist, during the April 16 shooting on the Virginia Tech campus there were more than 450 media representatives from around the world and 168 satellite trucks on campus. The intensity and stress this type of situation can create cannot be overstated.

The media interacted with many students, trying to get them to criticize the administration. During a meeting with students during that intense week, I asked the students what I could do to help. Their response? Tell the media to go away and leave us alone. Students, uncoached, were steadfast in their support of the university because of the positive organizational culture that had been nurtured there.

You will need to communicate simultaneously with internal and external communities. The information must be accurate and consistent for the two audiences, but often the message will be different. Having a well-developed website to provide updated information is a great asset that can help addressing proliferating rumors.

Notifications and warnings sent out as soon as information is verified must be carefully crafted. It is advisable to have a set of notifications already prepared. When an emergency has occurred, you can choose which is most appropriate. You will not have time for careful composition during the crisis.

Test Implementation Plans

Successful plans must be clear and tested. A great deal can be learned from both tabletop simulations and periodic full-scale simulations. My experience has been that by participating in and observing these exercises you can identify weaknesses in the decision-making process and structure. In addition, it is possible to identify key personnel who perform well in these stressful settings. Not everyone will.

These simulations, like all such organizational activities, require investment. It is easy to delay such expenditures, assuming that "it can't happen here." This is a big mistake.

Organizational Culture

While difficult to define, a resilient organizational culture is critical to managing and recovering from a major tragedy. It must be present in advance. Community response in the form of counseling by local religious groups and support from local charitable organizations such as the Red Cross and local police, fire, and rescue services are all critical factors in achieving success. After the emergency happens, it is too late. Having a resilient cultural infrastructure requires constant cultivation, communication, and cooperation. It requires a shared sense of community. This must occur both within the university and in collaboration between the university and the broader community.

Prepare for Litigation

Regrettably, there is a cadre of plaintiff's lawyers who see any tragedy as an opportunity to enhance their income. They combine negative publicity with massive Freedom of Information Act (FOIA) requests to create a level of distraction and harassment intended to generate generous out-of-court settlements. The suits will come, consuming many resources and distracting management from focusing on the real task of recovery. You must be prepared for this. The lawyers are not held accountable for false statements, but you will be.

When real-time decisions are made in emergency situations there is rarely complete information. Without exception, decision makers' judgment calls will be questioned. As we know, hindsight is always 20/20. Moreover, while it is easy to understand that the victims will be in a state of shock, this is also true for the staff who are attempting to deliver services and manage the crisis and indeed for the community at large. Memories of events will differ.

Consequently, it is important to carefully document decisions, verify actions, and review resource commitments. You must decide in advance who will carry out these functions and in what form they will be done.

Management during the Crisis

Perhaps it is self-evident, but the most significant emergency will occur without warning. A peaceful and predictable day can turn into chaos if you are not prepared. While there are dozens of activities to consume your time, during an emergency you must focus on the following four activities.

First, establish clearly that you are in charge of managing the crisis. Convene the appropriate task forces, and assign responsibility for key response functions.

Second, initiate communication plans, and establish communication to key constituencies such as the state governor and the governing board. Uncertainty elevates levels of fear and concern. People need to know what to expect. Establish a regular schedule of communication or press conferences. Tell the public what has happened and what you are doing. Depending on the situation, every four hours is not too often. You will be inundated with requests for information and interviews, and you must be careful to convey accurate information. All interviews should be cleared through a central office. Allowing contradictory statements will haunt you later if litigation ensues.

The press is not your friend. While there are exceptions, the majority of the media are interested in finding fault with your decisions and exploiting divisions within the community. Conflict drives up ratings. This is where prior investments in good community relations are of value.

Third, take care of yourself. One crisis management expert I worked with asked, how can you take care of others if you are not functioning at your best? The following actions are difficult but will enable you to serve others better:

- Get sleep.
- Set aside a period of several hours each day when you do not listen to media.

Fourth, make personal contact with victims. As president of the university or college, you are the symbol of the institution. It is essential that you are perceived to be in charge and are visible. In tragic situations where loss of life is involved, you should immediately communicate with victims—personally where possible. It is important for victims to know that you care and that they are important to you.

To ensure that each family received regular communications and that their specific needs and concerns were addressed, we assigned a liaison to each family. This involved 57 volunteers who had to be coordinated. This level of support cannot be sustained for very long and must be replaced by professional staff and effective organized structures. It is a difficult assignment. Even now, a decade after the incident, we have an Office of Recovery and Support that still interacts with the families affected by the April 16 tragedy.

The interaction with victims and their families must be done with care and understanding. Victims and indeed communities must go through a process of grieving before healing can occur. Different individuals go through this process at different rates and handle the various stages of grieving in different ways.* As you may already know, the stages are as follows:

*Julie Axelrod, "The 5 Stages of Grief and Loss," PsychCentral, http://psychcentral.com/lib/the-5-stages-of-loss-and-grief/.

1. denial and isolation
2. anger
3. bargaining
4. depression
5. acceptance

You will be the target of all of these emotions. Some attitudes toward you and your institution will change over time. Although the vast majority of individuals affected by tragedy are sincere and struggling to cope with loss, you can rest assured that some will be coached by their attorney. Considerable care is required when making commitments. You need to understand at what stage of grieving individuals might be; it will affect how you interact with them.

Continuous communication is crucial to helping victims move through the healing process. The initial demands on the president will be intense. Given all of a president's other responsibilities, this level of engagement cannot be sustained and must be supported by a professional organization.

Managing Resilience and Recovery

Recovering from a major emergency is a long and sustained process. It will test the level of resilience you have created in the university through preparation and organizational culture. Demands will be endless, but resources to accommodate them will be limited.

To manage the recovery process, it is necessary to create a formal though temporary organizational structure to

1. continue communication with the victims,
2. address litigation issues,
3. address compensation demands,
4. conduct a post-event study of the emergency,
5. implement improvements, and
6. manage the recovery budget.

Addressing these items associated with a major emergency is not a part-time job. The president has a university to run and cannot spend significant amounts of time both managing the recovery and sustaining the positive momentum of the university.

Post-Event Study and Evaluation

As part of the recovery process of the April 16 shootings at Virginia Tech four studies were initiated. Three were carried out by the university and one by a panel convened by the governor. The three studies by the university focused on

1. physical infrastructure,
2. communications, and
3. policies and procedures.

These studies resulted in 168 recommendations. The recommendations were implemented over a two-year period at a cost, as noted earlier, of more than $40 million. The panel appointed by the governor had good intentions, but the study morphed into a political document and as a result produced no useful recommendations.

Managing Donations of Material and Money

We are fortunate to live in a society that is generous to those affected by an emergency. The nature of our media landscape is such that the entire country is aware of virtually any major emergency that happens. Consequently, the inflow of donations of materials and money can be significant. While this generosity is much appreciated, it too can create post-emergency management issues.

Someone must be assigned to document the materials received. After the events of April 16, Virginia Tech received $8.4 million and 90,000 items. I personally received 9,000 letters. Hard to imagine.

Many positive motivations lay behind the generosity demonstrated by people and organizations across the United States. How these donations were distributed, though, was a subject of considerable controversy. The vast majority of the money was given to be used by the university. Because I knew virtually all of the major donors, I know this was the case. This was not the feeling of the families of the victims. They believed that all of the contributions were intended to be distributed to them. A small group of families, in fact, believed that all money raised by the university should be distributed to them.

Initially, the university attempted to distribute funds to families to meet immediate needs. I express no judgment when I note that the requests for support varied broadly. One family requested funds for a trip to Disney World, another wanted the university to replace the roof on their home, and another needed funds to pay rent. This was needed because the son who was lost in the shooting was using a portion of his assistantship to pay rent for his family. Despite the best efforts of our staff, it was quickly apparent we did not have the organizational capacity or experience to administer these funds.

To address this controversy we took two steps: First, we decided to distribute all $8.4 million to the families to dispel any sense that the university was exploiting the event to raise money. (The university actually suspended all fundraising for six months during the recovery period from the shooting.) Second, we secured the services of Kenneth Feinberg to administer the distribution of these funds. He was called upon to oversee the program for 9/11 victims in New York. He was kind enough to assist us pro bono. His past experience was of great value and assured us that we were handling this issue in the best fashion possible.

The principal lesson from this experience is that the institution should designate an established organization, such as the Red Cross, to receive and distribute donations. Do not accept donations directly. This will eliminate the sense of distrust and the questioning of the integrity of the university. It is important to note that over time these opinions change, but the victims and their families are in shock and experience anger that must be focused somewhere.

Hiring Crisis Management Consultants

Unanticipated emergencies present circumstances that the vast majority of organizations and their administrations have never experienced. Hiring an experienced consultant immediately brings a vast array of experience to assist in dealing with at best a difficult situation. As president, you are expected to bring the best talent possible to address the situation. It is wise to seek support of the governing board in this decision. Experience suggests that while some will applaud the decision, others will criticize it. The critics will cite the expense and accuse you of using consultants to cover up your weaknesses. Those who support the hiring decision will argue that it would be irresponsible not to seek expert help. Ignore the critics and employ the experts needed to help the university recover.

Conclusion

Many of the comments and recommendations contained in this chapter are simple common sense, but neglecting them can have serious negative consequences. The key lessons my experience offers are the following:

- Preparation is key to success.
- Organization and community culture enable a resilient response to an emergency.
- The president must lead the management of the emergency response and be visible.

What I Wish I Had Known When I Started I did not have a full appreciation of the impact of the symbol of the presidency and the value placed on commentary by the president.

What I Wish I Had Done When I Finished I wish I had written a book outlining many of the critical decisions and recognizing the dedicated people who contributed to the success of the university.

What I Wish I Had Not Done While in Office I took too long to remove dysfunctional people from their positions.

What I Wish I Didn't Know When I Finished How tough I would have to become to survive and move the institution forward.

How I Knew When to Stop When it became clear that solving the immediate strategic problems facing the university would take longer than the one or two more years I could reasonably remain in office.

12 How Tenuous Is Tenure?

Faculty Tenure in the Twenty-first Century

Ann Weaver Hart and Andrew R. DuMont

While the importance of academic tenure is often unquestioned in colleges and universities, tenure is not well understood or widely supported outside the academy. Often taken for granted as a feature of regular faculty appointments and perceived as enabling the freedom of teaching and research, tenure is also seen by many outsiders as a dysfunctional job guarantee of employment for life.

At its simplest, tenure is a tool, one that has enabled the perhaps unparalleled freedom of inquiry and teaching of the US system of higher education since its formalization in 1915 and solidification in 1940.* Yet, particularly in periods (like the present) when financial pressures are pervasive, defending tenure can be problematic, particularly with the seemingly endless difficulties of dismissing tenured faculty who have seriously relaxed their own standards of performance or who breech standards of conduct through, for instance, sexual harassment or plagiarism.† While many universities have successfully implemented post-tenure review to assure that faculty and academic administrators stay in touch with faculty performance, the bureaucracy that has grown up around employment action against tenured faculty (whatever the cause) is seen by many as a form of medieval guild

*We refer to the "1915 Declaration of Principles on Academic Freedom and Academic Tenure" of the American Association of University Professors (AAUP) and the "1940 Statement of Principles on Academic Freedom and Tenure" of the AAUP and the Association of American Colleges.

†For instance, a recent letter to the Joint Committee of the Administration and Senate of the University of California from University President Janet Napolitano illustrates the difficulties that face university administrators and other leaders when dealing with sexual harassment and sexual violence cases involving faculty (Janet Napolitano, Letter to the Joint Committee of the Administration and Senate, April 18, 2016, retrieved from ucnet.universityofcalifornia.edu).

protectionism. Whether or not these critiques are always warranted, defining and articulating what tenure does, how it allows faculty members and the universities and colleges at which they work to carry out their unique role in our society, and why this matters, as well as addressing concerns about undue protectionism, are crucial to efforts to adapt and sustain tenure to meet the challenges of the contemporary and future university.

This is a vivid, not a theoretical, discussion within the academy. In the remainder of this chapter, we address recent pressures on tenure, propose a context in which solutions can be found and that is mindful of the changing nature of faculty work and recent innovations being implemented, and suggest the implications of this context for the leadership of presidents and chancellors in American higher education.

Tenure and Growth in Student Enrollment

With the enormous post-World War II growth in enrollment at many universities and colleges—especially public institutions—the historic balance of research, teaching, and service in faculty roles has become increasingly difficult to maintain. For instance, total undergraduate fall enrollment at public land-grant universities in the US increased by 27 percent (1,003,479 to 1,275,315) between 1980 and 2014.* Other kinds of public colleges and universities have grown much faster, bringing new challenges in the sheer volume of credit hours as well as the increased need for differentiated instruction and academic support.† These changes have brought with them an increase in the need for well-qualified teachers, especially for the large general education courses required of all students, and for more academic support professionals dedicated to student success. This model of growth has necessarily put pressure on funding for traditional tenure-line jobs, especially when professors expect to teach courses in their specific area of expertise rather than general education courses. For example, 2011 data from the City University of New York show that 37.9 percent of "general education courses" were taught by full-time faculty and 54.7 percent were taught by adjuncts, while 53.1 percent of "other courses," presumably more special-

*US Department of Education, Institute of Education Sciences, National Center for Education Statistics, Integrated Postsecondary Education Data System: US Land-Grant Universities, 4-year or above, 2016, https://nces.ed.gov/ipeds/datacenter/login.aspx?gotoReportId=1.

†This growth and the accompanying change in proportions of students at different types of universities and colleges are well documented. See, for instance, R. P. Chait, "Why Tenure? Why Now?" in *The Questions of Tenure* (Cambridge, MA: Harvard University Press, 2005), especially pp. 18-20.

ized courses in majors, were taught by full-timers, with 42.7 percent taught by adjuncts.* (In both areas of coursework, a small number of courses were taught by "other employee types").

Ironically, analysts believed in 1976 that there was a need to reduce the percentage of tenured faculty because student enrollment was expected to level off or decline.† Perhaps because of this prediction as well as other factors, many colleges and universities expanded teaching capacity by hiring adjuncts, defined as short-term instructors contracted on a per-course basis, or through non-tenure-track faculty—full-time instructors. One report from the Association of Governing Boards of Universities and Colleges shows that 21.7 percent of faculty were non-tenure-track and 78.3 percent were tenured or tenure-eligible in 1969. By 2009, those figures had nearly reversed, with 66.5 percent of faculty categorized as non-tenure-track and 33.5 percent as tenured or tenure-eligible.‡

Graduate student enrollment further complicates the issue. When faculty positions were increasing apace with the number of graduating PhDs, the growth in enrollment was a means of filling tenure-track faculty ranks and an effective way to add to the teaching and research workforce generally. However, with many PhD graduates unable to find long-term teaching positions at colleges and universities despite the need for qualified teachers, change is clearly required.§ Creating new models of faculty employment will meet the needs of universities, colleges, and their students while also providing meaningful and rewarding employment for dedicated and talented expert teachers. If we recognize that tenure is a tool to enable the principles and goals of universities and colleges, and if other tools can be used for

*City University of New York, Office of Institutional Research and Assessment, "Percentage of Senior College General Education Classes Taught by Full-Time Faculty," April 29, 2011, retrieved from www.cuny.edu/academics/initiatives/pathways/about/archive/archive/gen_ed_classes_by _ft_faculty_sr_colleges.pdf.

†W. A. Simpson, "The Case for a New Tenure Policy," *Research in Higher Education* 5, no. 3 (1976): 223-231; John G. Kemeny, "The University in Steady State," *Daedalus* 104, no. 1 (1975): 87-96.

‡A. Kezar and D. Maxey, "The Changing Academic Workforce," *Trusteeship* (May/June 2013). The report cites both the National Center for Education Statistics' Integrated Postsecondary Education Data System and Jack Schuster and Martin Finkelstein's *The American Faculty: The Restructuring of Academic Work and Careers.*

§See National Science Foundation, *Doctorate Recipients from U.S. Universities: 2014* (Arlington, VA, 2015), retrieved from http://www.nsf.gov/statistics/2016/nsf16300/digest/nsf16300.pdf, especially pp. 7 and 8. For historical comparison, see Association of American Universities (AAU), *Committee on Graduate Education: Report and Recommendations* (Washington, DC, 1998), retrieved from https://www.aau.edu/sites/default/files/AAU%20Files/AAU%20Documents/GradEdRpt.pdf.

non-tenure- track faculty, then designing and implementing those changes should be a focus.

Tenure and Faculty Unions

Collective bargaining at universities and colleges is more common in some states than others because of labor laws. Where it exists, it can be a potent force that changes the relationship between faculty, administrators, trustees, and staff. Some commentators have argued that this change is positive, protecting the principle of academic freedom when other tools (including tenure and shared governance) break down. Others counter that unions violate the very nature of shared governance (and with it, the culture of collegiality) that shaped American higher education in the twentieth century, a view supported by the changes in membership in the American Association of University Professors (AAUP) after the organization added its Collective Bargaining Congress in 1976.*

The interweaving of collective bargaining, shared governance, tenure, and academic freedom is complex. In a 2013 article in *The Chronicle of Higher Education* Nicholas Burbules points out that if we are to claim that universities and colleges are unique places of work because of the collegiality and scholarly community that depend upon but extend beyond local institutions, then unions as local bargaining units cannot replace tenure and other traditional means of mediating the relationship between faculty and universities or colleges. One reason is that in some cases, unions simply are not a feasible option, regardless of the views regarding labor politics held by faculty and administrators on a given campus, because of state right-to-work laws that protect the right of employees to work independent of collective bargaining, as is the case in Arizona.† As Burbules argues, tenure and academic freedom also serve a different purpose than unionization and collective bargaining. One is geared toward the mission of the university and the unique combination of membership in a professional community and contribution

*On the changes in AAUP membership, see P. Hutcheson, *A Professional Professoriate: Unionization, Bureaucratization, and the AAUP* (Nashville, TN: Vanderbilt University Press, 2005), or W. P. Metzger, "The Academic Profession in the U.S.," in *The Academic Profession: National, Disciplinary, and Institutional Settings*, ed. Burton Clark (Berkeley, CA: University of California Press, 1987). More recently, the continuing issue in the AAUP's membership is covered in H. Reichman, "Professionalism and Unionism: Academic Freedom, Collective Bargaining, and the American Association of University Professors," *Journal of Academic Freedom* 6 (2015).

†See, for instance, N. Burbules, "How Unions Weaken Shared Governance," *Chronicle of Higher Education* (October 28, 2013), and S. Aronowitz, "Should Academic Unions Get Involved in Governance?" *Liberal Education* 92, no. 4 (Fall 2006).

to the work of the institution; the other is a means of protecting the rights of workers by guaranteeing adequate compensation and working conditions. Both are worthy goals, and they may align in some cases. However, one cannot be used in place of the other, and where they diverge institutions seldom adequately delineate the goals of tenure and academic freedom as distinct from those of collective bargaining and labor rights.

Tenure, Free Speech, and Professional Expertise

Defending tenure without a clear view of its history and its role in enabling academic freedom can erode its effectiveness as a tool to achieve important outcomes. Of particular importance is the relationship that experts (university professors among them) have with the general public. A strain of anti-intellectualism in the US, which is sometimes exacerbated by the fundamental tension between expertise and public communication or the use of technical or otherwise specialized knowledge, has always existed.* Tenure and academic freedom help to mediate this tension, but they do not resolve it.

Even from the AAUP's beginning, the nature of academic freedom has been complicated by the extent of its projections and its relationship to freedom of speech and citizenship. For instance, Edward Alsworth Ross's public statements ultimately contributed to his 1900 dismissal from Stanford University at the request of its cofounder Mrs. Jane Stanford. His case demonstrated the need for tenure and other mechanisms to protect academic freedom and helped lead to the AAUP's formation. However, some of his statements were also racist and xenophobic and would make many current AAUP members (let alone others) shudder.† Thus, the case should also remind us of the limits to academic freedom and the fact that citizens' First Amendment rights to free speech provide less complicated and ambiguous protections than an amorphous definition of academic freedom, whose defense would be eroded when the nature and quality of assertions are questionable, as with Ross.

Linking academic freedom and free speech too closely puts the justifications for the former into question and ultimately does nothing to protect the freedom of individual speech.‡ Similarly, taking academic freedom to

*R. Hofstader, *Anti-Intellectualism in American Life* (New York: Knopf, 1963), pp. 19, 36, and 151.

†See B. Eule, B. (2015). "Watch Your Words, Professor," *Stanford*. Retrieved from https://alumni-gsb.stanford.edu/get/page/magazine/article/?article_id=75857.

‡On the relationship of the First Amendment of the Constitution to academic freedom, see Mark G. Yudof, "Three Faces of Academic Freedom," *Loyola Law Review* 32, no. 4 (1987): 831–858.

extremes threatens tenure indirectly, because a too-expansive view erodes public and political support.* This problem is exacerbated by social media, which, while an important tool for communication, also makes internal debates among academics more public and provides a platform for speech that is more easily shared out of context. Recent controversies at universities around the United States—including Missouri, Yale, Illinois, and others—illustrate this potential for quick-moving debates that tend to be more inflammatory than in the past owing to the speed with which they occur. In this context, sustaining academic freedom and tenure means walking the line between scholar and public intellectual in a careful way that maintains the authority of the profession while still enabling its impact in the world outside the university, its classrooms, libraries, and laboratories.

Faculty Professionalization, Hiring, Promotion, and Tenure

The changes in universities and colleges over the past several decades bring with them changes in the nature of faculty members' daily work and, consequently, new complications in the nature of faculty training and evaluation. These changes include developments in the kinds of research that faculty members do (and how they are rewarded for it), an increased emphasis on teaching and mentorship, particularly at the undergraduate level, and changes in how each of these activities is evaluated by peers. All of these considerations must be included in any discussion of tenure and the future of the US academy.

Among the primary complications of tenure review and professionalization are the power dynamics of faculty peer evaluation, especially with regard to scholarship and research. Only faculty members of equal or higher rank are involved in evaluations or votes to grant tenure, creating a hierarchical power relationship between tenured and pre-tenure faculty members that has the potential to suppress creative and innovative but riskier research.† Such research includes translational work, which has often been considered less worthy of reward than basic research. As a result, at most universities and colleges, success with these kinds of faculty innovation was not admissible (or counted for very little) in promotion and tenure applica-

*Also see Chait, "Why Tenure? Why Now?" pp. 9-12.

†For a thoughtful discussion of this issue of power dynamics and tenure, see R. Mason, C. Casey, and P. Betts, "Toward Tenure: Developing a Relational View," *Journal of Educational Thought* 44, no. 1 (2010).

tions.* Recently, however, faculty senates at some universities—including the University of Arizona—have amended faculty bylaws to allow translational work as part of promotion and tenure evaluation. Similar considerations of the changes in faculty research and its relationship to other areas of academic work need to be included in discussions of tenure and its future.

Questions of evaluation and professionalization are equally fraught for non-tenure-track professors and, in some cases, for tenure-track faculty at teaching-focused colleges and universities. The traditional model of faculty training and evaluation at four-year universities and colleges largely emphasizes research and scholarship. The growth of regional comprehensive universities has changed this to a certain extent, but—anecdotally at least—hiring practices at many of these schools still privilege research production rather than teaching preparation and experience during the PhD or other terminal degree. With many professors charged primarily with teaching rather than with research or service as part of their responsibilities of employment, the traditional modes of evaluation—and the current organization of most PhD programs, focused primarily on research—may not be sufficient. Our point is not to question the importance of scholarship in the preparation of a university or college teacher—PhD graduates are qualified to teach at the university level in part because of their scholarship in content knowledge. Rather, given the changing nature of faculty work, we believe the importance of innovative and sophisticated preparation in teaching also is warranted. Inroads have been made in some areas, including teacher training in first-year writing and composition programs and orientations to teaching and American culture for international graduate students. Recent initiatives have focused on improving student outcomes through evidence-based faculty development programs; these include initiatives of the Association of College and University Educators and the undergraduate STEM (science, technology, engineering, and math) education project at the University of Arizona (with similar programs at seven other universities) funded by the Association of American Universities. With the growth of non-tenure-track faculty and the often poor oversight and mentorship that can go with those types of faculty appointments, these kinds of programs need to be expanded.

*E. L. Boyer, D. Moser, T. C. Ream, and J. M. Braxton, *Scholarship Reconsidered: The Priorities of the Professoriate, Expanded Edition* (Hoboken, NJ: Jossey-Bass, 2015).

Students and institutions undoubtedly benefit if non-tenure-track instructors, clinicians, or researchers are from PhD and other doctoral ranks, qualified for the full balance of faculty work by their degrees but hired to do specific critical academic work with a broad understanding of their field and specialized knowledge within certain segments of it. Thus, non-tenure-track faculty would be qualified to design and teach courses, exercise the "scholarship of practice" in Boyer's words, or conduct research in much the same way as their tenure-track peers. However, as Michael Bérubé and Jennifer Ruth point out in their book *The Humanities, Higher Education, and Academic Freedom,* the role of non-tenure-track faculty on campus complicates other traditional tools like shared governance, which have sustained the unique collaborative culture of colleges and universities. Many agree that in an inclusive academy, research, clinical, or teaching faculty who are not tenure-track must be included in shared governance for it to have meaning, but, as Bérubé and Ruth argue, because of their more tenuous status, their loyalties may be (understandably) divided.* Thus the corollary, what does meaningful shared governance, or, more broadly, academic freedom look like off the tenure-track?

Issues for Chancellors and Presidents

In the first two decades of the twenty-first century, colleges and universities have changed dramatically. Looking ahead, higher education leaders will need to preserve the best contributions of the last century's models of tenure—free inquiry and research (and publication) and teaching the results of that inquiry—while responding to and influencing judicially protected employment interests, the protections of free speech, and the rights and interests of people with protected differences (inclusion) in an environment where standards of excellence may be unclear or in dispute.

Financial Issues

The rapid rise in the cost of a college or university education to the student in recent decades affects the relationship of tenure and faculty status to the jobs of the future. While tenure came to represent lifetime employment in the absence of gross failure to perform or malfeasance, increased access to and enrollment in colleges and universities, the growing differences in

*M. Bérubé and J. Ruth, *The Humanities, Higher Education, and Academic Freedom: Three Necessary Arguments* (London: Palgrave Macmillan UK, 2015), pp. 107–112.

economic prospects among those with and without college educations, and the cost of the old model have all led to rapid changes in faculty roles and the relationship of old definitions of those roles with tenure. These developments are in addition to the growth of post-tenure review, faculty unions, and political involvement in governance beyond anything seen in decades (for instance, the recent turmoil at the University of Louisville and University of Tennessee), and the pressures for new leadership solutions that also preserve the core principles of free inquiry, publication, and teaching.* All of these changes and more will frame the search for financial solutions.

Expansion of Faculty Roles and Responsibilities

The rapid changes noted in the preceding section also have brought changes in the preparation of faculty and movements to advance high-quality teaching, research, and clinical/practitioner engagement. One of the primary ways in which higher education leaders can shape the future is to find ways to integrate the tenure or tenure-eligible tracks with the other critically important responsibilities of faculty, providing the same academic freedom to all full-time members of the academy that tenure alone used to provide.

Shared Governance

Faculty senates traditionally provided the most visible and influential contributions of the faculty to governance. Under old models of tenure, only faculty in tenure-track positions or holding tenure participated. Under the new definitions of faculty and structural changes in the nature of colleges and universities, leaders in higher education will need to find creative ways to preserve the unique and distributed contributions to governance of their institutions in an era where nothing is as it was—from student status, to political expectations, to sources of funds (such as philanthropy and other partnerships in addition to state appropriations and federal research funding).

All Things Digital (and Then Some)

In the past few decades, the rapid expansion of online education, blended delivery models, massive open online courses (MOOCs), and other structural innovations have completely redefined what tenure might mean for a

*At Louisville we refer to the changes in the governing board starting in the summer of 2016, and at Tennessee to the change in executive leadership in June 2016.

huge proportion of the academic workforce. Not only do faculty need to know new and sophisticated ways to teach, but the responsibility to succeed in teaching (as demonstrated by student learning and success) has shifted from the student to the teacher. In addition to changes in how students learn and are taught, particularly in the kind of general education courses often taught by non-tenure-track faculty, developments in the nature of scholarship and research through advances in computing have the potential to change the kind of independent, collaborative, or guided work that students conduct as part of an advanced course or degree program.

Conclusion

The future of tenure cannot be decided in the abstract. Each university or college in the context of its mission, its institutional culture, and the role of trustees or regents in its governance must address its relationship to the principles it protects. In every case, the challenge will be to sustain the conditions for success for the entire academic enterprise, including finding appropriate means to hire and retain qualified teachers, researchers, and clinicians as the number of students continues to rise and budgetary pressures remain strong. As Bérubé and Ruth point out, the fundamental feature that has distinguished the modern US university from other kinds of institutions is the self-regulating community of scholars who are at its core. We believe that these communities of scholars, and a strong understanding of and commitment to the principles of free inquiry and teaching that have been supported by tenure for a century in American higher education, are critical to preserving the advancements that colleges and universities have contributed to our society. These core principles, not the specific features of a tenure system, should be front and center as we address the needs of an expanded higher education community into the future.

The principal goals tenure protects are (1) preserving the free exploration of knowledge and ways of knowing in the academy, (2) promoting the free and broad distribution of that new knowledge, as well as opportunities for others to examine and critique it through widely available and dramatically expanded avenues in print, digitally, and in currently unimagined ways, and (3) protecting those who pursue that new knowledge from retaliation in the workplace for doing so. There are many ways to preserve rights and freedoms that stand as hallmarks of American society, but these three principles stand as enduring features of the quality and advancement of human knowledge, expression, and creativity. Tenure has served the purpose of protecting these goals. If we are to contemplate its demise—or even its revision—we must first have clear, concrete, and deeply imbedded mechanisms for preserving these goals to sustain the best of US twentieth- and twenty-first-century higher education.

Ann Weaver Hart

What I Wish I Had Known When I Started I wish I had known in my gut (rather than theoretically) that facts and rational argument are only part of the important work of a university president. The facts are necessary but not sufficient; symbolic, political, and sense-making activities are important!

What I Wish I Had Done When I Finished When I finished, I wish I had spent more time thanking all the people who had worked on the leadership team to make the university successful.

What I Wish I Had Not Done While in Office I wish I had not been so slow to recognize the immediacy of the fast-paced world of social media. News cycles and rapidly spreading stories create a very different social context than the routine work of research and teaching.

What I Wish I Didn't Know When I Finished I wish I didn't know how little of the work that feels so intense and deeply important that we do actually survives our leadership tenure for very long. Mistakes and failure to lead can sometimes have longer-lasting impacts than does success.

How I Knew When to Stop I knew it was time to stop when I had a strong feeling of completion, pride, and satisfaction and a vague sense of restlessness.

The Fragile Future of Academic Freedom

Cary Nelson

On January 3, 2017, 13 faculty members at the University of California at Berkeley sent a letter to their chancellor, Nicholas Dirks, with an unambiguous final line, isolated on the page above their signatures: "We urge you to cancel the planned speaking event for Milo Yiannopoulos as soon as possible."* Ninety-eight faculty members subsequently signed on to both the original letter and a January 4 supplementary one restating the demand after Associate Chancellor Nils Gilman wrote to say a public university "may not engage in prior restraint of speech based on concern that a speaker's message may trigger disruptions."

That was Gilman's conclusion, but he opened by pointing out that Yiannopoulos had been invited by a registered student organization, Berkeley College Republicans, which was exercising its right to invite speakers of its choice and to reserve space in which they could present their views. The university was hosting the event but in no way endorsing the speaker. Neither, as Gilman properly declared, was the university willing to block or censor the event: "The First Amendment prohibits the University from censoring those events or banning speakers based on the viewpoints that might be expressed. . . . There is no general exception to First Amendment exception for 'hate' speech or speech that is deemed to be discriminatory."

Gilman's arguments were both clear and definitive, but they did not dissuade more than 100 Berkeley faculty members from reiterating their call for the talk to be cancelled. A number of the faculty members who signed are scholars with national reputations well beyond their areas of specialization. News reports highlighted literary theorist Judith Butler among them. All were, I suspect, well aware of the issues Gilman raised. Indeed

*The original letter to the chancellor, along with links, the Gilman response, the expanded list of signatures, and the follow-up letter, is available online at https://docs.google.com/document/d/13mTOQ7wVst6voLMg6Pvr-3uJ2Fbn7zcXg_Bkx8mGDOk/edit. The two main faculty letters are also on the *Daily Californian* website in slightly edited form (http://www.dailycal.org/2017/01/10/open-letter-calling-cancellation-milo-yiannopolous-event/). The *Daily Californian* later reported Gilman's remarks at a Senate meeting discussing the events: "While I empathize deeply with and share the revulsion generated by Yiannopoulos' vulgarian pantomime, blocking his exercise of his constitutional rights only serves to endanger our own" (S. Cannestra, "ASUC Senate Hear from Associate Chancellor, Student-Athletes during Meeting," *Daily Californian*, February 16, 2017). A February 2 article in the *San Francisco Chronicle* opens with a photo of the peaceful demonstration in Berkeley that preceded the violent event. Two carefully lettered signs are held aloft: "NOBODY'S FREE UNTIL EVERYBODY'S FREE" and "HATE SPEECH IS NOT FREE SPEECH," the former one of the slogans used to link support for Boycott, Divestment, and Sanction Movement (BDS) opposition to Israel with the Black Rights movement in the US. The piece quotes one of the original Berkeley faculty signers: "'We can support free speech,' said Wendy Brown, a political science professor, 'without choosing to host those who gleefully attack our most vulnerable, seek deportations and bans of our students and faculty, trample the principles of equality and respect . . . and in other ways aim to destroy the institution'" (B. Egelko, "Milo Yiannopoulos' Speech Unwelcome in Berkeley, but Protected by Constitution," *San Francisco Chronicle*, February 2, 2017). That is a perfectly fair argument to use in seeking to convince a group not to invite someone, but it is not warrant for the administration to block a speaker.

they could be guaranteed to make Gilman's very arguments themselves in defense of a speaker whose politics they endorsed. That, of course, is the fatal distinction: politics in this case trumped principle. Some free speech rights were more equal than others.

In the rejoinder to Gilman, the 13 letter writers made an argument more appropriate to a private religious community or a self-help group than a university: "Just because behavior isn't illegal doesn't mean it's appropriate. **At the University of California, we hold ourselves to a higher standard** and strive to promote a culture where everyone is supported to reach their fullest potential. To do that, **we need to address problems before they hurt our community.**" One might well warn in response that these Orwellian standards could not be widely applied without suppressing much provocative campus speech, not only in public spaces but also in classrooms. One might also argue that it is controversial and even outrageous speech that challenges values and assumptions and helps people "to reach their fullest potential" by promoting understanding, critical analysis, and self-definition. The boldfaced passages, reproduced here as in the original letter, add an uncannily unstable element: do they express especially intense certainty or self-doubt?

The first letter is of note for piously intoning the very values the writers proceed to discard: "We support both freedom of speech and academic freedom on campus and realize that controversial views must be tolerated in any campus community dedicated to open debate and opposed to censorship." But "Yiannopoulos's views pass from protected free speech to incitement, harassment, and defamation. . . . Such actions are protected neither by free speech nor by academic freedom." This last passage comes from the third paragraph, but it is preceded by complaints clearly directed toward political opinion, including Yiannopoulos's castigation of Black Lives Matter and the fact that he "mocks campus cultures of inclusiveness." They go on to note his projection of images of audience members onscreen and assert a privilege that would disallow real-time news organization videos of campus audiences: "Students are not public figures, and they do not agree to have their likeness projected in public." Of course comedians do the same thing all the time, reasoning that audience members consent to be part of the show.

That Yiannopoulos, an alt-right provocateur and former *Breitbart News* editor, is an abusive speaker is not in question. He has been banned from Twitter and in February 2017 had a speaking offer withdrawn by the Conservative Political Action Conference (CPAC) after remarks that seemed to defend pedophilia surfaced. None of that, however, prevents a recognized campus group from inviting him. Some of his practices of singling out individuals might be considered intentional infliction of emotional distress or invasion of privacy, and legal remedies could be pursued after the fact.

But they are not typically enjoined in advance, as the group of Berkeley faculty urged. Slander is a subcategory of defamation, but it is not subject to prior restraint under the First Amendment. Insulting and vulgar language speech cannot be punished, let alone restrained, though it can be energetically condemned. Private universities hosting an event before an invited audience could prohibit some practices as part of contractual conditions for a speaking engagement, but an open event at a public institution is more difficult to constrain.

As widespread news coverage reported, the speech ended up being canceled on advice of the police. Students and faculty staged a large public demonstration against the February talk. That was a perfectly appropriate expression of opinion, protected both by academic freedom and by the First Amendment. But, as Thomas Fuller reported in the *New York Times* on February 2 ("A Free Speech Battle at the Birthplace of a Movement at Berkeley"), more than 100 masked, black-clad off-campus political activists showed up to throw rocks, smash windows, and launch Molotov cocktails. At that point public safety required that the event be canceled.

I expect that the 100-plus Berkeley faculty members who had urged that the speech be canceled would almost all reject violence as a tactic and decry the events as they unfolded. But one may argue that their letter provided unintentional justification for closing the lecture down by other means. With Berkeley administrators unwilling to listen to reason, the argument might go, demonstrators had no choice but to intervene with force. After all, Butler and her coauthors had detailed the harm the community faced if the speech were permitted to occur as scheduled.

If, as reported, the ninja-style rioters at Berkeley came from a Bay Area anarchist collective, we can assume similar occurrences at that level of violence are unlikely elsewhere in the country. The same prediction does not apply to the protest letter from Berkeley faculty. That letter represents the leading edge of a national and international campus trend. It is the most recent—and perhaps decisive—component of a long-term series of developments collectively undermining academic freedom on campus.

Part of what we are seeing is the overlap or intersection of long-running and apparently unrelated trends in higher education. The first of these trends, over 40 years in duration, is the gradual and seemingly inexorable adjunctification of the professoriate. In 1975 roughly two-thirds of American faculty were eligible for tenure. Now the percentage has dropped to a third, with fully two-thirds employed either part time or on short-term full-time contingent contracts not eligible for tenure. That trend is at work in Canada and Mexico as well, where such faculty, respectively, are called sessional or precarious. Because such faculty members are hired at will, they are subject to summary dismissal (with or without cause, depending on their contracts) or, more important, to what amounts effectively to dismissal: the simple nonrenewal of their employment.

As every such faculty member knows, they either have limited academic freedom or none at all.* The necessary link between job security and academic freedom has been severed. While tenure remains the ruling principle for faculty hiring at elite institutions, it no longer operates as a nationwide principle at the majority of US colleges and universities.

Contingent faculty are easily eliminated if they become politically controversial, the object of criticism from administrators, politicians, religious leaders, or the press. Thus we should not expect them reliably to defend academic freedom principles when they are embedded in political controversies. Unfortunately, there is now another addition to the list of players who may compromise the academic freedom of their most vulnerable colleagues: tenured faculty whose political views take precedence over respect for academic freedom.

That new and genuinely alarming threat to higher education's fundamental principles is a consequence of another long-term trend, also of several decades' duration: the gradual politicization of the humanities and soft social sciences, a trend that also puts both contingent faculty and graduate students at increased risk. That trend is dramatically on display in the Berkeley letter, though some of the faculty signers are also from other disciplines. What is of special note in the Berkeley effort to cancel a properly scheduled speech is that it did not occur on the expected political terrain.

*Tenure is the gold standard for protecting academic freedom. The only realistic alternative for contingent faculty is a strong collective bargaining agreement. Unfortunately, many faculty collective bargaining agreements do not have sufficiently nuanced and detailed academic freedom guarantees. The most common such clause simply incorporates the "1940 Statement of Principles on Academic Freedom and Tenure" issued by the American Association of University Professors (AAUP) and the Association of American Colleges. That was a compromise document, which served its purpose of codifying the principle of tenure but left faculty vulnerable to sanctions for some speech that academic freedom should protect. The AAUP issued a clarification in 1970, which helps, but collective bargaining agreements generally omit the clarification.

It migrated from the usual current arena of the heckler's veto, the Israeli-Palestinian conflict, to empower a quite different political agenda: the silencing of the alt-right.

Of the 13 signatories to the original Berkeley faculty letter, 5 had previously signed public petitions endorsing boycotts of Israeli universities. A sixth signed a petition objecting to the University of California Statement on Intolerance because of its inclusion of some forms of anti-Zionism as examples of prejudice. The opposition to Yiannopoulos's appearance on campus has no direct relation to debates about the Israeli-Palestinian conflict, but those debates have given faculty opposed to the Jewish state a more general warrant to shut down events sponsored by those they perceive as their political opponents. Since 2014, Boycott, Divestment, and Sanction Movement (BDS) supporters both within and without the academy have been repeatedly exposed to the idea that dialogue with political opponents is politically and ethically misguided and unprincipled. It is to be resisted.

So far as I know, the Berkeley events are the first time recently that the impulse to oppose campus speakers has triggered a major incident quite separate from the Israeli-Palestinian conflict. But I expect the impulse to spread and the Berkeley letter to be replicated and adapted. Indeed on March 3, 2017, hundreds of students at Middlebury College joined forces to shout down the conservative writer Charles Murray and prevented him from presenting his invited lecture, largely because of lingering anger at his widely criticized 1994 book *The Bell Curve*, which promoted the claim that there are inherent race-based differences in intelligence. After he was moved to a secret location where he was interviewed livestream as an alternative, students saw his car attempting to leave campus and surrounded it, jumping and pounding on it and blocking its progress. In this case it was hundreds of Middlebury alumni who had signed a letter declaring there were no free speech issues at stake in blocking Murray's lecture. If this becomes a trend—and widespread campus opposition to Trump administration policies may encourage it to become a trend—the impact on academic freedom will not be good. By the time this essay is published, I expect there will have been other allegedly principled faculty efforts to shut down campus lectures.

Students and faculty should be able to stage a noisy protest before a lecture begins—and to stand silently with opposing posters throughout an event—but to repeatedly interrupt an invited lecture or to compel its cancelation is a violation of academic freedom. For the administration to have honored the request the 111 Berkeley faculty members made to cancel the lecture would have been a clear and unequivocal violation of academic freedom as well. In all honesty, there are many people among the 111 that I would not have expected to sign such a letter. I take my personal surprise as some evidence the academy's commitment to academic freedom is changing.

Understanding how that change has occurred requires some historical background, first in terms of how the suppression of opposing viewpoints was elevated from a violation of principle to become a principle on its own. One may begin with one of the first of these Israel-related episodes in the US, when Michael Oren, a historian serving as Israel's ambassador to the US, was repeatedly interrupted with shouted slogans and epithets at the University of California at Irvine in 2010. Oren was blocked from offering more than fragmented portions of his lecture at a time, though he did eventually complete the presentation. The incident was widely condemned, however, and 10 protestors were later found guilty of disrupting a speech and directed to perform community service as a consequence.

In the years since, a concept originating in the Middle East, "anti-normalization," has gained currency in the West. Anti-normalization stigmatizes any collaborative dialogue, interaction, or negotiation between Israelis and Palestinians on the basis that it "normalizes" the prevailing power relations and injustices. The concept has had violent consequences in Palestine, especially on the West Bank, where Palestinians who engage in dialogue with Israelis can face both intimidation and genuine threat. After the BDS movement began to actively promote anti-normalization in July 2014, the tactic gave theoretical warrant in the US to the impulse to set aside academic freedom in favor of goals seen as morally and politically superior. As a consequence, efforts to silence Israel's supporters on campus gained a sense of moral urgency and ethical superiority.

Anti-normalization is a basis for some faculty and students to reason that targeting Israeli speakers for silencing does not constitute a general assault on the principles of free speech that underlie both liberal democracy and academic freedom. It serves as an intellectual justification for separating the Israeli-Palestinian conflict from all other political issues. In Palestine it can subject those who engage in empathy-building dialogue to both threat and assault; in the US instead it stigmatizes efforts at campus dialogue between pro-Israeli and pro-Palestinian constituencies.

Incidents soon proliferated. In October 2015, former Israeli Supreme Court chief justice Aharon Barak, noted for his support of Palestinian rights and his sympathetic handling of Palestinian appeals to the court, had his own UC-Irvine talk interrupted and curtailed. The following month the world-renowned Israeli philosopher Moshe Halbertal, an authority on Maimonides, coauthor of the Israeli army Code of Ethics, and New York University faculty member, had a University of Minnesota lecture disrupted. In February 2016, Israeli Arab Bassem Eid, a radio analyst and human rights activist, was relentlessly heckled by BDS activists at the University of Chicago; in April, they blocked Jerusalem Mayor Nir Barkat from speaking at San Francisco State University.

In retrospect, it seems fanciful at best to have supposed that a special justification for setting academic freedom aside in one political context would not encourage setting it aside in others. Moreover, increasing political polarization in the US generally can also be expected to have campus consequences, especially since the campus is not broadly polarized in the same way the country is. Opposition to the hard Republican right largely unifies the campus, and rejection of right-wing spokespersons' political positions will garner wide consensus. That in turn will give credibility to a significant minority that actually wants to see hard-right speakers barred from campus. Whether that minority expands on various campuses partly depends on political developments in the country as a whole. But proactive support of principles of academic freedom now is clearly a priority.

The importance of proactive measures in support of academic freedom is highlighted by the other decades-long trend in the academy cited earlier: the gradual politicization of humanities and soft social science disciplines. A series of intellectual and social movements that began outside the academy led their constituencies within the academy to coalesce in new research and teaching initiatives beginning in the 1960s and 1970s. African American studies and women's studies were the first such research initiatives to gain programmatic status, and these projects succeeded in revolutionizing and democratizing both faculty research and the curriculum. Gradual growth in other areas, including Native American studies, followed. The foundational role that social and political activism played in these new academic areas, however, made them vulnerable to alliances with other political movements and to far less fully examined political commitments outside their areas of academic expertise.

At the same time, other departments and their academic associations, most notably American studies and Middle East studies, but also smaller identity and ethnicity-based disciplines, some of which began as broad-tent enterprises, became narrow-tent ones quite willing to take political stands that would alienate many members. The largest humanities and soft social science disciplines—anthropology, English, and history—developed noisy constituencies for political activism that on occasion could create coercive standards for political correctness within particular departments or transformative movements in national disciplinary associations.

The roots of these developments go back decades, and they are not yet fully understood. They have often evolved, moreover, in partly discipline-specific ways. Once devoted to studying primitive and indigenous cultures, anthropologists eventually began to feel responsible for advocating for them. Middle East studies was inevitably drawn into the very political conflicts it was studying. The identity-based mission of African American, Asian American, Chicana/Chicano, Native American, and women's studies programs in the US, all carrying historical experience of discrimination, gave them a potential basis to identify with disadvantaged populations elsewhere. The theory of "intersectionality," which served in the 1960s and later to explain how different social categories overlapped and interacted in peoples' lives in specific cultural contexts, evolved in the new millennium to warrant connecting injustices across time and space. Plus, to a significant degree the sense of political solidarity among different groups was grounded in and enhanced by cross-disciplinary theoretical work in areas such as race, colonialism, and postcolonialism.

Once again, those changes coalesced around the Israeli-Palestinian conflict. They began to come to a head in 2013 and 2014. At that point graduate students and contingent faculty in those areas became vulnerable to political intimidation. In 2017 I met a contingent faculty member who had recently published a book about an internationally respected Israeli Holocaust poet; within weeks of its publication, she received letters from five faculty members pledging to boycott her book and encourage others to do so, all because of its subject matter. Beginning in 2015 I started to meet graduate students and young faculty who were persuaded they shouldn't specialize in Israel studies if they wanted to have any chance at an academic career. All were from the range of disciplines cited here. Academic freedom means that people should be able to follow their hearts in deciding what work they will do. It will not survive as a universal principle if it is undermined in a series of disciplines.

The fact that fewer and fewer young faculty are winning tenure-track appointments exacerbates these development. It means that many graduate students and many contingent faculty will be subject to political intimidation or coercion throughout their professional lives. While it is good that the hard sciences and the professional schools have shown none of these tendencies, that offers little in the way of reassurance about the role the humanities and soft social sciences can play either in academia or in the culture as a whole.

Willingness to fund politically corrupted disciplines, disciplines that cross the line from political advocacy to indoctrination, will inevitably decrease. And the influence that such disciplines can have on public policy and debate will suffer as well. Can this problem be addressed? Only if administrators are willing to make certain that a sufficient degree of political balance and range of political views obtains in the curriculum as a whole. So long as faculty members welcome student expression of dissenting views, they cannot be prevented from teaching on the basis of politically biased syllabi. And individual departments cannot be mandated to mount a politically balanced curriculum. But administrators can give other departments hiring opportunities that would make for more campus diversity. Then at least the campus as a whole can be defended.

The other lesson that can be learned from this story is that it is not a good idea to wait until Milo Yiannopoulos is scheduled to speak on your campus to educate students and faculty about the nature of academic freedom and encourage them to honor it. I don't think Judith Butler and the other signatories to the Berkeley letters were likely to admit they were wrong after they initiated a campus-wide campaign. The Berkeley events have been described as a teachable moment, but that hopeful claim has only limited validity. Most of the teaching needed to have taken place long beforehand.

Understanding of academic freedom is not incorporated into faculty DNA. It has to be learned. Some faculty do not understand that academic freedom does not give them the right to refuse to teach the courses they are assigned. It does not give them the right to belittle students for their beliefs. But in the current campus climate it is much harder still to get humanities faculty to understand that academic freedom should trump their political passions.

Half a century ago, when the head of the American Nazi Party spoke at Antioch, my undergraduate college, I learned that there is educational value to experiencing monsters in the flesh, at least if they have national constituencies. George Lincoln Rockwell lost control and began angrily cursing the audience of 600 who silently declined to ask him any questions. That performance taught me more about anti-Semitism than anything I might have read about him. Does Yiannopoulos fit into the same category? One thing at least is certain about both speakers, only one prevented from speaking: neither had any potential to rally students and faculty behind them, either at Antioch or at Berkeley. That eliminates any claim to urgency behind the faculty project of suppressing academic freedom in the service of a more self-gratifying agenda. And that, at least, makes the Berkeley incident a teachable moment for the rest of us.

What I Wish I Had Known When I Started What we do not know when we start is how things will work out. The science fiction film *Arrival* asks whether we would proceed if we did know. It's not an easy question to answer. But I cannot imagine we would proceed in exactly the same way. Some conflicts we would avoid if we knew the consequences in advance. Seemingly modest commitments can have huge unforeseen consequences.

What I Wish I Had Not Done While in Office Although I paid a high price for some decisions, I cannot say for certain I would choose not to make them again.

What I Wish I Didn't Know When I Finished There are some betrayals one might be better off never learning about.

How I Knew When to Stop We do not always have agency, and we do not always get a choice about when to stop. Sometimes others decide; sometimes rules set term limits. But it is also the case that organizations and institutions change and require quite different leadership.

III EXTERNAL CHALLENGES

13 Working with Elected and Community Officials

"All Politics Is Local"

Christopher Howard

It is your turn to address the governor. A small group of independent university and college presidents, rounded up by the state association's executive director, have worked feverishly for the past several weeks to salvage the portion of the state budget dedicated to funding schools like yours. Though these dollars make up only a small portion of total spending for the upcoming year, they are critical to the financial health of your institution. You clear your throat, smile, and pray—that's right, pray—that this is not the first time you have ever spoken to the governor.

In the case of government and community relations, emphasis should be placed on the word "relations." It is critically important to build rapport and, even better, a relationship with your government counterparts and local community leaders the day you begin your tenure as president. By doing so, you gain the opportunity to learn the priorities, agenda, and concerns of these individuals without being in the awkward position of having to ask for something shortly after being introduced.

A few points are relevant as we begin this chapter. First, I have served as president of two independent or private schools, though I did hold an executive position at a flagship state university where I worked closely with the head of government relations, who was the former state house majority leader. Therefore, I have not had to lobby state officials directly for the lion's share of my institution's operating budget. However, government officials play a key role in how independent colleges and universities are governed, funded, and regulated—perhaps to a greater extent today than in any time in recent history.

From my vantage point, there are five areas of consideration when it comes to optimizing relations with government and community officials for a college or university president.

1. Learning the lay of the land: Who's who and what do they really want?
2. Just say yes to the Rotarians, Kiwanians, and some (but not all) of the rest.
3. You are not alone: Working with state, regional, and national organizations.
4. Know both of your "top fives."
5. A warm call always beats a cold one: Never miss a chance to say hello and thank you.

Learning the Lay of the Land: Who's Who and What Do They Really Want?

The life of a new college or university president may seem complicated enough as he or she tries to learn the campus organization, climate, culture, and personnel issues. The calendar appears as though it may implode of its own weight with internal meetings, meet and greets, and briefings. It is at this time that someone on the staff or board mentions the name of an elected official you must meet with immediately. Before this happens, try to get ahead of the game by having a member of the staff brief you or at least provide material about the government officials who most affect your institution. It may seem somewhat prosaic, but start with the local folks. The late Tip O'Neill, speaker of the US House of Representatives, once quipped, "All politics is local" and he was right. The "town" in "town and gown" represents the local government entities that quite often literally touch your institution. Towns, cities, and counties often have overlapping and confusing jurisdictions that your staff needs to help you understand as soon as possible. Who controls the school's water and sewage? Does the county sheriff's department work with your local campus police? Does the local school board work closely with faculty at your institution? What governmental body must approve the physical growth of the campus?

Even before the new president can recall the name of the mayor, county commissioners, head of the school board, sheriff, and city council members, someone from the state senator's office has invited him or her to a fundraiser. Obviously government does not stop at the local level. The state representative and state senator play a key role in determining an institution's success with budgetary matters, among others. In addition, the chairs of the education, appropriations, or budget committees can either help or hinder your chances at achieving the school's goals and aspirations. The legislators of course only make the laws. The executive branch, led by the governor, will likely have a secretary of education devoted to managing issues that impact your school daily, though they will likely be responsible for elementary and secondary as well as higher education. Many states also have a commission on higher education with a mandate that differs from yet overlaps that of the department of education.

No sooner does the state senator's invitation hit the president's desk than the local congresswoman decides to visit her alma mater for a previously scheduled symposium and to shake hands with the new president. With our federal system of government and the increasingly intensive oversight in areas like Title IX, federal loans, and Pell Grant and research funding, it is imperative for presidents to know their member of Congress and hopefully both senators.

In many ways determining the lay of the land is much easier than discerning what officials really want—as opposed to what they say they want. Every elected official the president meets has an agenda, stated and unstated. The president's job is to identify that agenda with the aim of leveraging areas of agreement to benefit the school and minimizing the downside when elected officials' agendas are at odds with those of the school. But how to accomplish this unseemly task? As you develop your group of trusted advisors, ask them to be both candid and comprehensive when describing the school's work with elected officials. This recommendation is not meant to turn staff meetings into reality television shows but rather to build the expectation that your briefings will include the good, the bad, and the ugly when it comes to elected officials.

To recap: There are several levels and layers of government and elected officials that can help or hinder your chances for success, whether at private or public institutions. Identify a member or members of your staff to brief you early on the following:

- Organizational chart noting municipal and county government positions
- Explanation of which entity has authority over issues germane to your school

- Names of the officials and their connection to and history with the school (they should refrain from including sensitive material in a presentation and save it for oral discussion)
- List of key issues currently in play with elected officials

Finally, though presidents naturally devote time to learning about and cultivating relations with elected officials responsible for budgetary affairs, they should not forget those who enforce the law. I am thinking here specifically of the district attorney. Often an elected official, the DA has the authority to prosecute members of your student body, faculty, and staff, though students are more likely to find themselves in his or her crosshairs than anyone else. I met with our DA on a regular basis simply to let him know that I was in the business of developing young people who would no doubt make mistakes. As they made mistakes, our student judicial system was equipped to mete out justice and offer opportunities for redemption on a case-by-case basis. What I could not or would not do was serve as judge, prosecutor, and jury for legal matters that, in my estimation, were the DA's purview. Once our dean of students or campus security got wind of criminal activities, we would take what we knew to the DA and let him proceed as he deemed appropriate, all the while conducting our student judiciary proceeding. I made my philosophy known to the board, administration, parents, students, and faculty early in my tenure, and I can't say everyone agreed with me, though they respected my approach. But as difficult cases arose, and they inevitably do, I developed a reputation for consistency and fairness—two traits a president can always use when dealing with elected officials.

Just Say Yes to the Rotarians, Kiwanians, and Some of the Rest

After transitioning from the military and corporate America to higher education, I contemplated the prospects of one day becoming a college president. My work as a vice president at a large flagship school had gone well, and several executive search firms approached me about the prospects of interviewing for a presidency. It was at that time I decided to determine the type of school I wanted to lead. A brief Google search resulted in a list of schools aligned with my interests. I then printed the biographies of the presidents of 130 schools and found something interesting: a significant number of them were members of the Rotary Club. Though not surprising, this fact is quite useful. College and university presidents must be "glocal"—both local and global simultaneously. Rotarians are by design rooted in the local affairs of their community but always concerned about issues facing our world, such as education and eradication of diseases such as polio.

I encourage new college and university presidents to discern the issues and ideas he or she finds most stimulating and to use this understanding to navigate the world of community leaders. There will be no shortage of organizations vying for your time. You should of course prioritize building relations with those community officials whose organizations will have the greatest impact on the school but a close second should be those places with which your interests and passion most closely align. For me, connecting young leaders worldwide to my campus was a must, so the Rotarians (of which I used to be a member) were high on the list.

For a new president, connecting with local community leaders is paramount, but connecting with community leaders who have a mission that extends beyond the town's borders is even better. I found that Kiwanians, along with Rotarians, keep one foot in local affairs and another on the global stage.

Because a president's schedule is so hectic, I advise being strategic about which local groups to invest one's most precious resource: time. Though others may have alternative litmus tests, I have always tried to spend time with community leaders who have mission statements that extend beyond the town's borders. That said, I encourage new presidents to develop a framework for determining with which community leaders they will spend the most time. It may be proximity to the campus or a shared academic focus or a historical affinity. At my previous institution we identified three organizations that had historic ties to the school and whose goals aligned with our strategic plan. In fact, the chief executives of these three organizations participated in our strategic planning process. Our trio consisted of a food pantry, a civil rights museum, and a nonprofit dedicated to providing job opportunities for the mentally disabled. The types of community organizations was perhaps less important than providing clarity to our faculty, staff, and community that our schools would try to say "yes" to their requests. Whether it was granting requests for meeting space, participating in programming, or just offering words of advice and support, after vetting these organizations, we made them our partners. Partnerships with community officials and organizations afford the school the opportunity for robust curricular, co-curricular, and extracurricular activities that can make a deep impact on all parties involved.

All presidents must foster productive relationships with myriad community leaders and weigh depth versus breadth as they manage their overloaded calendars. My recommendation is to identify in a transparent manner the handful of groups where the school is willing to go deep. Doing so increases the chances of making a real impact.

To recap:

- Try to identify community organizations with both a global and local outlook.
- If global affairs are not of interest, focus on those entities aligned with your interests and passions.
- Focus your energy on building a few strategic partnerships.
- Ensure that university constituents understand the rationale for and upside of working with your strategic partners.

You Are Not Alone: Working with State, Regional, and National Organizations

Although presidents of colleges and universities are leading during a time of increased scrutiny and criticism by virtually all members of civil society, the disdain cuts across all of higher education. The old saying that "misery loves company" is apropos. The good news is that schools are working together to create and communicate their agenda through state, regional, or national coalitions, associations, and consortia. New presidents should get to know which of these groups is best advancing their school's agenda and get involved.

Both the Association of Independent Colleges and Universities of Pennsylvania (AICUP) and the Council of Independent Colleges in Virginia (CICV) serve as exemplars of how statewide associations can help presidents by keeping them abreast of all the legislation that may impact their respective member institutions. More important, staff members from both of these groups and their counterparts in other states can mobilize the membership to support or reject measures in a timely manner. Every bill has a history, and it is the state associations that know that history. As a result, they can direct the new president to the appropriate elected officials (and their staffs) to make their case. Membership dues can be high, but I submit they are well worth the price. Whether it be funding for capital projects, tuition, or research, state organizations are the principal guides for new university and college presidents as they unpack their legislators' dense agendas.

At the national level both the American Council on Education (ACE) and the National Association of Independent Colleges and Universities (NAICU) do a fine job keeping track of the major legislative, judicial, and legal affairs affecting higher education. I served on the board of ACE, whose mandate is to serve both public and independent schools. ACE and NAICU let the membership know about everything from Supreme Court rulings, to Department of Labor regulations, to congressional bills that might make a difference in the world of higher education. But because the Higher Education Act of 1965 has not been significantly modified since 2008, the impact of state budgets often trumps that of the federal budget. At times, smaller institutions may feel overwhelmed by their larger counterparts when it comes to the national organizations; however, ACE, NAICU, and their public counterparts work diligently to ensure all schools have a say in shaping the lobbying agenda.

New presidents should consider serving institutions like ACE, NAICU, CICV, or AICUP, whether as a member of the board of directors or as a member of task force or advisory board. The payback and professional satisfaction are immense. Opportunities to meet with key elected officials on a regular basis abound as well as interacting with a top-notch professional staff often comprising graduates from the schools being served.

Finally, each day presidents receive a multitude of newsletters on myriad topics. Be sure to at least skim those sent by state, regional, and national organizations that lobby on the school's behalf. Your board members likely have a cursory understanding of how government funding affects your school and will expect you to be an expert. These newsletters and other "news flashes" are an excellent way to stay on top of the issues and build relations with elected officials.

To recap:

- Remember that other schools are also experiencing difficult times.
- The state association is laser focused on governmental matters that will impact your campus.
- Regional and national organizations also focus on legislative, judicial, and executive actions that affect higher education.
- Get involved with these groups early in your tenure as president because doing so increases the frequency and quality of your interactions with elected officials.

Know Both of Your "Top Fives"

One cannot browse the internet, scan radio stations, or surf television channels without encountering a "top-five," "top-10," or even "top-100" list of virtually every endeavor known to humankind. But top-five lists can serve a useful purpose by forcing individuals to focus and prioritize.

Five years into my first presidency, I scheduled phone calls with my three predecessors asking them to offer any advice they thought would be important at this point in my tenure. Without hesitation all three said, "Focus on your priorities." When it comes to optimizing relationships with elected and community officials, it is imperative that a new president determine his or her priorities. I like to call it my "top-five" list, and it includes the five most important actions the school could take to ensure our success. In many ways the list serves as a filter as I determine how I will schedule events for the day, week, month, or even the year and also an agenda for meeting with elected and community leaders. The list is not static, and a new president should not expect to have it ready on day one. Over time, however, every president who is leading his or her institution effectively should have a "top five" and strive to align his or her actions with its content.

It is not enough for the president to know the "top five"—the staff, and especially the president's scheduler-cum-assistant, must know it as well. Members of presidential staffs or cabinets often live hectic lives trying to determine how presidents want them to spend their time. Top-five lists afford these vice presidents a lens of sorts when it comes to their activities, including in the realm of building and sustaining relations with elected and community officials.

A second top-five list is crucial as well: the names of those individuals (in this instance community and elected leaders) who can help the school address the priorities noted on the top-five list. Though this idea is simple, it is surprising how many administrations are not aligned this way when it comes to using the president's time effectively and efficiently. When the board has authorized the administration to, for example, build a new sports center, there are inevitably certain community and elected officials who can help make it happen. When the president's assistant knows that list, he or she can shape the president's calendar in a way that dedicates as much time as possible to building relationships with these individuals without the president having to micromanage the scheduler. The result is an aligned organization that optimizes the president's time and energy.

To recap:

- Know the top-five actions that will have the greatest impact on the school.
- Know the top-five community and elected officials who can influence those priorities.
- Ensure that your staff and assistant know both lists.

A Warm Call Always Beats a Cold One

I opened this chapter with the story about a meeting that included the governor and statewide association of college and university presidents regarding a key budgetary issue. The story is true. Luckily, my prayers were answered as I had already built a relationship with the governor well before that day.

Though college and university presidents would like to describe their work as both analytical and intellectual, often it is simply about relationships. People tend to react more favorably to those they know and like than those they do not know and dislike. This is not rocket science, nor is it meant to be a euphemism advocating backslapping and secret handshakes. Instead, these words are meant to encourage presidents to get to know elected and community officials starting early in their tenure. Do so with no agenda other than simply getting to know the human beings across the table. Ask open-ended, Socratic questions to learn how they see the world. Talk less and listen more, saving your agenda for later in the meeting or, even better, at a different meeting altogether. Invite officials to participate in events on your campus or that include constituents from your institution, regardless of venue. Say what you will about college athletics, having a state senator spend three hours on your campus for a football game interacting with members of your community goes a long way. Over time you will build a rapport with the very people your institutions depends upon. They will in turn take your calls and respond to your questions. If you are lucky, they will gain a keen understanding of your agenda and try to help. This is not to say that they will obey your every wish or even agree with you on every important matter, but they will at least hear what you have to say and give it serious consideration. At the end of the day, getting others to understand what a school needs is paramount for any president to succeed, from the smallest liberal arts college to the largest flagship public university, especially when those "others" are community and elected officials.

What I Wish I Had Known When I Started I wish I had known what a high number of community and elected officials I would interact with on a regular basis when I started.

What I Wish I Had Done When I Finished I wish I had sent a thank-you note to every community leader and elected official I had worked with when I finished my first presidency in order to assist my successor with the transition.

What I Wish I Had Not Done While in Office While in office, I wish I had established my "top-five" list of priorities and "top-five" individuals to assist with addressing these priorities earlier in my presidency.

What I Wish I Didn't Know When I Finished I wish I didn't know just how small-minded and parochial some politicians could be, especially when it came to their pet projects.

How I Knew When to Stop I knew it was time to leave after my administration had achieved about 90 percent of the objectives in our strategic plan.

Becoming an "Engaged University"

Robert A. Scott

An important but little-understood role for campus presidents, especially at independent colleges and universities, is to work with elected officials and the community. The former include not only state and federal officials, in both the legislative and executive branches of government, but also village and county officials as well neighbors. In some cases, these local entities also include neighborhood associations, which are the sources of candidates for "city hall" elections and the school board. The "community" includes these groups as well as campus neighbors, the area historical society, the local and regional chambers of commerce, and others. Each group is a stakeholder in the college or university's mission and strategic plan, often with a critical role to play with regard to campus safety, construction approvals, and assistance with temporary parking or sports fields.

While I have always believed that a campus must be a good neighbor, it was in my first months as president of Adelphi University, when I met with the president of the Long Island Association, that I formulated my notion of "the engaged university." I asked about the distinctive features of the 18 other campuses in the region, and he complained that they were too involved in their own identities and not sufficiently engaged in regional issues. I asked for an explanation and decided that, for these contemporary reasons as well as for Adelphi's historical priorities, my mantra would become "Adelphi: The Engaged University."

By this I meant that Adelphi as an institution, as well as individual Adelphi faculty, staff, and students, would be involved in community initiatives for the betterment of the region and that we would actively invite the broader community to attend campus events of all types:, including drama, dance, music, theater, lectures, and so on. Some events, of course, feature elected officials, and the campus thus serves as a neutral forum for discussing issues important to the community and the region. In these ways, I underscored the role of president as conductor of external as well as internal affairs.

At my first meeting with the New York State Chair of the Senate Higher Education Committee, who happened to be an Adelphi alumnus, I was asked point-blank why I didn't want to buy the derelict but iconic 100-year-old former boys school, a brick edifice of High Victorian Gothic Design in Garden City. I already knew the estimate for bringing the facility up to code was north of $50 million. The senator said I could ask alumni for donations, something I did not want to do given the programmatic and facility priorities on campus. Thus, my first meeting with someone who became a friend and supporter started off in a different direction.

For a campus, critical issues involving elected officials and local, county, state, and federal administrators include regulatory approvals, discretionary or competitive grants, academic program and zoning or construction approvals, professional degree certifications, student aid advocacy, and, for public institutions, trustee approvals, often in the state capitol or the district offices of officials. While I was president of Ramapo College of New Jersey, for example, I worked with state department heads on construction regulations, trying to change the regulation for "lowest bidder" to "lowest responsible bidder" in order to avoid having a paving contractor qualify to build a residence hall.

The other presidents and I also worked with state senators who had used their "senatorial courtesy" option to hold up appointments of college trustees at a local campus, even when the new trustee was needed to have a quorum on a board. This often happened when one senator needed the vote of another for his or her favored constituent, even when the college was not actually in the middle of the policy discussion, but merely a pawn in the negotiations.

Again in New Jersey, presidents had to devote time to meeting with the governor's staff on trustee appointments, labor contract negotiations that were handled centrally, budget appropriation implications, and capital budget priorities. Once a former attorney general told a group of us to be on friendly terms with state legislators because this would make it easier to seek "forgiveness" in cases when "permission" had been neither requested nor received.

I had become a college president to be an educator, but my colleagues and I had to devote a great deal of time to fiscal and labor issues. So, three of my fellow presidents at colleges in other states with similar missions decided to create a new subgroup of institutions—public liberal arts colleges. We persuaded *U.S. News and World Report* to create a separate category for ranking these institutions, set about to recruit additional institutional members who met our criteria, and then resolved to ask our state legislatures to designate each member campus as "the" public liberal arts college in the state. I did this with relish, telling our state senators and assembly members that Ramapo was a real college, not a "pretend" university. Our arguments prevailed.

In New York, when I started at Adelphi, the primary issues, even at private colleges and universities, concerned teacher education program regulations, which were overly restrictive; inadequately funded student financial aid programs; and a stalled capital project funding program, all requiring trips to Albany and local legislative offices. In each case and at each level there are points of leverage. The first point of leverage is a personal relationship with the official. This is essential, and it can help if he or she is an alumnus or an alumna. A second point of leverage is the campus staff dedicated to government relations.

These newer positions, often at the vice president level, sometimes puzzle critics of college costs who do not appreciate how much time and talent it takes to understand proposed and actual government regulations and the process to influence or amend them. A third point of leverage at the state level is the association of college presidents, because state officials listen when many voices speak in unison. Government relations lawyers, also known as lobbyists, can also be helpful. While lobbyists in general have a tarnished reputation because of the actions of a few, in my experience they are mostly honest, earnest professionals whose expertise in the workings of government and whose personal relationships can help open doors for campus presidents to make their case.

At the federal level, personal relationships, associations of colleges and universities, and lobbyists are also integral to the process of government. I have engaged all three at different times to advocate for improvements in federal work-study funds, changes to the proposed College Scorecard and federal loan program regulations, and the establishment of the twenty-first-century G.I. Bill.

As part of a president's role in becoming known by elected officials, he or she will be invited to fundraising events and to contribute to campaign funds. This can be treacherous territory. Tax-exempt colleges are prohibited from giving to political accounts, so the burden falls to the president. My advice: give modestly and selectively, and keep records. I received a letter of inquiry from the New York State attorney general once alleging that Adelphi had contributed to a political action committee. With my record in hand, I could prove that the donation was personal, not institutional. Without a copy of the record, the university could have faced further scrutiny. This is, by the way, another way in which lobbying firms can be helpful. They can contribute to political events and invite institutional representatives as guests. This helps the campus representative further personal relationships without crossing the legal line.

The approaches to take in working with elected officials and the wider community are the same as working with other campus constituents. We must be persistent but principled, and know when to be patient. We should show up and stop by—engaging in friendly conversations even when business is not urgent.

Having a friendly relationship can help improve the reception of an urgent request. As always, listen. Show respect. Know the person's interests and priorities, so that conversations can be interactive, not just one way. Invite officials to celebratory events; ask them to offer remarks; take pictures and place them in the media.

Keep your contacts informed of your progress—and problems. Remember: no surprises. The odds are that the elected official has constituents who are in the neighborhood or are alumni. It is better for you to tell them about an issue than for them to be told by someone else or read about it in the newspaper. At Adelphi, we kept neighbors informed of campus plans by inviting them in for tea and briefings, inviting village officials to tour campus facilities and review project plans, attending meetings of the local property owners association and village board of trustee, and participating in local chamber of commerce meetings and activities. We invited the local sports teams and clubs to use our facilities.

We also sponsored an annual prize for leadership to recognize high school juniors from Garden City, but not necessarily at Garden City High School, for their voluntarism. The 10 or so winners each year were selected by a committee consisting of the local school district superintendent, the village administrator, and me. Each student winner earned a cash prize, invitations to meet with major speakers brought to campus, and free tuition for two credit-bearing courses. This program was our PILOT (Payment in Lieu of Taxes), a modest solution to an increasingly contentious topic between campuses and communities.

In 2001, we submitted a request to the village to construct a new residence hall on the west side of campus, adjacent to neighbors' homes (and the president's house). Through the property owners association and at a meeting with the village board of trustees, nearby neighbors told lies about the qualifications of Adelphi students and complained about drug paraphernalia and liquor bottles on the property line separating their homes and the campus. When I looked at the site the next day, I found early childhood play equipment that showed signs of active use. I had photographs taken of the site and showed them to the village trustees, informally, asking if I should bring the pictures to the next public hearing. The point was made, and the board approved our plans without another hearing. The neighbors had become accustomed to a campus with declining enrollment and talked openly about their uninterrupted walks in the part-like setting. They did not want a revitalized campus neighbor. The mayor had even stood up at a public hearing when I was at a podium and interrupted me by saying, "Scott, we will never approve this project." Well, they did, and two years later the now-former mayor called asking me for help in finding a job. He had been laid off from his position on Wall Street. I wrote a letter of reference for him.

At a tea for neighbors from the property owners association at the President's House, I noticed that one of the women looked sad and tense. When I asked if she was okay, she replied that her husband needed a heart transplant, and his employer wanted him to have it done in Illinois, where the firm was located. They lived in Garden City. I asked for the details, contacted the state senator who chaired the Senate Health Committee, and our neighbor got his new heart 30 miles from his home. In these various ways, the campus president plays a "retail" role, becoming directly involved, and a "wholesale" role, as speaker or champion.

The campus is both a community and a part of the larger community. Alumni, students and their families, and faculty and staff are constituents of legislators. These campus stakeholders can often be even more persuasive than the institution's president in making the case for a policy, a program, or a change that will help the college or university fulfill its mission of service to society. The president is the conductor of this symphony with many parts.

What I Wish I Had Known When I Started Before assuming my first presidency, at Ramapo College of New Jersey, I asked the experienced president of Purdue University, Steve Beering, for advice. He emphasized the need to work closely with the board of trustees. However, even with this advice, I did not realize how time consuming board work would be. I wanted to be a campus president because of my commitment to the transformative powers of education, so I was surprised by the amount of time spent discussing fiscal and labor issues. To help compensate for this, I helped cofound the Council of Public Liberal Arts Colleges (COPLAC), which still flourishes.

What I Wish I Had Done When I Finished After I announced my decision to leave Ramapo College after 15 years, I was consulted by several of the candidates who were in line to succeed me. When I realized that two of the four would not accept the post if offered and that a third had withdrawn, I talked to the board chair about the fourth candidate. I wish I had been more forceful in encouraging him to continue the search instead of settling on a doubtful candidate, who was forced to leave before his third year started.

What I Wish I Had Not Done While in Office About 8 years into my 15 years at Ramapo College, I succumbed to an invitation to be a candidate for the presidency at the University of Rhode Island. I was intrigued by the opportunity to lead an institution with doctoral programs and a robust research agenda, but anxious about my candidacy becoming known on my home campus. Well, it became known; I withdrew from the search, and I convened a faculty meeting to explain and apologize. I didn't want my colleagues to feel that I valued another institution more than Ramapo. My focus on the topic gave it more attention than it deserved.

What I Wish I Didn't Know When I Finished One May, when I was preparing my annual report, I created a thought puzzle. I asked my vice presidents to take a piece of paper and write down the top three actions they would encourage a new president to take during his or her first three to six months on campus. To my surprise, each had the same number-one item, to dismiss a midlevel administrator who was known to be insubordinate in a variety of ways. I said, "Why wait for a new president?" I denied the person's reappointment, was sued for four forms of discrimination and one form of defamation, and spent 20 hours on the witness stand—after I had already started at Adelphi. After eight years, with four lawyers, the plaintiff's claims were denied by a Superior Court jury. While I am glad I did what I did, I may have chosen a different course if I had known the toll the case would take on my staff.

How I Knew When to Stop After 13 years at Ramapo, and considering a number of invitations to be a candidate as campus president elsewhere, I decided that there was no other campus I wished to serve. However, I did want to pursue a position at an organization serving higher education and was delighted when I received an invitation to be interviewed as executive vice president and heir apparent at a large, prestigious nonprofit testing company. During the interview process, I realized that I would not want to report to a CEO and could not work in an organization designed as a matrix, with no one directly responsible for his or her portfolio or the overall results. Then I received a call about Adelphi, a doctoral-level research university with a high priority on teaching. It was a dream come true.

14 Exercising Institutional Autonomy

Entrepreneurship in Higher Education

William R. Harvey

Institutions of higher education—since the time of the first formal institution, the University of Bologna—have always had and will continue to experience challenges and changes. A number of these challenges exist because of the many unpredictable changes that occur in society over time. These include increased competition for faculty, staff and student talent; technology advancements; economic pressures; societal expectations; globalization; and the creation of new funding opportunities. As a result, universities all over the globe are having to adjust their educational business models. Because of the pressures to identify new and additional sources of revenue, many institutions have begun to pursue entrepreneurial activities as one of the solutions.

The importance of the revenue side of the budget cannot be overstated. When mention is made of a "budget," many people think only of expenses, forgetting that a budget is comprised of two sides of the ledger, i.e., revenue and expenses. Those who manage the higher educational enterprise must constantly think about ways to secure sufficient resources to support required and approved expenses. This means that college and university administrators who value entrepreneurial activities as a new source of funding must create an environment that promises, supports, and rewards new and innovative thinking and practices.

As an entrepreneur and educator, I have long appreciated the benefits that these two powerful enterprises can produce by working together. Having served as president of Hampton University (HU) for nearly 40 years and having been 100 percent owner of a Pepsi-Cola bottling plant for 34 years, I make this assertion not as a theoretical construct, but as a working reality.

In the early 1980s, long before the concept of entrepreneurial activities became as popular as it is today, I presented a plan to Hampton's trustees for our university to become entrepreneurially active. Initially, some pushed back, some called for more information, and at least one member declared that colleges are in the business of providing education and not running businesses. Even though a majority of the trustees were in favor of moving forward, not all of them were convinced at first. Instead of calling for a vote, I chose to continue to educate the members on the benefits of an entrepreneurial mindset.

The rationale for the plan was that we needed to be forward thinking because society, higher education, and demographics were changing. These developments were going to require Hampton, as an institution, to be prepared to change its business model. We could not and should not rely on the traditional revenue streams of tuition, public and private grants, and income from our modest endowment. Therefore I proposed that Hampton adopt a strategic plan that increased the endowment, with the understanding that part of the increase could, with board approval, be used for entrepreneurial and strategic initiatives. After a great deal of discussion over several meetings, the board of trustees voted unanimously to approve this concept. Hampton's endowment, which stood at $29 million at that time, stands at approximately $280 million today.

Our first business development was the construction of a small shopping center and apartment complex named the Hampton Harbor project. This investment totaled $12.3 million, of which $2.2 million came from the US Department of Housing and Urban Development in the form of an Urban Development Action Grant (UDAG), $700,000 from a grant from the City of Hampton, and the remaining $9.4 million from the university's endowment fund. The complex, with a square footage of 54,645, is 100 percent owned by the university. The shopping center—located adjacent to downtown Hampton, Interstate 64, and the university—spans more than 25 units and houses a Burger King and other restaurants, dry cleaner, bookstore, barber shop, insurance office, and a continuing education unit. As of June 30, 2015, this investment had earned more than $26 million to support student scholarships. This project was an instant success, realizing more than $1 million in profits in the first year of operation, and every year thereafter.

The success of this first project gave the trustees and the administration more comfort with the concepts of risk and reward. Hampton's next projects involved partnering with several municipalities in Virginia and a construction company to build hotels. This arrangement was unique: Hampton University provided the financing and charged the market interest rate during construction. This meant that the interest and fees that a financial institution would have received instead went to HU's endowment. Additionally, upon completion of the construction, we required an equity interest of between 37 and 40 percent in the sale proceeds of the property.

The university's first hotel project came in 2002. In May of that year, we financed the $17.5 million construction loan for the Hilton Garden Inn project from the university's endowment fund. This complex, comprising 100,000 square feet, is a 176-room, limited-service hotel located in Virginia Beach, Virginia. In 2003, the loan, interest, and fees were paid in full.

In December 2004, the university joined forces with the Armada Hoffler Construction Company and the city of Newport News to construct a premier Marriott hotel and conference center in the City Center at Oyster Point. Hampton University provided the full financing of $24 million for this project from our endowment fund. The 200,000-square-foot construction project included a full-service hotel with 256 rooms. In early 2008, just three years after providing the construction loan, the university received all of its funding back and earned a $3 million profit on this investment.

HU entered into an agreement in January 2006 to invest $5 million from the endowment fund in the Westin Hotel. This hotel, which has 236 rooms and five levels of parking with 950 parking spaces (totaling 339,000 square feet), is part of the Town Center project in Virginia Beach, Virginia. The hotel sits in a 40-story tower that also houses retail space on the first floor and upscale condominiums on the top 21 floors. With a 20 percent ownership interest, the university has earned $707,000 on its investment to date.

In March 2008, the university, along with other investors, entered an agreement to construct a Hilton Garden Inn in Blacksburg, Virginia. The university's investment was $736,640 from the endowment fund. The project cost was $13 million for the construction of 137 hotel rooms with a total square footage of 76,400. In 2015, this loan was closed, with the university earning $600,000 on this investment.

Recently, the university partnered with the Armada Hoffler Construction Company to construct a 156-room Hyatt Regency on the beach in Virginia Beach. The hotel has approximately 20,000 square feet of high-end retail shops, along with a 322-space structured parking garage and 9,000 square feet of complementary retail. The total cost of this project is estimated at $77 million. The university's portion of the investment is $13.5 million from the endowment fund. Construction was completed in March 2017, and the project is now open to the public.

Another business venture that Hampton University engaged in was the building of the Williams Mullen Law Center in Richmond, Virginia. In February 2008, we provided financing for the first new high-rise office tower located in downtown Richmond in several decades. The tower comprises nine and a half floors of office space consisting of 207,000 square feet; first-floor retail space of 5,100 square feet; and a 114-space parking garage. This new tower adjoins an existing parking garage owned by the Richmond Metropolitan Authority, which is available for office tenant use. The university's investment was $7 million from the endowment fund. In the latter half of 2009, the loan was paid off and the university earned more than $2.2 million from this investment.

Because of Hampton's innovative, entrepreneurial spirit, the total profit realized from its real estate investments is approximately $34 million to date. This is phenomenal for an institution the size of Hampton. As mentioned, all of the profits from the Hampton Harbor project went into a student scholarship endowment, while the other realized gains were placed into the nonrestricted endowment fund. Not only did Hampton's endowment grow by more than $34 million, but some young man or woman was able to attend Hampton on a scholarship because of the entrepreneurial aggressiveness on the part of the trustees and administration.

It took courage and confidence for the Hampton's board of trustees to make these investments. To university leaders pondering these kinds of actions, my advice is to take the time to bring your trustees along with you. Even if you initially have the majority of the votes on this or other issues, be sure to address all questions and concerns. Patience is truly a virtue in these situations, as the payoff will usually be positive. Thus far, every entrepreneurial venture that Hampton University has undertaken has turned a profit. As a result, students have benefited from scholarships received, jobs have been created, services have been rendered, economic development has been achieved, and Hampton's endowment has grown. All of this was made possible through the entrepreneurial mindset of one modest-size university.

In addition to participating directly in business ventures, Hampton initiated an academic entrepreneurial program housed in the School of Business. It is designed to provide students with an understanding of general business practices, risk taking, ownership, technology transfer, and opportunities. From its inception, however, the primary theme of this academic entrepreneurial program has been one of economic development.

I firmly believe that the chief reason for being of any college or university is the promotion of learning. Entrepreneurship not only serves that function, but adds to it the promotion of services. One good example of the value of service can be seen clearly in the transferring of intellectual property rights by faculty and students into business development. Perhaps the most well-known example of student entrepreneurship to commercialization can be found with the social media phenomenon of Twitter and Facebook. Jack Dorsey cofounded Twitter when he was a student at New York University, and Mark Zuckerberg cofounded Facebook during his student days at Harvard.

Although Hampton University's thrust has been one of direct involvement as an entrepreneur, an entrepreneurial university can include a broad array of activities, such as the transfer of new technology; commercialization of any conceivable business, including intellectual properties; new startups; promotion of social change; innovations that lead to teaching students, faculty, and community residents about the risks and rewards of starting or owning a business; business and industry partnerships; and participation as the entrepreneur.

Different universities, and even different countries, use innovative approaches to starting or increasing entrepreneurial activities. In the European model, entrepreneurship is embedded into all aspects of universities, including leadership and government, opportunities for learning entrepreneurship in and out of the classroom, and interdisciplinary interaction among faculty and students that create new knowledge. The prevailing view is that to be successful, an entrepreneurial university must not only have the support of leaders at every level, but it must employ individuals who can serve as entrepreneurial role models.*

The Europeans believe it is imperative for an entrepreneurial university to build a community of faculty, staff, and students who are willing to take risks. Once these foundational elements are in place, an entrepreneurial university is in a position to engage in entrepreneurial ventures, such as empowering faculty and students to capitalize on university research by developing new products and technologies, creating new business ventures, and enteing into economic partnerships with public and private entities.†

*P. Coyle, A. Gibb, and G. Haskins, eds., *The Entrepreneurial University: From Concept to Action* (Coventry, UK: National Centre for Entrepreneurship in Education, 2013).

†Ibid.

Universities in Europe have implemented entrepreneurialism on their campuses in several ways. The University of Oxford has established a technology transfer company designed to transform research projects from all disciplines into technology and expertise that can be used by clients. The company helps researchers secure patents, license products, and establish companies as well as providing consulting services and advice on technology transfer to public and private clients. In addition, Oxford has created an interdisciplinary research unit that seeks to address global challenges and answer the questions that will be important to the world's future. The goal is to one day use this research for technology transfer and establish companies that would create financial income for the university.*

The US model of entrepreneurship can be divided into five categories: student entrepreneurship, faculty entrepreneurship, technology transfer, industry collaboration, and engagement in regional economic development. These five categories were identified in a 2011 letter from 142 university presidents and the National Advisory Council on Innovation and Entrepreneurship (NACIE) to the US secretary of commerce, requesting that the federal government partner with the universities in the areas of innovations and entrepreneurship.†

As a result of this letter, the US Department of Commerce and NACIE undertook a two-year study to understand what America's colleges and universities were doing in the areas of "innovation, commercialization, and entrepreneurship." The resulting report, *The Innovative and Entrepreneurial University: Higher Education, Innovation, and Entrepreneurship in Focus,* found a great deal of interest, discovery, and activity on many of the campuses. Specifically, the report stated, "Hundreds of colleges and universities across the U.S. are creating entrepreneurship programs with short-term objectives of creating educational value for the students and long-term objectives of driving economic growth in their communities through locally developed enterprises."‡

This report also highlighted the fact that some universities are investing heavily in entrepreneurial skills for students. For example, the University of Colorado system's Innovation and Entrepreneur degree program offers a bachelor's degree in Innovation; the University of Illinois's Intellectual Prop-

* Ibid.

† US Department of Commerce, *The Innovative and Entrepreneurial University: Higher Education, Innovation and Entrepreneurship in Focus* (Washington, DC, 2013), p. 4.

‡ Ibid., p. 9.

erty Clinic arranges for law students to help student inventors draft patent applications; Washington University in St. Louis gives 25 of its students the opportunity to receive paid internships in startup companies; and the University of Florida's "INSPIREation" Hall is an academic residential community for entrepreneurially interested students.*

Another approach can be found in the University of Virginia's July 2016 announcement that it had established a $2.2 billion fund for strategic initiatives. This multibillion-dollar fund is above and beyond the university's approximately $6 billion endowment. This strategic initiative fund reportedly is to be used for support of technology, scholarships for students, recruiting of faculty talent, and the like. Presumably, this initiative may also be used for innovative and entrepreneurial activities as well.

These few examples show the wide range of activities that American colleges and universities are employing to emphasize innovation and entrepreneurship. In my judgment, this trend will only become larger and more directed. The economic and intellectual benefits are too great for it not to expand. Historically, the business models for colleges and universities have been highly dependent on securing appropriate and adequate resources, and the federal government has been the main driver.

Perhaps the first tangible sign of support from the federal government came with the enactment by the US Congress, in 1862, of the Morrill Act. The legislation for this act was proposed by Representative Justin Smith Morrill of Vermont to establish land-grant industrial colleges. It designated land to be allocated to each state based on its number of US senators and representatives. In addition to scientific and classical studies, the schools were to teach military tactics and "agriculture and the mechanic arts." Based on the 1860 census, eligible states received 30,000 acres of federal land per member of Congress. The proceeds from the sale of the land were used to establish and fund land-grant institutions. Under this act, 17,400,000 acres were allocated, and the sale of the land resulted in $7.55 million in endowment funds.†

The Morrill Act of 1890, or Second Morrill Act, was designed to include former Confederate states and allow them to establish and operate institutions with the same rights as 1862 Act institutions, although no federal land was given to them. This Second Morrill Act also required states to provide

*Ibid., p. 10.

†1890 Land-Grant Universities, The Morrill Acts of 1862 and 1890, www.1890universities.org/history.

educational opportunities for newly freed slaves by requiring the states to prove that race was not a criterion for admission to their land-grant institutions. The passage of this legislation opened the door to the recognition of public historically Black colleges and universities and the Tuskegee Institute as land-grant institutions with the benefits that designation entailed.

The next significant change in the educational business model came in 1944, when the G.I. Bill was enacted. This bill gave veterans assistance with expenses if they wished to attend an institution of higher education. The law allowed millions of veterans, including me, to attend the college or university of their choice to receive bachelor's, master's, and doctoral degrees.

In 1978, the passage of the Middle Income Student Assistance Act established Basic Education Opportunity Grants (BEOG) for low-income students and increased eligibility limits for others. The eligibility changes were enormously helpful to middle-income families. In 1980, this program was renamed in honor of Senator Claiborne Pell of Rhode Island. Pell Grants continue to be a major source of support for many students today. These federal support programs, along with state aid to public colleges, have been of great assistance to millions of students, and correspondingly to the revenue side of the economic business model for all colleges and universities.

Whether an institution serves as an entrepreneur itself, as Hampton University does, or employs another approach, it is clear to me that colleges and universities need new business models to successfully cope with the economic changes that they will continue to face. I remain convinced that entrepreneurial activities are a major solution to the challenge of creating new funding opportunities to sustain those necessary economic business models.

What I Wish I Had Known When I Started When I began as the president of Hampton in 1978, I was prepared. My previous higher education experiences at Harvard, Fisk, and Tuskegee Universities had given me insight into the demands and challenges inherent in the presidency. As a result, I knew what to expect. Therefore, I was not surprised by any of the issues I faced; I expected them.

What I Wish I Had Done When I Finished Because I have not finished the job, my goal each day is to ensure that Hampton University remains *the* standard of excellence.

What I Wish I Had Not Done While in Office Though I have not yet left office, I have no regrets. By no means was every decision I made the best decision, but it was the right decision to be made at that time, based on the information available to me. When in the process of making a decision, I get as much information and input as possible from my colleagues. Then I make the decision and let the chips fall where they may.

What I Wish I Didn't Know When I Finished I am not finished, but I wish I didn't know that many people focus more on the negative than the positive. Instead of lighting a candle, they curse the darkness.

How I Will Know When to Stop I will know it's time to stop when I no longer enjoy doing the work.

Mythical Beasts and Real Challenges

Gerald B. Kauvar, Stephen Joel Trachtenberg, and E. Gordon Gee

Although many claim to have seen them, unicorns remain a mythical beast: a chimera.

So it is for institutional autonomy.

Traditionally viewed, autonomy often refers to "independent" institutions in distinction to those that are state supported. Autonomy also refers to the hoped-for flexibility that branch institutions of a state system try to maintain over their academic and non-academic offerings, choices, and policies. In fact, no matter how an institution is chartered or funded, it is not autonomous. It swims in a sea of competing interests.

Simply put, all are at the mercy of mysterious and rapidly changing demands—for example, the demand that more university offerings be geared to obtaining jobs in lieu of those in the liberal arts. All are at the mercy of state, local, and federal government rules and regulations that govern (whether wisely or not) how they compete for and offer financial aid, how they implement Title IX, whether and which weapons may be brought to campus, how they meet the concerns of various regional and accrediting associations, where they may operate, whether there are caps on enrollment or barriers to enrolling foreign students, how much they spend on research, and what their priorities for research should be. To these, add pressure from trustees, alumni, unions, neighbors, city council members, mayors, clergy, fraternal organizations, and vendors.

Each institution is subject to the wisdom and whims of boards of trustees or regents, as well as state boards of education. Many are subject to ossified union agreements, faculty handbooks, and forms of faculty governance that take little account of changing patterns of hiring, transformations in the environment for how and when and where students can enroll in courses, and the disruptive forces of virtual reality, artificial intelligence, and other tools that may revolutionize patterns of teaching and learning. Independent institutions must follow legislative dictates on such issues as the open carry of guns on campus.

Institutions are in competition with each other, for students, faculty, staff, athletes, musicians, deans, and presidents. They compete for the loyalty of alumni who have attended more than one institution. They compete for higher rankings in publications that rank institutions for academic reputation as well as for non-academic success in job placements for their graduates. They compete for federal and foundation grants. They compete for funding from state and local governments. The competition that gets the most attention occurs in athletics, where abundant scrutiny and embarrassment have resulted in no significant changes being undertaken. All compete for "reputation." All wish, and many claim, to be the Harvard of their niche (though rarely is Harvard envied for its athletic prowess despite its justifiable pride in many of its teams and players).

Choices and decisions are constrained by the competitive environment. What an institution might wish to do it may be unable to do because of lack of internal and external support and the simple fact that there is more good to do than can be financed.

Some of you reading this chapter may aspire to become college and university presidents or vice presidents or deans or department chairs. You may achieve your ambitions only to find out, if you had not figured it out already, that you don't rule, you lead; you don't govern, you inspire; you don't have enough non-discretionary money to achieve your goals; you can't raise money quickly enough to meet even a small percentage of the demands for more funds for both questionable and meritorious proposals. Every decision displeases a lot of people and gratifies few—most of whom are ungrateful that they didn't get all they asked for.

Today's university presidents lose their First Amendment rights. Students today have little sense of humor or irony or history. Words take on meanings you never contemplated. Suggestions that reasonable parents might make to protect their children, if made by a university president, may be misconstrued as "blaming the victim." Students pushing against authority figures may target you simply because you are the president. They are not yet clear about who are their friends and who are their enemies. Inexperienced, they do not yet fully understand that the life of a university student may turn out to be as good as it gets in an imperfect world. They want a better world, and they want it now. Race, gender, sexuality, ethnic background, and religion are all tinder awaiting a spark. You have to provide leadership without being a mug while the world watches, wonders, and opines.

Autonomy is an illusion. Institutions are like the surface of a doorknob at an elementary school: swarming with unseen life forms. They are complex organisms—not simple or clear or clean. Universities are constantly reacting to forces known and unknown, internal and external. As a university president you will find that almost every article on the front page of your daily newspaper raises issues. A police shooting of a black man on the West Coast impacts every campus. The rise and fall of the dollar relative to the pound or the euro says something about the ability of international students to pay tuition. Middle East wars have students coming and going. Almost anything reported has to be considered for its possible consequences: electric rates, elections, bombings abroad and in the US, US visa policies, Title IX, appointments to the National Labor Relations Board and other federal agencies. Need more to brood about? OK, interest rates, team sports, particularly basketball and football, alcohol abuse, helicopter parents.

A university president who does not perceive the intersectionality of all things will make mistakes and miss opportunities. The job is one of anticipation. Preparing in every possible way for the unknown. Buying real estate when it is available to be used by your successor for who knows what. Putting funds away against a tomorrow that may never come. Making friends with a backbench politician who might one day chair the higher education appropriations committee of your state senate. Befriending a young reporter who turns out to do a major piece on your administration in your tenth year.

Ask not for whom the bell tolls. You are never off duty. You cannot go to the supermarket unshaven or disheveled on a Saturday. You cannot have another drink at a social event if you flush or slur your speech. You cannot give a lift home to a faculty member of a different gender whom you run into coming out of a restaurant during a downpour—unless you are with others or have a driver. You must not have ad hoc conversations with untenured faculty about their circumstances unless you are prepared to be deposed about your comments in the event they do not get tenure. Don't speculate on the possible value of a property in a public place where word might get back to the seller, who uses those comments in later negotiations. Think twice about granting awards (for teaching, for example) to untenured faculty, who may use them against you when they sue the university for denying them tenure. All acts or non-acts, decisions and indecisions, have consequences. You are not a feather in the wind of circumstance, but you only seem to have free will. Keep that in mind at all times.

How then to cope while tied up like Gulliver? Reread Kipling's poem "If." Remember, it begins "If you can keep your head while all about you are losing theirs and blaming it on you." If you don't read the whole thing, here's the last stanza:

> If you can talk with crowds and keep your virtue,
> Or walk with Kings—nor lose the common touch,
> If neither foes nor loving friends can hurt you,
> If all men count with you, but none too much;
> If you can fill the unforgiving minute
> With sixty seconds' worth of distance run,
> Yours is the Earth, and everything that's in it
> And—which is more—you'll be a Man [or Woman] my son [or daughter]!*

Or you can recall the modern parody: If you can keep your head while all about are losing theirs, you don't know what the hell is going on.

*Kipling made a tad less insensitive.

15 Managing Donor Relations

Fundraising Is a Relationship, Not a Transaction

S. Georgia Nugent

When you become a college president, you begin to have strange new experiences. Suddenly, all of your jokes become funny. When you speak in a meeting, folks often actually stop and listen to you (a particularly novel experience if you're a woman). Your sartorial choices may become trend setting (if you sport bow ties, for example, you may begin to notice that the distribution of bow-tie wearers on your campus is disproportionate to the distribution in the population at large).

One of these new experiences is that virtually everyone who knows you're a college president (your former faculty colleagues, your neighbor, your brother-in-law) will volunteer, unasked: "Well, I could never do the fundraising." Typically, this is asserted with a mix of incredulity and sympathy. It's pretty clear that the image your interlocutor has in mind is that of a panhandler or a pickpocket.

So the first thing that needs to be said is that fundraising is fun! And the second point—even more important, but more difficult to convey—is that working in philanthropy is *not* about taking but about giving. I know, I know, that sounds hokey. But the fact is that the last thing a successful fundraiser wants to do is reach into a donor's back pocket and grab their wallet. The real objective of a great fundraiser is to offer donors an opportunity to accomplish something that feels important, that resonates with their values, and that they will feel great about doing.

I learned this the hard way. In my first presidency, I inherited a head of development who was extremely bright, great at producing work products, and terrible at fundraising. I still shudder to think of some of those early mistakes. I was sent out to ask the grandparents of students who had already graduated to fund a facility in which they had no interest. The lowest point was when I was scheduled to have lunch with one of the college's most generous and loyal major supporters. My marching orders were to show him the development office's "gift pyramid" of amounts needed to complete the campaign and ask, "Where do you see yourself?" I cringe even writing this. Never, never is that the way to approach a donor.

Happily, I was able to bring into the college a new leader for development who was a gem. It is no exaggeration to say she taught me everything I know. Successes in our campaign included coming in over the goal (during the Great Recession), garnering the only grant our state's public facilities commission had ever given to a private institution, and receiving a total of 15,000 individual gifts from an alumni base of 17,000. We conducted, at that time, the largest private college campaign that had ever taken place in our state. How did we do it? Here are some tips gleaned from a quarter of a billion dollars of fundraising.

First, as I mentioned, it's not about asking but offering. In meeting and cultivating donors, the goal is to find a match between an aspiration that's important for your institution and an objective that touches a chord in the prospective donor. When that match has been properly made, it's really not a matter of urging the donor; it's a matter of true partnership between the donor and the institution in bringing about a result (whether a facility or a program or an endowed chair or a scholarship or . . .) that both donor and institution truly care about.

How do such happy marriages of donor intent and college or university need come about? The first answer is thorough, meticulous, even obsessive research. When I went out to meet with donors, I was almost embarrassed because I had such a great research team that I felt I knew what the prospective donor's pets' names were, what they liked for breakfast, and where they last vacationed. That's the position you want to be in. If you don't have a great research team, begin to build it; they are one of your most valuable assets.

Of course, a caveat is that it's crucial to be selective and discreet in using the research. Few of us really want to be aware of the extent to which institutions (even our alma mater) are tracking us. So it is the role of the research team to be relentless in finding information (yes, there was the death of a child or an SEC investigation or a messy divorce), and then it's the role of the president to be discreet and exercise judgment in how he or she treats this information.

Armed with information from the research team, the president meets with the prospective donor. This is both an extension of the research effort and a "first date." Where the meeting takes place is significant.

If the meeting is scheduled in the prospective donor's home or office, the prospects for research are further extended. Be curious. Notice everything about the donor's environment. Are there works of art? If so, of what quality? What are their subjects? Are there trophies or mementos? Are there photographs of family members? Are there certificates of accomplishment (diplomas, recognitions from organizations)? Does the space hold other indications of interests important to the donor? What does the environment tell you about his or her style? Hobbies? Pets? Politics? Each of these can contribute toward building an authentic relationship, perhaps through common interests or experiences—or, conversely, by offering an opportunity to learn more about a topic with which you're not familiar.

If the meeting takes place in a less personalized space, such as a restaurant or club, take note of the implications of that non-personal space and draw out, in conversation, some of the donor's more personal commitments. As in most relationship building, it is more important to listen than to talk. If at all possible, do *not* make a first meeting the occasion for an "ask." Rather, take it as an opportunity to get to know the individual as a person: What's important to them? What are their preferences and predilections? How close is their relationship to your institution?

In some cases, you may be meeting with someone who has been disaffected from your college. That's OK. The simple fact that they have accepted a meeting with you means that you are being offered the chance to rebuild a relationship. Listen especially attentively to their gripe. It may be personal or political or even puerile. It doesn't matter. Do not attempt to explain why your conversation partner is mistaken. Simply listen, with all the empathy you can muster. So often what a person wants is simply to be heard, without interruption, without objection, without correction. For the most part, the facts of the matter are beside the point. This person has felt wronged. Perhaps a child or grandchild was denied admission. Perhaps a gift wasn't properly acknowledged. Perhaps the institution has changed in ways that the individual doesn't appreciate or accept. In any of these cases, you are dealing with an emotional wound. You have the opportunity to offer healing.

In my early days in the president's office, I found it difficult to understand the intensity of feeling with which alumni can react to a change in their alma mater. Sometimes the change seems trivial to you; sometimes it seems self-evidently necessary. No matter—among some graduates, irrational anger may erupt. Over time, I've developed a theory about this pattern of reaction. For the college student of traditional age (say, 18 to 22 years old), these late adolescent/early adult college years are—as we know—an extremely important, formative period of life. The graduate may look back on that time in his or her life as an idyllic moment, the proverbial "best four years of my life." For some, a change in the life of the institution today feels as if it somehow reaches back into their own past and questions, rearranges, or discredits their life story; it can feel emotionally wrenching. The good news is that the stronger this reaction, the greater the graduate's emotional tie to the institution. Relevant here is the old adage that the opposite of love isn't hate: it's indifference. The alum who reacts strongly to change isn't indifferent; he or she is a lover spurned. There is a great opportunity to woo that individual and reestablish loyalty and commitment to the institution.

But what about a potential donor who's disaffected because of a perceived personal harm or slight by the institution? In my experience, there is only one way to deal with that situation. It is simple, and I have known it to be remarkably effective. Identify fully with that person's perception of pain. In her groundbreaking book *The Body in Pain,* Harvard scholar Elaine Scarry foregrounded one undeniable truth: there is no way we can experience the pain that another is feeling. Despite Bill Clinton's famous phrase, it is literally impossible for another to "feel your pain." What we *can* do is express our understanding and acceptance of the fact that another is in pain. The person who feels he or she has been hurt by your institution is in pain. You may not fully understand why and you may not be able to fix the situation, but actively acknowledging what the person is feeling can often go a remarkably long way toward undoing the harm.

Let me offer an example. During a prize ceremony, a student's name was mispronounced, and the student's family was outraged. Their angry phone call made it seem as if the student's entire college career had been undone by this faux pas. Their wrath knew no bounds. Logically, we can recognize that, in the course of pronouncing perhaps hundreds of proper names, it is fairly likely that an announcer will make one or two gaffes. But logic is beside the point. What's at stake here is pure emotion. Freud coined a term for this phenomenon: the narcissistic wound. This needn't imply that the person in question is a narcissist. Rather, a narcissistic wound results when something is perceived as a threat to one's self-esteem or self-worth.

Like pain, this kind of wound is an irreducibly subjective experience. It is impossible for me to have access to your perceived experience—but I can acknowledge the truth of your experience for you.

So, in this case, even if the reaction to a mispronunciation might have seemed to me excessive, I have learned that responding along those lines (what we might think of as trying to "reason" with the aggrieved individual) leaves no way forward but continued confrontation and perhaps even escalating bitterness. A much better way, I have found, is to simply step from a position opposite the person (confrontation) to a position alongside them (empathy). Accept and share in their frustration or grief. Express your understanding of how devastating this error must have been, how badly it must have made their child feel, perhaps how hurtful or embarrassing it may have been for family members attending the ceremony. Apologize deeply and profusely for the institution's error. Many, many times the feeling of being truly heard, of being understood will open an entirely new channel of communication. In this particular case, the family—having felt that they were heard—in fact became quite warm, and we developed a particularly friendly relationship through the rest of that student's time at the college.

It is important to say a word here about sincerity. For the shift from confrontation to empathy to be successful, it must be authentic; it must be genuine. I'm not recommending a kind of pandering lip service to an individual who feels wronged. Ostensibly agreeing with a complainant while in fact continuing to harbor the view that he or she is completely unreasonable and misguided will quickly be perceived as the bad faith that it is. Rather, for a president dealing with a "difficult" person to successfully find a way forward from argument to acceptance—even if not agreement—requires a certain capaciousness of sensibility. It isn't necessary for your views or perceptions to be just the same as the other person's; what is necessary is to recognize the validity of their perceptions to them in a way that is not condescending but rather appreciative of the varieties of human experience.

Let's assume that you have now begun a positive relationship with a prospective donor. How might things proceed, beyond that "first date" to courtship and, perhaps, ultimately to the happy marriage of institutional priority and donor intent? I mentioned that it's desirable to avoid at all costs "making an ask" in your first meeting with a donor. Here, I'll go further. In my view, the ideal fundraising scenario is one where the president doesn't actually make an "ask" at all. And I don't mean that he or she delegates everything to the advancement team—far from it.

Ideally, the president's role is to excite the potential donor about the possibility—so important and even transformative for the college, the students, the faculty—that his or her gift can bring into being. The president isn't asking for money but giving the donor the priceless opportunity to make a difference. Again, authenticity is crucial. The project you bring to a donor must be something you truly believe in, something where the depth of your understanding and the vividness of your enthusiasm will lead the donor to say, in effect, "Wow, how can I help you do that?"

Sound unlikely? Not at all. Time and time again, I have had donors ask that very question: "How can I help?" This isn't accomplished in a day. Typically, it's the fruit of a relationship built over some period of time in which trust and mutual respect are nurtured and the seeds of a personal friendship grow. One of my favorite donors was an interesting and interested businessman with whom I simply enjoyed having great—and usually fairly extended—conversations. Eventually he began to kid me, saying, "Aren't you going to ask me for money?" I usually deflected the question and simply spoke about the exciting plans we had for the college (plans that, of course, I knew from our research accorded well with his interests). Not only did he give multiple gifts to inaugurate new programs on campus; when I stepped down from that presidency, he anonymously gave a million dollar scholarship in my name.

Of course, not all donor relationships will advance so happily. But I would maintain that this is the ideal. Key ingredients include a genuine and trusting relationship between the president and the donor, the president's being truly committed to the project, research showing the donor's capacity and interests to be well aligned with the project, and the project's being so well formed that the donor spontaneously wants to be a part of it.

I also mentioned the relationship "advancing." Those "great conversations" that I had with my favorite donor? They were not without purpose or plan. Perhaps the most important recent advance in advancement, if you will, is the introduction of a process known as "moves management." Too often in the past, college development officers simply "stayed in touch" with alumni without actually moving them closer toward making a gift. Moves management is an intentional process in which every "move" is a step in the process of ultimately securing a commitment. Conversations provide opportunities to learn more about the donor's interests—and perhaps to focus and refine the project the president will bring to the donor in light of those interests. Arranging for alumni to visit campus or host a student intern are means of bringing them into closer touch with the contemporary institution. Careful records are kept and data are mined. While moves management is undoubtedly oriented toward the institution's goals, it is also a way of being respectful of the donor's time, preferences, and interests. Everyone benefits.

A final word to the wise president: aim high, but not too high. We come full circle to the importance of research. You need sound, reliable information about a donor's capacity. Asking for a gift either too small or too large can be a source of embarrassment for the donor—and a loss for the institution. If a donor immediately and eagerly assents to your request, you've probably aimed too low. Take note; accept the gift graciously; and return later. Perhaps more problematic is an ask that is wildly out of range for the prospective donor. While occasionally someone may feel flattered by the miscalculation, more often this can be a source of embarrassment and even shame. Should a request be met with stunned silence, the wise president will take pains to emphasize the value of the person and their continuing relationship to the institution. Recall that it's not about taking but giving—in this case, giving the individual a clear affirmation that the institution values them for their self-worth, not their net worth.

What I Wish I Had Known When I Started Developing donor relationships, at its best, is actually developing friendships; it's both gratifying and fun.

What I Wish I Had Done When I Finished We probably never say "thank you" enough. Of course, the college thanked donors at the conclusion of our campaign, but it would have been classy for me to have personally written to our many donors.

What I Wish I Had Not Done While in Office Early on, I made some real errors in bringing potential donors projects that weren't an appropriate match for them.

How I Knew When to Stop I believe a leader probably has the opportunity (and the capacity) to bring about a half dozen to a dozen major improvements for an institution. When you're fortunate enough to have accomplished those, the institution—and you—need a change.

When a Gift Brings Controversy

Ángel Cabrera

You would think that the announcement of a $30 million gift would be a cause for great celebration at a university. But when George Mason University announced a gift of that size to name our law school, glee was hardly the response. Instead, we became involved in a controversy of national proportions that forced us to confront our values as a university. This story may serve to illustrate the complexities of philanthropy in today's universities and the difficult decisions university leaders increasingly face.

On March 31, 2016, our board of visitors (as public university governing boards are known in Virginia) voted in favor of my proposal to accept the largest gift in Mason's history to name our law school after the late Supreme Court Justice Antonin Scalia. Two-thirds of the gift came from an anonymous donor, and the other third came from businessman, philanthropist, and political activist Charles Koch through his foundation. The entirety of the gift would fund scholarships for law school students.

Reactions on social media even before the board meeting adjourned made it clear that the decision was about to generate one of the most intense and public controversies in George Mason history. Some thought Scalia's views conflicted with those of the largest public university in Virginia, which prides itself on diversity and accessibility. For others, the source of the gifts raised concerns. They wondered if it would give donors a say in the future of the law school and compromise our university's sacrosanct academic independence. Still others wondered whether the name of a perceived conservative jurist would be accepted in academia.

I knew that accepting the gift would not receive everyone's approval. But I also knew it was the right decision for our university. What might have come across to some as a contradiction really was no contradiction at all. Our university values declare that "diversity is our strength" and that "we honor freedom of thought and expression." Rejecting a major gift that would have an immediate impact on our students on the basis that some do not agree with the opinions of the jurist being honored, or the political activities of the donor, would contradict those values. As our rector, former Virginia

Congressman Tom Davis, would later tell the *Richmond Times-Dispatch*, "You think this is controversial? Try turning down $30 million."*

In addition to pitting law school faculty members against colleagues from around the university, the decision sparked a spirited debate about academic freedom, the realities and perceptions of donor influence, and the increasingly vital role of philanthropy at public universities. The decision evoked a torrent of reactions from social media, the late-night comedy shows (watch your acronyms!), and the news and opinion pages of the *New York Times*, *Washington Post*, *Wall Street Journal*, and other major media outlets.

Nerves were thin, and irony was thick. By naming a school after a Supreme Court justice, we put ourselves on trial in the court of public opinion. And the many critics who denounced the decision on the grounds that Scalia was a narrow-minded jurist had to ask themselves if they harbored ideological biases of their own.

We buckled up for a bumpy ride.

The Decision

Our law school dean, Henry Butler, had been working on a major gift since he was appointed in June 2015. The preceding years had not been kind to law schools. Between 2010 and 2015, the number of LSAT test takers—the best proxy for applications to law schools—had declined by one-third. To preserve student quality, many schools were forced to reduce enrollments, with a subsequent hit in tuition revenue and financial resources. Dean Butler's plan, which I fully supported, was to make a major injection of scholarship dollars to help attract top talent and increase enrollments to pre-financial crisis levels.

The Charles Koch Foundation, a traditionally generous supporter of our university's work in law and economics, had agreed to match the contributions of other donors up to $10 million. The plan materialized when Dean Butler identified a second donor willing to donate $20 million on the condition of anonymity and in honor of the legacy of Justice Scalia. The combined $30 million would mark the largest gift in our university's relatively short (independent since 1972) history, and it would be a transformative investment in our law school.

The gift ultimately would be structured to fund three scholarship programs, one in particular geared toward students from traditionally

*J. Schapiro, "Bid to Name Law School for Scalia Triggers Injudicious Debate," *Richmond Times-Dispatch*, April 12, 2016.

underrepresented groups. The scholarships would enable us to recruit more of the best and the brightest students and faculty to what already is a top 50 law school in the *U.S. News & World Report* rankings.

Scalia's opinions may have been divisive, but he was undoubtedly deserving. Appointed to the Court with a Senate vote of 98-0, he served 30 years before his death in February 2016. Legal experts praise his acumen in interpreting constitutional law. His fellow justices, including his favorite sparring partner, Justice Ruth Bader Ginsburg, hailed his style and his wit. President Barack Obama said Scalia "influenced a generation of judges, lawyers, and students, and . . . will no doubt be remembered as one of the most consequential judges and thinkers to serve on the Supreme Court."

As I would later write in a letter to the *New York Times,* if someone who served our country for 30 years at the highest level of government—and who is considered by experts of diverse political leanings to be a distinguished jurist who had a profound effect on the legal field—is not good enough to be recognized in this way by a university, I am not sure who would be.

Scalia was not officially affiliated with our law school, but he had long lived in Northern Virginia, not far from our campuses. He spoke at the opening of our new law school building and had been a guest lecturer at Mason, regularly visiting law classes when his schedule permitted. He had a visible presence in the region and strong family ties to the community. Mason theater professor Edward Gero got to know the justice when he portrayed Scalia in *The Originalist,* a drama performed at Arena Stage in Washington, DC.

We were not the first university to honor a Supreme Court justice. Arizona State, Louisville, and Texas Southern have named law schools after former justices. Stanford and Arizona have a courtyard and center, respectively, named after conservative justice William H. Rehnquist, whom Scalia replaced.

Criticisms of gifts from the Charles Koch Foundation to Mason weren't new. Charles Koch has been one of our most generous donors, especially in support of economics and related disciplines. He has appreciated the caliber of our work in this area. Our Economics Department had built an enviable reputation very early on, with two of its members earning the Nobel Prize—James Buchanan in 1986 and Vernon Smith in 2002.

Henry Manne, widely considered a father of the law and economics field, joined the law school as dean in 1986 and turned it into a powerhouse in his field. Today, our law faculty is ranked twenty-first in the nation in terms of scholarly impact, the youngest university in that top tier.

Our success in economics has been the result of strong academic leadership, strategic focus, and generous philanthropy. Our donors know that their gifts do not entitle them to influence our work or to decide what faculty we hire or promote. They understand that any threat to our academic integrity would jeopardize the quality and impact of the very work they support.

Clearly we need to make sure any gift agreement safeguards our academic independence. But many of the criticisms of our Scalia decision were cloaked in an outright rejection of the donor for what he represented. As a university leader, I believed this gift would help students and uphold our values as a place that welcomes a multitude of opinions.

The Reaction

We planned to announce the gift and law school name on March 31, after our board of visitors voted their approval. Word leaked, however, with an early afternoon tweet from National Public Radio legal affairs correspondent Nina Totenberg: "George Mason renaming its law school The Antonin Scalia School of Law. The late Justice, a genuinely beloved teacher, must be on cloud nine!" In my statement to the *Washington Post* and other media outlets, I called the gift "a milestone moment for the university," and another way for us to "deliver on our mission of inclusive excellence." We received a statement from Justice Ginsburg, who called it "a tribute altogether fitting that George Mason University's law school will bear [Scalia's] name."*

The elation of announcing the largest gift in university history was fleeting. The negative reaction was swift. A Virginia House of Delegates member immediately circulated a petition to block the naming that was contingent of the gift, calling it "so transactional, so crass." Late that afternoon, a few senior leaders and I gathered in the office of our vice president of communications and marketing. Each of us had our phone in hand, reading aloud the comments flooding social media. They were like punches to the gut.

Mason also became the butt of jokes. Literally. Not because we decided to name the law school after Scalia, but for the name we gave it. During our conversations prior to accepting the gift, we referred to the impending name as the "Scalia School of Law"—just like our "Volgenau School of Engineering," named after a donor. But for the formal name of a school, we use the

*S. Svrluga, "George Mason Law School to Be Renamed the Antonin Scalia School of Law," *Washington Post*, April 1, 2016.

honoree's full name. So while conversationally we'd be known as the "Scalia School of Law," formally we'd be the "Antonin Scalia School of Law."

Routine, right? Well, not exactly. The formal name made for an unfortunate—and unrealized—acronym. The national media, including the late-night talk shows, had a field day at our expense with their "ASSOL" and "ASSLAW" jokes. The *New York Times, Wall Street Journal,* CNN, Fox News, and NBC News were among the many media outlets to weigh in on the acronym story. Days later, we tweaked the name to the Antonin Scalia Law School.

A few days after the gift announcement, I took the opportunity to address the naming decision at a campus event called "Doing What Matters: Pathways to Inclusive Excellence." I had been scheduled to offer opening remarks, but I wanted to address the elephant in the room—questions about whether the acceptance of the naming gift was at odds with our efforts to strengthen our culture of inclusion. I explained the logic of the gift while emphasizing my unwavering commitment to diversity and inclusion at Mason.

That same day, 10 Virginia Democratic lawmakers sent a letter to the State Council of Higher Education for Virginia asking them to not approve the naming of the school. "We have received pleas from alumni who are deeply concerned that this decision will undermine their ability to find future employment or undermine their professional reputation," the letter stated.* In addition, about 140 of our 2,600 faculty members signed a petition denouncing the naming of the law school because it "tarnishes our reputation."

I spent many hours taking calls from elected officials and entertaining informal conversations with faculty colleagues and university friends. Some called to offer support. Some called to express disappointment in me and the university. Some called to express disappointment about those expressing disappointment.

Leadership Team's Response as Pressure Mounts

My leadership team, highly diverse and seasoned in making difficult decisions, also grappled with the naming and what it meant. Regardless of our personal views, we were all under constant criticism and pressure to explain the reasons behind the decision.

*M. Barakat, "Democratic Lawmakers Oppose Renaming Law School for Scalia," Associated Press, April 6, 2016.

The uproar brought out the best in our team. I am proud of the open and trusting culture we have created in our administration. I didn't realize how crucial that would be until we were in crisis mode. The fact that we were able to share openly how we each felt and what pressure we were under gave us the strength we needed to convey why we made the decision.

We needed that cohesion. A few weeks after the announcement, our Faculty Senate approved a resolution that criticized the naming, calling Scalia "a significant contributor to the polarized climate in this country that runs counter to the values of a university that celebrates civil discourse." The Faculty Senate also questioned the transparency and long-term financial feasibility of the gifts in regard to the two new centers and 12 new law professors we would add through revenue generated by the increased enrollment the scholarships would create.*

I welcomed the Faculty Senate's engagement and feedback. I responded in writing to its resolution, a letter that the *Washington Post* ran in full on its website, detailing how donors do not influence faculty selection and promotion, student admissions, or curricular choices.

That same week, the *New York Times* ran a front-page story about the law school gift and other gifts the Koch Foundation has given Mason over the years. I felt the article misrepresented Mason, making it seem as if the Kochs, who donate to many colleges, had built our university into what it is today. I expressed my opinion in a letter to the editor, detailing how philanthropy accounts for about 5 percent of our budget and that no donor poses a threat to our academic independence.

For those trying to brand us as a "conservative" university, I pointed out that we have received equally intense criticism for opinions expressed by faculty members on the opposite end of the political spectrum, including climate change scientists and others who have delved into sensitive political topics. We are a space where scholars of all backgrounds are free to voice their opinions.

In a specially scheduled meeting, our Faculty Senate sharpened its rhetoric in passing two additional resolutions, requesting that we suspend the name change and show how the gifts come with no academic influence, citing American Association of University Professors standards. One of the student protestors given a forum to speak at the meeting referred to the law

*Faculty Senate of George Mason University, "Proposed Faculty Senate Statement Regarding Law School Gifts," April 26, 2016.

school name change as "a symptom of a much deeper problem: undue donor influence and our university's lack of consultation with important university stakeholders, such as faculty and students."*

As a response to the Faculty Senate, the Mason law faculty unanimously passed a resolution endorsing the new name and expressed "its regret at the unprofessional and dissembling conduct of the Faculty Senate," which it accused of ideological bias.

Meanwhile, an editorial in the *Washington Post* said that Mason officials "aren't fooling anyone if they contend that naming the school after such a polarizing figure doesn't give it an ideological brand," adding that the naming could have long-term implications in regard to applicants or future donors.† We also received support. Two Georgetown University professors wrote an op-ed in the *Washington Post* favoring the decision. A Mason law professor did likewise in the *Wall Street Journal*. The Republican leadership in the Virginia House of Delegates weighed in with their support.

The Takeaway

Eventually, some detractors began to focus on the real meaning of the gift—the students who would benefit from the scholarship money. For example, Diverse: Issues in Higher Education, a media website that covers colleges and universities from the perspective of people of color and underrepresented groups, took a more nuanced look at the gift through the eyes of a second-year law student who accepted one of the scholarships. The student, Jacquelyn Branscomb, acknowledged concerns about the name but also remarked that law school has become very expensive. She then thought about the benefits that would come by taking advantage of the scholarship. "I figured, why not use the money to improve diversity at the school? Because I feel like I have a different political background than most people at the school," said Branscomb, a board member of the Asian Pacific American Law Students Association and a member of the Black Law Student Association at Mason. ‡Her comments went to the heart of our original intent of the gift and the broader mission of the university. Diversity is one of our greatest strengths, and these scholarships stood to bolster that diversity.

* George Mason University, "Minutes of the Faculty Senate, April 27, 2016, Continued May 4, 2016."

† Editorial Board, "A Polarizing Name Change at George Mason," *Washington Post*, May 7, 2016.

‡ J. Abdul-Alim, "GMU Law School Renaming a Possible Roadblock to Diversity," Diverse: Issues in Higher Education, July 24, 2016.

Many college presidents will face difficult decisions and controversies like ours. As taxpayer support drops, philanthropy continues to grow as a necessary source of funding in higher education. According to the Council for Aid to Education, in 2015 Americans gave more than $40 billion to universities, a 7.6 percent increase over 2014 and double the figure 10 years prior.

In our case, we were well prepared to press on despite the controversy because we had grounded our decision in core values: serving students, preserving academic freedom, and promoting freedom of speech. We also had no illusions about the potential reaction. We knew that the decision would be controversial, and we didn't try to fool ourselves into thinking that there would be an easy path forward. Finally, we embraced the dialogue engendered by our decision, and we didn't shirk from the tough conversations that ensued.

I believe we emerged from our challenge a more robust university. We engaged in difficult but necessary conversations. We listened to each other and came away with a greater understanding of academic freedom and diversity. We put our values into practice. Best of all, we created a life-changing educational opportunity for hundreds of students who might otherwise not have been able to afford law school. And that is why we are in this profession in the first place—to change lives and better society through education.

What I Wish I Had Known When I Started The advice a CEO I admire later gave me: "If nobody is upset with you, you probably aren't doing your job."

What I Wish I Had Done When I Finished Not stay too long after announcing I was leaving.

What I Wish I Had Not Done While in Office I wish I hadn't failed to find the time to continue with my writing.

What I Wish I Didn't Know When I Finished That I had fewer friends than I thought I did before announcing my leave.

How I Knew When to Stop I felt I had made a difference and things were going well. Quit while you're ahead!

16 Dealing with the Changing Landscape of Accreditation

Judith S. Eaton

I was chancellor of the Minnesota State Colleges and Universities System when I got a call from a headhunter, one of the very few I have ever received. Did I want to be a candidate for the presidency of a newly formed organization, the Council for Higher Education Accreditation (CHEA)? It was 1997, and CHEA was recently created as an institutional membership organization to provide, on behalf of institutions, national coordination of accreditation.

My first response was "no." I told the headhunter that accreditation wasn't interesting enough. Having it was unremarkable. Earning it was a fair amount of work, but not intriguing. It became a bit challenging only if you needed and couldn't or didn't have it. Please find someone else.

It's 19 years later, and I have been president of CHEA all of this time. What happened? Why did I take the job, after all? What about accreditation, its past, present, and future, can help explain at least this CEO's varied reaction here?

Accreditation Past

Accreditation, higher education's primary means of assuring and improving quality, is higher education's very own creation. More than 100 years ago, a few leaders came together and established accreditation, initially to distinguish "college" from secondary school and to address transfer of credit. Since that time and into the present, various institutional and programmatic accrediting organizations have been created, funded, and governed by colleges and universities. Accrediting organizations are now 85 in number, and all are nongovernmental, nonprofit membership bodies.

The bedrock of accreditation is a small set of core, vital commitments. When an institution commits to accreditation, it is taking these on. First, accreditation was initially developed as a form of self-regulation: To achieve quality, we are committed to academics reviewing academics, professionals reviewing professionals, a process of self-reporting about our work accompanied by peer review. Second, accreditation is above all committed to quality improvement—your institution getting better in quality. This is beyond a focus on accountability—your institution meeting minimum expectations of quality, as important as accountability is. Third, accreditation is committed to the value of a diverse, mission-driven higher education enterprise, with many types of institutions serving many types of students, accompanied by a strong commitment to academic freedom. In this context, institutional autonomy is vital.

For a president or chancellor, it was agreeable to buy into these commitments. For me, they were part and parcel of the values that made higher education so attractive. Yes, accreditation also had a bureaucratic dimension. The review process was time-consuming and annoying and, anyway, who likes to be regulated, even in this collegial, formative way? Yet, as any number of presidents have told me over the years, for any college or university that was reasonably healthy financially, the likelihood of failing with accreditation was very low. It was worth it to go through an institutional review and the various reviews for the programs for which accreditation was available.

Accreditation past was about a low-stakes affirming or reaffirming of the basic academic legitimacy of an institution and its role in the community of respected higher education. The investment of time and effort almost always paid off. And, if an institution had to be examined, accreditation was far preferable to other forms of external oversight from sources with less experience or understanding of higher education, such as government or the business sector.

Accreditation Present

Accreditation present is about trying to maintain the core commitments that characterized accreditation past while sustaining an all-important relationship with the federal government. This relationship began in the 1950s, decades after accreditation itself had started operating, and continues. It is often called "gatekeeping." The federal government, as a condition of making federal funds such as student grants and loans available to institutions, requires that the institutions be accredited by an accreditor the government deems acceptable. Accreditation present is about a partnership with government and how it has both been maintained and evolved over the years.

Throughout much of accreditation present, maintaining this partnership has not been difficult. The federal government was initially comfortable deferring judgment about academic quality to accreditation; officials did not want to develop a federal capacity to do this work. Accreditation not only provided reliable information about the quality of traditional institutions, but was also essential for future quality as higher education embraced both change and innovation—from the major growth in community colleges in the 1960s to the advent of distance learning in the 1990s to today's world of internationalization in higher education.

When it comes to dependability of accreditors, government at first confined itself to a cursory review of the accrediting organizations with which it worked, e.g., are there sufficient resources and is a sound organization in place?

However, as we are seeing now, this partnership is changing. Events throughout accreditation present have had a cumulative impact on the relationship. The advent of the Higher Education Act in 1965, the subsequent development of a complex range of student grant and loan programs, the enormous growth of higher education enrollments, the ever-increasing importance of federal student aid to access to higher education, and the need for at least some higher education for jobs, economic security, and mobility—all coalesced to heighten both the federal government's interest and concern when it came to the accreditation partnership.

As the sense of urgency around quality as essential to the success of higher education continued to grow, so did the attention to accreditation as of paramount importance to government, students, and the media. Today, the federal investment in higher education is considerable, some $170 billion annually and growing, justifying federal concerns and increased attention to accreditation. As part of responding to the growth of both higher education and federal expenditure while retaining quality, the government expanded its cursory review to an increasingly in-depth, periodic examination of accrediting organizations, based on a regularly growing body of law, regulation, and guidance.

Yet, for presidents and chancellors I've talked to during these years, the changes in the accreditation-federal government relationship and the growth of the federal role have had limited impact to date. Accreditation remained relatively low stakes and familiar, based on the commitments described above, dedicated to self-review and peer review leading to quality improvement. Typically, little that was dramatic was expected to happen. For example, regional accreditors did not deny accreditation to any school in 2015 and withdrew accreditation in only 2 instances out of more than 350 actions. For the programmatic accreditors with more than 2,900 actions, accreditation was denied in 13 instances and withdrawn in 110.* For example, I can recall sitting down with accreditors who, with great gravitas, told me that this or that program was deficient as they saw it. I had only one question: Of the concerns that an accreditor had, what was essential and required to be done to remain accredited and what, on the other hand, might be desirable but not required? Once I had the answer, it was not difficult to address the essentials of accreditation.

Accreditation present is about trying to stick to accreditation as we have always known it, but now accompanied by more and more federal requirements influencing what accreditors do.

Accreditation Future

If accreditation present was about managing a partnership, accreditation future is about managing the increasingly influential federal role or, if you will, an emerging new boss. The approach of partnership with government is giving way to an approach of oversight and control by government. The federal government has begun investing even more in time in examining in even greater and greater detail how accrediting organizations operate, the standards they maintain and how accreditors carry out the responsibility of assuring that institutions are providing quality education to students using federal funds.

The federal government's current concern is grounded in an appropriate desire to accelerate student success and the use of federal funds in achieving this objective. Three issues are paramount: What is considered quality and are accreditors' judgments still reliable here? How can the accreditation process be made more uniform and, for some, thus viewed as more dependable and understandable? What additional federal scrutiny is essential to assure accreditation's effectiveness? These issues as paramount mean that government is now looking not only at how accreditors operate, but at how well the individual institutions that are accredited perform. If there are questions about the adequacy of performance, e.g., students graduating or level of student earnings following graduation or students amassing large amounts of debt, government has questions about the effectiveness of the accrediting organization itself.

*Council for Higher Education Accreditation, Almanac Online, http://www.chea.org/4DCGI/cms/review.html?Action=CMS_Document&DocID=29&MenuKey=almanac, accessed July 11, 2016.

In this context, government has decided what quality is, defining this as graduation, earnings, and indebtedness—in contrast to how most accreditors define quality in terms of meeting the diverse array of standards that they have established. Armed with extensive amounts of public data made easily available on various interactive federal Websites, the federal government is starting to raise questions about the reliability of the individual judgments that accreditors make when awarding accredited status. In the face of, e.g., low graduation rates or high levels of student debt, how can accredited status be justified?

We all know that predicting the future is at best hazardous. For accreditation and the institutions that are accredited, however, there are several fairly safe bets about what we can expect.

The first bet is that the expanded, influential role of the federal government in accreditation will become a permanent feature in the life of accreditors and accredited institutions and programs going forward. The initial deference demonstrated by the federal government about how accreditation did its work, how quality was defined, and the judgments accreditation made about quality has been dissipating and is pretty much gone. This was made clear at a recent meeting of the national advisory committee that advises the US Secretary of Education on approval of accrediting organizations, with a member saying that everything that accreditors do was within the purview of the committee and thus the federal government. If this scrutiny demonstrates that accrediting organizations fail to meet some of the many pages of law, regulation, and guidance to which all accreditors are currently subject, accreditors must act to conform with federal expectations.

The second bet is that the accrediting organizations themselves will adjust to serving, in essence, as arms or agencies of the government, not as independent membership organizations making independent judgments about quality and accredited status. They will adjust to an increasingly intrusive form of oversight. Just about any major decision an accrediting organization makes will continue to be influenced or will be newly influenced by federal law or regulation.

Does a college or university want to add new degree levels, establish new online programs or open a new location? Accreditors will accommodate the expanding scrutiny of the federal government as they go about approving such changes, deemed major or "substantive." Accrediting organizations that want to make significant changes in their governance structure will turn to government first to learn whether the changes are likely to be approved.

The federal government tells accreditors whether their standards and policies are acceptable, whether the composition of their decision-making bodies is acceptable, and whether their due process procedures are appropriate. If accreditors once asked forgiveness with regard to standards, policies, or practices that did not exactly meet federal expectations, they now ask permission prior to developing them.

Moreover, the government will expand the extent to which it holds accreditors accountable for how well institutions are monitored when it comes to use of federal funds, in addition to judgments about quality. This includes, e.g., the decisions that accreditors make when the ownership of an institution changes, when institutions are accused of misrepresenting themselves to students, and about the institution's role when students cannot find appropriate jobs. It is quickly becoming commonplace, for example, for federal officials to be critical of individual institutions' high levels of student debt or default on loans, even though an institution has little control over either. If these rates are high, there are also questions about whether the accreditor is doing its job. And, as government considers expanding access to student grant and loan funds to new, innovative providers, as it at least explores investing even more federal funds in higher education through free tuition, free college, and expanded loan forgiveness programs, accreditation's obligations will increase.

The third and most important bet is that the accrediting community will find ways to carry out its work now so dominated by the federal government while simultaneously seeking to sustain those initial core commitments of self-regulation, peer review, institutional autonomy, and academic freedom discussed above. This is the greatest of the challenges and the central issue for the future of accreditation.

Accreditation will find a way to sustain its commitment to self-regulation and peer review, even with the federal constraints about how both are carried out. For example, accreditation will continue its reliance on the integrity of data and information from colleges and universities that are both self-reported and peer-reviewed, although it is likely that external judgment and verification of this information, whether by government or other sources, will be required. The heretofore typical accreditation self-study and team report will no longer be considered solely adequate and reliable indicators of institutional or program performance. Institutional autonomy will remain as well, although the commitment to mission will be weakened as accreditors are likely to be required to use national quantitative data to judge graduation rates across all accredited institutions or all accredited institutions of a specific type, driving uniform expectations of quality. Government will also likely press for uniformity of process across all accreditors, e.g., common terms for formal actions, common procedures, that will have a similar impact.

For a president or chancellor, accreditation future will mean that accreditation has moved from a low-stakes to a high-stakes endeavor. Accreditation will be a more regulated industry, and institutions cannot escape the reality that the regulation will be visited upon them. Given the increased scrutiny and constraints resulting from the additional federal oversight, given the standardization of quality emerging from government, a college or university will be examined more, will be required to meet more exacting standards, and will be judged based on these national considerations.

Accreditation future means that an enterprise with its roots as a nongovernmental activity initiated and still financed by higher education, gives way to a significantly federalized activity. The difference between accreditation present—managing a partnership—and accreditation future—managing a new boss—is profound. The definition of quality will no longer in the hands of higher education or accreditation. Direct federal scrutiny of major magnitude is the emerging norm for all accreditation. Additional federal review of accreditation decisions about the status of individual institutions will become commonplace.

So—it's 2016 and I took the job at CHEA because the commitments on which accreditation was created align with my strongly held values about the role of higher education and especially the need for autonomy and self-determination of colleges and universities when it comes to academic quality. I stayed in the job to address the challenge of the changing relationship between accreditation and government that I saw, early on, as undermining, perhaps not fatally, those commitments. I didn't want these commitments to lose out to bureaucracy. I don't want academic self-determination to become the victim of expanding regulation. At the same time, as I consider the likely future, I ask: How do I frame and respond to the emerging leadership challenge here, so different from accreditation past and present?

What I Wish I Had Known When I Started I wish I had better understood the extent of the gap between accreditation and presidents. While presidents often acknowledged the importance of accreditation, I quickly learned that this was not accompanied by an ongoing willingness to personally engage and invest in accreditation to any appreciable extent.

What I Wish I Had Done When I Finished I haven't finished—but hope that when I do, I will have made a significant contribution to accreditation's maintaining the core commitments of independence and self-determination when it comes to academic quality. I believe that an autonomous academic enterprise is essential to the best we can achieve for intellectual development in our society.

What I Wish I Had Not Done While in Office I wish that I had not so often found myself on the outside of what most people in the association world, in accreditation, and in government were thinking about accreditation. I perpetually found myself in an "other than" role, and it was perpetually uncomfortable. I worried all the time about the impact of this on CHEA.

17 Litigation or the Threat of Litigation as a Constraint

John M. McCardell Jr.

The question was astute: why are more and more colleges and universities considering attorneys as candidates for a presidency? The answer was insightful: "There's a good reason for it. . . . There's so much more litigation than there used to be. A university president these days really has to have a lawyer at his side."

"These days" were in fact three decades ago. The respondent was none other than the estimable former president of the University of California, Clark Kerr. And the story appeared in the *New York Times* on Christmas Day, 1987.

The question is no less apt today, though the so-called "nontraditional" candidate is likely to come from a much wider range of occupations. (I have often, as an aside, wondered why major corporations do not populate their boards, never mind their executive offices, with "nontraditional" candidates from, say, academia. But that is for a different essay.)

The essential point is clear. The threat of litigation is not a new problem. It has long been a serious challenge confronting higher education leaders. Indeed, a 1984 report of the Commission on Strengthening Presidential Leadership, directed by President Kerr, noted that "over the past 20 years" the presidency has been "weakened" by "more constraints," including "more participation by the courts in academic decision making."*

To recognize that higher education institutions have for a long time been vulnerable to legal challenges is hardly a source of comfort. Presidents can count on regular—at least weekly in my experience—discussions with university counsel on the current state of legal actions pending, in various stages of discovery or investigation, in arbitration or negotiation, or actually in court. These cover the spectrum from frivolous to serious. They involve some plaintiffs with legitimate grievances. They also involve at least as many

*Clark Kerr, *Presidents Make a Difference: Strengthening Leadership in Colleges and Universities* (Washington, DC: Association of Governing Boards, 1984), p. 99.

hoping to reach into the institution's supposedly deep pockets for a settlement that might leave them some found money after paying their selfless attorneys' contingency fees, which can run to 30 percent or more of a settlement amount. (These angels of justice spare no expense in advertising their services. Prospective aggrieved clients, according to one such commercial, should get in immediate touch with a "client intake specialist.")

All of this would be (barely) tolerable if a whole new set of expectations and requirements, largely in the form of nonlegislative yet binding directives from federal agencies, had not also materialized in recent years. These well-meaning guidelines, meant to address serious issues and often set forth in a "Dear Colleague" letter, have imposed a quasi-judicial role on entities ill-trained or equipped for the task, with the implication that "justice," however defined, can be satisfactorily rendered through processes that cannot possibly replicate a genuine legal proceeding.

Examples abound. One such letter indicates both the degree of detail expected of an academic institution's resolution of a complaint and the implications of falling short of the agency's expectations. It prohibits an institution from turning a case over to law enforcement or to the courts; that is the plaintiff's choice. It also prohibits an institution from delaying its own investigation until a court of law has heard and settled a case:

> Schools should not wait for the conclusion of a criminal investigation or criminal proceeding to begin their own . . . investigation and, if needed, must take immediate steps to protect the student in the educational setting. For example, a school should not delay conducting its own investigation or taking steps to protect the complainant because it wants to see whether the alleged perpetrator will be found guilty of a crime.*

In conducting a hearing, moreover, the institution's finding must be based not on "reasonable doubt," the standard in a court of law, but rather "preponderance of evidence," or, as the letter puts it:

> The school must use a preponderance of the evidence standard (i.e., it is more likely than not that [the offense] occurred.) The "clear and convincing" standard (i.e., it is highly probable or reasonably certain that [the offense] occurred), currently used by some schools, is a higher standard of proof. Grievance procedures that use this higher standard are inconsistent with the standard of proof . . . and

*US Department of Education, Office for Civil Rights, "Dear Colleague Letter," April 4, 2011.

> are thus not equitable . . . . Therefore, preponderance of the evidence is the appropriate standard for investigating allegations.*

Finally, if the federal agency "finds that a school has not taken prompt and effective steps to respond . . . [the agency] will seek appropriate remedies for both the complainant and the broader student population. . . . When a recipient does not come into compliance voluntarily, [the agency] may initiate proceedings to withdraw Federal funding . . . or refer the case to the U.S. Department of Justice for litigation." In May 2014 the Department of Education released to the public the names of 55 institutions that it was currently investigating in the hope of achieving "appropriate remedies."

One could argue that setting forth such elaborate procedures for internal resolution of complaints might in fact reduce the constraint imposed by formal litigation. One would be wrong. The cost in time and effort required to comply with these exacting standards in the case of every complaint brought forward is a genuine constraint. Nor does the search for internal resolution reduce either the threat or the eventual reality of litigation. Indeed, it often heightens both: the possibility that some internal procedural error might occur or that some perceived unfairness in the conduct or tone of a hearing (which is of course recorded in its entirety) might be discerned at once creates the mistaken impression that what is taking place is in some sense a legal proceeding.

A wise and experienced colleague once noted (in language I have shamelessly claimed as my own many times since) that an academic institution should be neither an arm of, nor a haven from, the law. That has always struck me as a sound principle for determining how to deal with violations of institutional policies, which, since they are developed by fair and reasonable if also imperfect human beings, most of the time set behavioral standards virtually identical to those expected of any citizen in any community. Put another way, if, on a college campus, a member of the college community violates an institutional policy or rule, the institution is obliged to deal with the alleged offender and enforce the policy. This in no way prohibits any individual member of the college community from seeking justice in court. By the same token, if a member of the college community is charged by law enforcement with a violation of the law, it is not the place of the institution to protect or defend that individual from the judicial process, but it is also the prerogative of the institution to take whatever action it deems

* Ibid.

appropriate to ensure the safety of its community and the integrity of its policies.

Unfortunately, and increasingly, members of college communities, especially students and their parents, do not understand this simple principle. And a president, fearing and thus constrained by the threat of litigation, may think himself or herself powerless. Here is where the "bully pulpit" can be a most effective instrument.

To be sure, rhetoric alone will not guide the way back to an unfallen world. But it can help. Several examples come to mind. The first is the eminent nineteenth-century statesman Daniel Webster. In a speech late in his life, Webster declared that "liberty can exist only in proportion to wholesome restraint." These are wise words, and their effect on an audience of students or parents ought not to be underestimated. What Webster is saying is simply that liberty without restraint is anarchy, chaos. Restraint without liberty is tyranny. The challenge is to find the balance between the two. Restraint must come. It will come either from without or above, in the form of a lengthening list of rules and penalties, or it will come from within. Our hardest task is to develop in our students a mature and consistent sense of responsibility and accountability and self-restraint. But if we mean truly to lessen the constraints of litigation, Webster offers a way forward.

To this might be added the words of Edmund Burke. "Men are qualified for liberty," Burke wrote, "in exact proportion to their disposition to put moral chains upon their own appetites. . . . Society cannot exist unless a controlling power upon will and appetite be placed somewhere, and the less of it there is within, the more there must be without. It is ordained in the eternal constitution of things that men of intemperate minds cannot be free. Their passions forge their fetters."

William Blake saw it, and put it, a slightly different way. "You never know what is enough," he wrote, "until you know what is more than enough." Could there be a more succinct, or accurate, description of so much of what constitutes student life on a college campus than that? He went on to write, "The road of excess leads to the palace of wisdom." The work in which these statements appear is entitled (appropriately) *Proverbs of Hell.*

The threat of litigation we shall always have with us. Our best hope of coping with it and minimizing its constraining presence is to do the hard but necessary work of strengthening community. Our campuses are now more diverse, more aware, more self-preoccupied than ever before. Financial pressures, the prospect of employment, and family interference and dysfunction do nothing to diminish students' impulse to identify sources of offense or discomfort or threat, call them out, and bring them to justice. An increasing, and increasingly byzantine, set of federal requirements or conditions inclines a community to succumb to the mistaken belief that academic judicial processes are in some way the equivalent to a court of law.

All this need not be a constraint, or at least not a debilitating constraint. Develop reasonable policies and then live by them. Build the building. Let the underperforming faculty or staff member go. Above all, work hard to create and maintain an atmosphere of trust—by what you say, by what you do, by where and how and with whom you spend your time. Model your rhetoric. And never forget what a blessing it is to be leading an academic institution, with all its warts and all its charms, at such a time as this.

And finally, I offer some free advice:

1. The worst number of attorneys to have on your governing board, like the worst number of obvious internal successors, is one. None or more than one are preferable. Boards tend to defer to the expertise around them. Better to have in-house or external counsel with true expertise in higher education issues.
2. Consider assigning the task of risk management to a single individual or office and insist upon regular review of the most important institutional policies. At many institutions this has become a full-time job. Prepare for allegations of "administrative bloat." That is one of the risks to be managed.
3. An entire campus should be a "safe space." To set aside particular places as "safe" surely suggests that all other places are "unsafe." Safety for what? Safety from what?
4. Think carefully about what you put in writing and especially in emails. Documents and emails are subject to discovery disclosure, and "reply all" and "forward" can compound your troubles.
5. An immediate response is unlikely to be the best response. Think, consult, digest. Only then speak or write.
6. There is a difference between the need to know and the desire to know. Don't confuse the two.
7. When a legal issue becomes public, designate one person to speak on behalf of the institution. No one else—and especially members of the governing board—says anything.
8. Do not let the fear of litigation become a paralyzing constraint.

The great American historian David M. Potter more than a half century ago observed an ongoing tension in American life between freedom and security. The more of one, he contended, the less of the other. Many college campus communities might choose to deny that simple truth. But there is no such thing as a risk-free environment. The best that can be hoped for is an environment where the possibility of risk is acknowledged and a prudent set of policies mitigates. In that dynamic pull and tug, litigation may threaten to constrain, but it will neither stifle liberty nor impose unwholesome restraint.

What I Wish I Had Known When I Started That so much of my time would be occupied by personnel issues—not just performance-related but organizational. Creating a table of organization, or changing one, can be enormously time consuming; sensitivity over titles, duties, and reporting lines are more acute than I had anticipated; and there seems always to be a position that needs to be filled (and, often and concomitantly, duties to be reassigned).

What I Wish I Had Done When I Finished I am not finished yet in this second stint. But at the very start of the new presidency, I issued new letters of appointment to all members of the senior staff, thereby (I hope politely) reminding them that they now worked for me. I will advise my successor to do the same.

What I Wish I Had Not Done While in Office Signed a petition. I did not make this mistake a second time. My rule is not to sign anything that someone else has written. So long as a president is consistent in this view, he or she will be spared considerable stress.

What I Wish I Didn't Know When I Finished That a presidency that had been characterized as wonderfully transformational on my last day in office could so quickly become the reason my successor had to fix so many problems left behind. Successors need to understand that they, too, will someday be the "old regime." That can be an antidote to any impulse to gracelessness.

How I Knew When to Stop When I stopped the first time, it was after 13 years in office and a successful capital campaign. The prospect of another round of strategic planning, feasibility study, and a comprehensive campaign held little charm. Five years later, I got back in harness, at a different institution. The change had a tonic effect. But I suspect the same warning signs will eventually reappear.

18 Balancing Systemwide Needs with Institutional Autonomy

Why Public Universities Need Greater Autonomy

Rebecca Blank

In the past decade, there has been a growing conversation about the extent to which public universities—and particularly the flagship research universities that often compete with peer private institutions—should have more autonomy from state oversight. This issue raises a couple of central questions: What is a public university? And what is the appropriate relationship between state oversight and university operations?

Public universities in the United States were established as state-supported entities (with a bit of help from the federal government through the Morrill Act of 1862). Because states wanted their citizens to have the skills needed to attract businesses and provide crucial services, these universities not only offered a liberal arts college education but over time became the location of state-supported professional schools in areas such as engineering, business, law, medicine, and veterinary medicine. As a result, flagship public universities look quite different from their private peers. They are bigger, with far more schools and colleges and a much broader mission. This different structure and history is why the models to fund and organize public institutions are different from the models used by private universities.

In many cases, because these universities are state institutions, this has meant extensive state involvement in their operations beyond just budgetary support. Public universities are governed by publicly selected boards. University employees are often tied to state compensation and benefit systems. The state is frequently involved in regulating construction and facilities management. The university often must follow state rules on purchasing and is subject to multiple statutory requirements. Most notably, states require public universities to offer substantially subsidized tuition to state residents, often regulate the share of residents they must admit in their student body, and are frequently involved in setting these in-state tuition levels.

The University of Wisconsin-Madison, where I work, is an extreme example of this type of control. We are a state agency and largely subject to the same requirements as the Wisconsin Department of Motor Vehicles. We have no independent ability to provide across-the-board employee raises unless the state approves this. All facility renovations or construction must go through a state approval process, and we have no independent bonding authority. Even though the state provides only 15 percent of our funds, any dollar that we spend counts as "state money" and is subject to all the controls placed upon any state expenditure.

Trying to run a modern research university under the same rules as the Wisconsin Department of Natural Resources can be challenging, and we have recently received some flexibility in our human resource operations and our facility construction requirements. But the lack of operational discretion within the university in many areas is constantly frustrating.

For instance, a few years ago the state audit agency decided that we were misinterpreting the state statute governing how parking revenues collected by the state should be spent. We had long been using our parking revenues to support transportation broadly across campus, including funding our bus system and our biking infrastructure. This ruling would force us to use parking revenues only on automobile-related transportation, leaving us without funds to support our buses or our broader transportation infrastructure. It took more than a year and an extensive amount of time on the part of myself and my senior team at the state capitol to get the state legislature to add three words to the statute allowing us to continue using parking revenues to fund transportation needs. Of course, most other universities would have no restrictions on the use of parking revenues at all and could count them as general revenues for use throughout the institution. This level of university micromanagement by state statute is an extreme example of the sheer waste of time and effort sometimes created by state oversight.

The extent of state control over public higher education varies widely across states. Many universities are public institutions but not state agencies, giving them more operational freedom. In a few states, universities have quite limited public oversight. For instance, the University of Michigan was created when the state was formed in 1837, and although it is governed by a publicly elected board, its freedom to operate autonomously was written into the state constitution. Other Michigan public universities created later do not have this degree of independence.

While public university leaders have probably always grumbled about the problems of working under state oversight, these complaints have become more extensive in the past decade, with increasing calls for greater autonomy of public universities. This debate over greater autonomy in public universities is being driven by at least three major changes in the higher education environment.

First, state support for higher education has declined precipitously; for most flagship public universities state support accounts for less than 20 percent of their budget. As states become less important as funders of public universities, their high levels of statutory and regulatory control seem less reasonable. As my alumni frequently say when I talk about some of these challenges, "Why should the state regulate 100 percent of your operations when they provide only 15 percent of your funds?"

Second, higher education has become a much more competitive industry, both for students and for faculty. Flagship universities can no longer assume that the top students in the state will attend, as universities compete for students from around the country and even around the world. Top students, particularly those in middle- or upper-income families, now do a national search to select a college.

At the same time, the market for top faculty has become more competitive as well. The growing financial resources available to the top private research universities has led them to bid more aggressively for top scholars, and public universities—often facing budget constraints—have had to deal with more outside offers for faculty and sometimes found it hard to retain them. In addition, faculty now operate not in a national market, but in a global one, as universities in Asia, Europe, and the Middle East expand aggressively. As universities compete harder, both for their students and for their faculty, they need to move faster and be more flexible in providing the resources and the work environment that will keep them competitive.

Third, technological change has hit campuses in a variety of ways. The internet provides students anywhere with information about any university in the world, widening their potential choices about where to attend. Potential students can compare the food, the sports facilities, and the social scene across campuses, as well as the curriculum. At the same time, new technologies are changing the ways that educational information can be delivered. Increasingly, schools need to compete not just for residential students, but also for distance learners. And even among residential students, classes are expected to use new tools that engage students more actively in learning. This, too, requires institutions to change and adapt to this new environment.

To compete in this changing market, universities must be more entrepreneurial and more nimble. And this makes the cost of extensive state control over public universities more apparent, since public control and regulation often substantially reduce an institution's ability to respond nimbly or act entrepreneurially. Furthermore, these changes require investment in new technologies and new management systems. The decline in state funding, which has left many public universities struggling to maintain their existing quality, much less invest in new areas, makes the extensive state control over operations even more burdensome.

Let me give an example from Wisconsin. One new initiative we are working on is an expanded summer semester. This initiative will provide students with more curricular choices; it will allow them more flexibility if they want to spend a semester abroad or in an internship; it can help them get through school more quickly and with less debt; and it can allow us more flexibility to bring nontraditional students to campus for short-term certification or specialized learning opportunities. It will also expand our tuition revenues without raising tuition levels.

But this requires that we change a human resource system that is set up to schedule teaching across two semesters to one that might now allow someone to fulfill their teaching requirements across three semesters. This turns out to be quite difficult. We are limited by certain state statutes that affect timing of semesters and the structure of our human resources system; we are limited by board of regents policies that prevent us from changing the structure of faculty compensation; and we are limited by an outdated information technology (IT) system that has little flexibility in how we can track work and pay faculty and that will require substantial upfront investments of money, time, and training to improve and expand. All of this makes it difficult to undertake a sensible and creative change that will serve existing students better, attract new students into nontraditional courses, and increase our revenues.

The debate over autonomy has been particularly acute around questions of tuition and student access. As state dollars have declined, universities have sought to make up the lost revenue in three primary ways: through tuition increases, enrollment growth, and changes in the mix of in-state and out-of-state students.

States such as California, Iowa, Ohio, Pennsylvania, and Wisconsin have recently adopted in-state undergraduate tuition freezes for one or more years. A number of states impose rules regarding in-state student access, while states without such rules debate the pros and cons of growth in out-of-state students in their state universities. These restrictions make dealing with state funding cuts particularly challenging, since they limit the opportunities to expand other funding sources.

Here in Wisconsin, the state legislature has frozen in-state undergraduate tuition for the past four years. At the same time, state funding for UW System schools (which include UW-Madison) declined substantially in these four years. The board of regents had also imposed a rule that the share of out-of-state students could not exceed 72.5 percent at any school. Faced with this constraint, I approached the regents and asked for a deal around the student mix. I agreed to take a minimum of 3,600 students from the state of Wisconsin in every freshman class. This was slightly above the average number of Wisconsin freshmen we'd had over the past 10 years. In exchange, I asked to be exempted from the 72.5 percent cap. Essentially, if we chose to grow our class size, this new policy would allow us to do so by expanding out-of-state students.

The regents approved this solution for UW-Madison, in part because of the difficult financial situation facing the university. But also important was the changing demographics in the state of Wisconsin. Across the upper Midwest, the number of graduating high school seniors has been declining for a number of years, and that decline is expected to continue in the near future. At the same time, UW-Madison has had ongoing increases in the number and quality of out-of-state applicants. With a stagnant or declining in-state young adult population, I could make a strong commitment to the citizens of Wisconsin—actually admitting a growing share of the declining class of high school graduates—while taking advantage of my strong out-of-state application pool with a little growth in the entering class.

These debates about tuition and access and regulation raise questions about what a public university is and how it should be expected to operate. We all owe our existence and our growth over many decades to the support of our state and its citizens. As state institutions, we have a responsibility to provide affordable and accessible education to as many state citizens as we are able to admit. But to serve the citizens of the state effectively, we also have to be financially stable institutions with the resources to provide a high-quality education. Starving higher education and forcing it to lower quality and cut programs is a no-win choice for the state and its universities.

A variety of public universities have engaged in conversations about greater autonomy and flexibility. A report at the University of Virginia several years ago suggested a series of steps that would provide greater autonomy. Greater autonomy efforts have been discussed in Louisiana and Oregon. In Wisconsin, two previous efforts have proposed greater autonomy for different parts of the higher education system. While a number of universities have negotiated slightly more flexible arrangements with their states around certain issues, no public university of which I am aware has been able to substantially change its relationship with the state.

What might such substantial changes involve? We have to think outside the structure of public higher education that was created more than 100 years ago. What worked in 1900 just doesn't work as well more than a century later, when states have permanently reduced their commitment to higher education and a much higher share of the population is pursuing post-high school education.

For instance, here's an idea that makes enormous sense but is radical in comparison with past practice: eliminate the concept of a single in-state tuition rate. At a time when incomes have been stagnant or shrinking for many in the lower half of the income distribution, rising tuition causes serious concerns. But incomes among families in the upper part of the income distribution have grown strongly. Rather than charging a one-size-fits-all tuition level, why not calibrate tuition to income for in-state residents in state institutions? We could offer even lower tuition to low-income families, if we could raise tuition for others. Everyone would still receive a substantial subsidy relative to what they would pay at a private school. But UW-Madison currently charges everyone in the state about $10,500 in tuition. This amount is too much for some and too low for others. And it's far below the cost of providing the high-quality education that is available at UW.

Or, in a time of shrinking state commitments to higher education, some have proposed that the state simply pay the difference between in-state and out-of-state tuition for in-state residents. State dollars would be just another part of tuition in this case, with no additional dollars to support overall university services or special projects. In this case, in-state tuition would be set at whatever subsidy level the state was willing to provide. This is a very different financial model than in the past, where state dollars were considered important in funding the entire university, not just in subsidizing in-state students. But such a model would allow citizens to see exactly what type of subsidy the state is providing and to debate whether they want that subsidy to be bigger or smaller.

Access and price issues will continue to be a point of hot dispute in public higher education, because there are no easy solutions. Most state citizens still want the university to provide them with low-cost access to high-quality education, because that's what public universities have always done. But that model of public universities requires a level of public funding that many states no longer provide. This disconnect between expectations and reality drives much of the dysfunctional state policy around higher education.

One of the conundrums of modern public education is that the decline in state funding has not lessened the taste of state legislators to regulate higher education. In fact, there appears to be almost no interest in reducing the management oversight of public universities, even as state dollars have fallen. But perhaps this is not surprising. It is difficult to implement substantial change in the operational model of any public institution. Legislators like being able to score political points by "managing" public entities. They want to identify problems and then get credit for "cleaning them up"; they want to show they are actively running government; and in many cases they don't trust these institutions to run themselves effectively.

The biggest contradiction I experience regularly from publicly elected leaders is their demand that I run the university more like a business, coupled with their unwillingness to provide the management flexibility that any well-run business requires. In Wisconsin, we need to be more nimble in decision making, with less state control over how we manage staff, faculty, and facilities. This requires the ability to make management decisions about the day-to-day operations with some of the same freedom that private businesses have available to them.

The key question is how we create the political environment in which states are willing to cede greater management control and greater autonomy to higher education leadership. Even if state political leaders want to have an ongoing voice in tuition levels and class composition—issues that directly affect their constituents—they should be willing to talk about greater autonomy in institutional management.

But creating a political environment that makes greater autonomy possible will be difficult. My best suggested approach right now is to educate and look for windows of opportunity to implement change. That means talking regularly with political leadership about the limitations we face, the ways in which these limits affect our ability to operate efficiently and effectively, and alternative ways of operating. In most cases, change will occur only if a senior and relatively powerful state political leader takes up this cause and spends the political chips necessary to fight for greater discretion by higher education leadership. With the many political demands facing any governor or legislative leader, it will be a rare individual willing to take on this fight.

Ultimately, if state universities are going to stay competitive in a rapidly changing environment, their leaders must be willing to lead change inside the institution. But this requires the ability to generate new revenues and implement new programs as well as to control and manage expenses. Universities must have the autonomy that allows their leaders flexible managerial control. This is increasingly necessary to assure that our public universities remain effective and high-quality institutions that can compete with institutions around the world for good students and top faculty.

What I Wish I Known When I Started I grew up in the upper Midwest and have been amazed at the extent to which state higher education institutions are no longer a source of state bipartisan pride, but are instead used regularly as a punching bag in order to score partisan points. While many good folks in elected office don't do this, there are far too many who do.

What I Wish I Had Done When I Finished I'm not done yet, but I greatly appreciated the vocal support and good advice my immediate predecessor gave me when I started. I hope I can do the same when I'm ready to leave.

What I Wish I Had Not Done While in Office During the four years I've been in this job, at least three of those years have felt like a constant state of crisis, with one difficult issue after another either emerging on campus or coming at us from off campus, each generating substantial press, social media, and email attention. I'm still trying to figure out how to keep myself and the senior staff focused on the long-term strategic changes we need to be making while also dealing with the constant weekly crises.

What I Wish I Didn't Know When I Finished I continue to be amazed at the lack of understanding most of our stakeholders have about how things are done on campus. In the past six months I have received lists of various demands from students, from faculty, and from alumni groups. Almost none of them bothered to talk with anybody in a leadership position about what we're already doing or what's realistic in terms of budget and organization. Some of these groups just want to protest, but others honestly believe they are "helping."

How I Will Know When to Stop I'll know it's time to go when I feel like I can't help move this institution forward any more.

Working the System: Cultivating Personnel Partnerships to Optimize University Systems

Nancy L. Zimpher

In the most straightforward terms, public universities exist to serve students, to educate the populace, and to create an informed, skilled citizenry. To do this, legions of staff are required at every level: chancellors and presidents, provosts, faculty, and support of all kinds. Personnel are mission critical.

The State University of New York's (SUNY) mission has been, since its founding in 1948, to provide a world-class higher education to the broadest possible base of New Yorkers. The challenge is to stay at the leading edge of how. How can we always do better so we can meet our responsibility to society in a fast-changing, ever more complex world? For SUNY—and, I would argue, for any institution looking to execute big change—it has meant following a five-step leadership strategy:

1. create a vision;
2. generate buy-in;
3. facilitate action with accountability;
4. secure funding; and
5. spread the word

The success of each of these steps requires people power and partnership building. In this essay I discuss how we at SUNY engaged people in new ways over the eight years of my leadership there to create and reach our systemwide goal of educating more people, and educating them better.

Creating a Vision

When I came to The State University of New York as its new chancellor in 2009, leading a university system was a fresh challenge for me. I had spent several years at the head of the University of Wisconsin-Milwaukee and the University of Cincinnati, both mega-institutions in their own right, but still single institutions within systems. But being at the helm of SUNY is a different story. The largest comprehensive public university system in the United States, it is made up of 64 institutions of the broadest variety: doctoral-granting research universities, community colleges, liberal arts colleges, technical colleges, and health science centers (figure 18.1). The system enrolls more than 460,000 students a year, and, remarkably, every New Yorker lives within 30 miles of a SUNY campus. Among all of SUNY's programs and initiatives—whether its full-time enrollment, employment, online learning, Educational Opportunity Programs, campus-based childcare, alumni

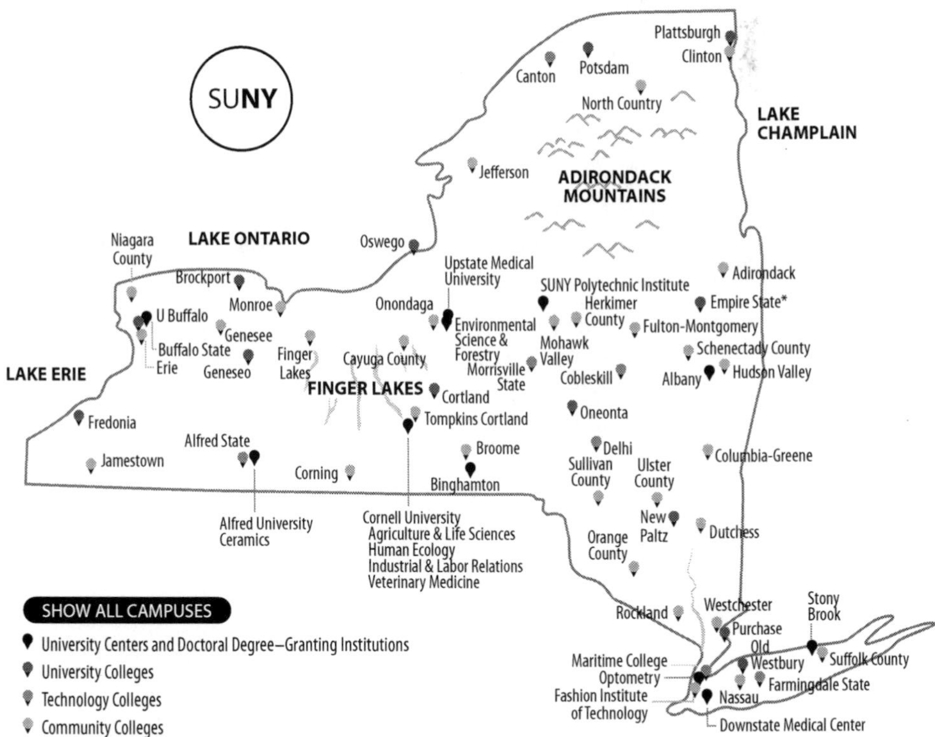

Figure 18.1. Campuses of The State University of New York (SUNY). *Source:* The State University of New York.

engagement, or countless other ways—we reach and in some way shape the days and lives of 1.3 million people each year.

I gathered some of my first impressions of SUNY on a statewide tour that took me to every one of our campuses in my first 100 days on the job. In that time I came to see that every institution in the system is distinctly different and has its own personality, its own history, and its own specialties. Of course I assumed this to be true before I ventured afield, but to see it for myself, as it played out on the ground, was something else—and it was inspiring in a way I had not expected. Crisscrossing the state and meeting with campus leaders and community members jogged a flood of ideas about SUNY's potential to do more, better, bigger in service of the state and the people of New York. Experiencing the structure of our system embedded in every region of the state, I became sure that SUNY was uniquely primed to function as the state's (much-needed) strongest economic and quality-of-life driver.

To become the reliable, unified education and economic powerhouse SUNY aims to be, I concluded that nothing short of an identity change was in order for the system. For the sake of strength, SUNY needed to think and act more like a single cohesive entity and less like a loose confederation of distantly related institutions. To illustrate this point I've often referred to an age-old Aesopian fable about a fractured family and a bundle of sticks. As the story goes, an old man, near death, summons his sons, who had fallen out. The man asks his sons to bring with them a bundle of sticks and in turn commands each of them to try to break the bundle. None is able to do so. But when he instructs them to untie the bundle, they can easily break each individual stick. The moral of the story is that there is strength in unity.

Historically, there was certainly no discord between SUNY's campuses, but there also wasn't a palpable sense of unified identity from which the system could draw strength to meet ambitious goals. So this is where we focused our energy: shifting mindsets toward a sense of unity and designing a strategic plan to articulate and drive it this shift—both monumental tasks that would take the concerted energy of many.

Generating Buy-In

Altogether, SUNY employs nearly 90,000 staff and faculty. And because personnel are indispensable in meeting any university's mission, cultivating and engaging talent at every level is a main element in what we call systemness. If a system is a set of connected parts that form a complex whole, systemness is the essence of it—how the various parts, partners, departments, and institutions work together to make the system successful and strong. Systemness, to return to the metaphor of the fable, is the both the rope that ties the bundle together and the concentrated strength itself, harnessed by the rope, that creates the unbreakable bundle. Over the past eight years, the systemness concept has been both our guide and our goal: focus on what can be improved upon to make a more perfect system, and do it together.

In 2009 and 2010 we undertook to create a strategic plan for SUNY, one that would articulate this new, unified vision. We knew from the outset that the process must be inclusive in a way that would be groundbreaking for New York. Building out from the 100-day tour, we held eight public conversations all over the state that sought input from a cross-section of SUNY stakeholders—200 faculty, staff, students, alumni, and community leaders—on what they thought the university should be and how it should change in order to best serve students, communities, regions, and the state.

I first turned to our presidents to gather the support and buy-in we'd need at the top to create the systemic mindset shift we sought. Each of SUNY's 64 institutions has its own president.* As a system leader, and a leader new to an institution, it is no small task to win the confidence and support of other leaders within a system who are successful in their own right, who have long histories with their institutions, who have their own vision and goals, or who are content with business as usual.

I was pleased to discover early in our strategic-planning process, as we began to identify a system-wide agenda, that many of our campus leaders were immediately receptive to the changes we proposed, even enthusiastic. They saw the value in the vision; they were willing partners. Some of them were themselves new to the system. Others had been in their positions for 20, 30, even 40 years. All of them brought invaluable perspectives that shaped our plan for SUNY's future.

In 2010 we launched *The Power of SUNY*—the result of more than a year of rigorous and inclusive conversations across the institutional and literal landscape of New York. In it we articulate what we together identified as six "Big Ideas"—SUNY's particular pillars of strength that would support our mission going forward. Everything we have done since 2010, everything we have accomplished—instituting a five-year rational tuition plan, creating

*The exceptions to this are SUNY's four land-grant institutions at Cornell University and the New York State College of Ceramics at Alfred University, which are headed by deans, not presidents.

seamless transfer policies that save students time and money, creating strategic enrollment policies and the best tools to sharpen student financial literacy, devising new ways to create efficiencies, making a system-wide commitment to cultivating the richest possible diversity at every level of the university, and more—goes back to the fulfillment of these six ideas:

- SUNY and the Entrepreneurial Century
- SUNY and the Seamless Education Pipeline
- SUNY and a Healthier New York
- SUNY and an Energy-Smart New York
- SUNY and the Vibrant Community
- SUNY and the World

To formulate this vision, getting buy-in from presidents was the beginning, but it wasn't enough. Systemic change requires leaders, but the seeds of new ideas must be planted deep within the institution and grow from there. Within the SUNY system, as with any other, you can draw lines around sectors, geographic regions, or schools according to size. But system goal setting must exceed those boundaries. Since 2009 SUNY has striven, and continues to strive, to cultivate a whole-system identity and with it views and approaches that meet state-sized and even broader demands: workforce preparedness, economic development, research and innovation. At SUNY, our ability to become better at those deliverables has, in large part, been powered by expanding the university's governance platform.

Every one of the more than 75 public university systems in the country, regardless of size or structure, is governed by some kind of board. In SUNY's case we have an 18-member board of trustees, 15 of whom are appointed by the governor, with the consent of the State Senate. In addition to the board of trustees, SUNY also has a University Faculty Senate (UFS) and Faculty Council of Community Colleges (FCCC). Created by the board of trustees, these two bodies represent the system's faculty at our state-operated and community colleges.

In 2006 the president of the University Faculty Senate was, for the first time, made a member (nonvoting) of the board of trustees. In 2011 the governance table was further expanded to include the FCCC president, also as a nonvoting member. The president of SUNY's Student Assembly, the official body for student representation and participation in university governance, is a voting member of the board.

So in addition to convincing our presidents and board that the direction we wanted to take SUNY was best and necessary for the university and the state, we knew that we needed to add more voices to that board. I cannot emphasize enough the importance in having faculty and student representation on a university system's governing body. There's the practical matter of the direct, live links it creates to our key constituents. The uppermost level of leaders need to be kept constantly aware of faculty and student issues, and they—we—need to hear it right from the source. But there is also the matter of the respect shown by including them at the table, and that is invaluable, too. To meet audacious goals, such as SUNY's aim to grant 150,000 degrees a year by 2020 (we currently award about 90,000), it takes unified system buy-in and support from all corners and levels. We simply could not even attempt such a heavy lift without the added strength and support of faculty and students, so it follows that their designated leaders must be at the table with us as we devise strategies to meet our goals.

I have also added these faculty and student leaders to my own cabinet for the same reason they are on the board—their insights are absolutely necessary to the policies and programs we shape in service of our mission and our motto: To Learn, to Search, to Serve.

Facilitate Action and Accountability

Systemic change within a large, complex organization like a university system requires sweeping cooperation. At SUNY, what we began to attempt in 2008 was unlike anything the system had attempted since its founding in 1948.

When we were in the process of creating *The Power of SUNY* plan we were committed to the idea that this would be a working, living plan, not something that would languish forgotten on a shelf. To ensure that the plan remained active, we needed to create a separate performance plan that would keep the entire SUNY enterprise on track as we strive to meet our goals.

As mentioned, SUNY set a major goal of awarding 150,000 degrees or credentials a year by 2020. We drew this number from projections showing that in the near future about 70 percent of jobs in New York State will require the kind of training and knowledge that come with a college degree, but that currently only about 46 percent of New York adults hold a degree beyond high school. That's a large gap, and SUNY, owing to its size, scope, and mission, is obligated to be a leader in closing it.

To meet our goal, we developed a performance system, SUNY Excels, created in a broadly inclusive manner similar to the strategic plan. Collaboratively, we agreed upon the key measures of SUNY Excels, which represent the university's commitment to continuous improvement and excellence in five key areas: access, completion, success, inquiry, and engagement. To ensure accountability, for ourselves and the public, each campus was asked to develop comprehensive performance improvement plans that include a narrative about their strategic priorities, as well as data commitments through 2020–2021 on a standard series of metrics.

The plans are working documents that are updated annually to reflect new developments and to report on progress. The commitments in the plans represent a true elevation of the SUNY system and our commitment to the state. It shows the maturity of the system, moving toward working together at a new level in support of New York.

In creating the performance plans, our guiding principles were that all metrics and indicators should

- be mission critical, understandable, and widely inclusive;
- be easy to track on a regular basis and aligned with existing assessments;
- maintain sensitivity to external conditions and mission;
- drive continuous improvement; and
- be ambitious and visionary.

Together we identified and committed to 17 points against which we continually measure our success in the five priority areas (figure 18.2).

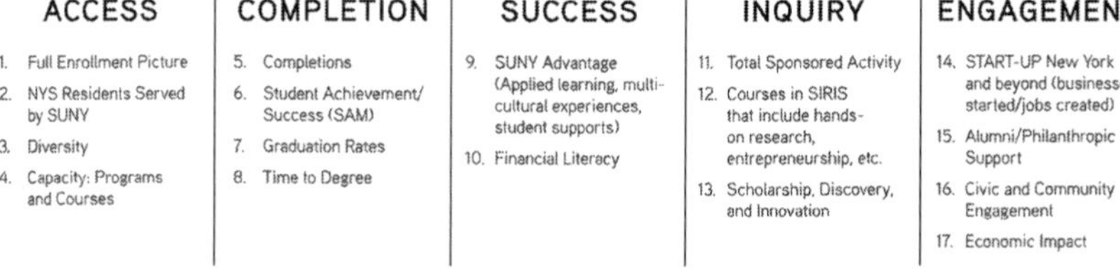

Figure 18.2. Indicators for measuring success in SUNY Excels. *Note:* SIRIS = SUNY Institutional Research Information System. START-UP NY = SUNY Tax-Free Areas to Revitalize and Transform Upstate New York. *Source:* The State University of New York.

SUNY Excels was implemented in 2015, so at the time of this writing it is still new to SUNY. But it is a process to which we are committed, and we are confident that it will cultivate our systemness and continually drive us to be a stronger, better university system.

Secure Funding

In my first year at SUNY, the country and state were approaching the nadir of the Great Recession, and SUNY, like so many universities across the country, was facing an uncertain financial future. Concerns about the economy were prevalent in conversations we had at every campus stop. In a single year, 2008, SUNY went from having its highest-ever level of direct investment by the state to crashing waves of cuts that led to the loss of more than $340 million in annual state support over the next four years.

The resulting belt tightening was acutely felt as the cuts were translated into eliminated programs and faculty positions and the threat of steeply and erratically rising tuition to close the funding gaps. All of this came at a time when we knew we needed to educate more people than ever before to prepare them for twenty-first-century careers. The strength of New York's economy, like any state, depends on the education sector—from K-12 through higher education—to get this right.

Until 2011, one of the biggest and most stubborn challenges SUNY faced for decades was that its tuition-setting ability was shackled by outdated state legislature regulations and budget practices. When SUNY had been allowed to raise tuition, it was sporadic and almost always dealt a huge blow to students and their families. In the university's 60-year history, SUNY had raised tuition only 13 times—a pattern that sounded good on its face, but that upon investigation revealed grave instability. Between 1964 (the first year SUNY charged tuition) and 2011, students in 17 entering classes never had to pay a tuition increase during their college careers; 19 entering classes saw one tuition increase; 8 entering classes saw two tuition increases; and the class entering in 1989-1990 saw three tuition increases. The smallest increase was 7 percent (2009-2010), and the highest was 43 percent (1991-992). The process was anything but fair.

Beginning in 2008 we launched an unprecedented campaign for regulatory change that would untie the university from the state's yearly budgeting process, where it was not unusual for the legislature to use tuition sweeps to close state budget gaps. In other words, the legislature would raise tuition and then use those dollars to plug holes in the budget that had nothing to do with SUNY, or even with education.

With all that SUNY needed to do to best serve New Yorkers, we needed reliable funding. It costs money to provide a modern, competitive education. It costs money to attract the best faculty and to maintain campuses, classrooms, and labs worthy of our faculty, students, scholarship, and research in the twenty-first century. It costs money to discover, implement, measure, and track programs and approaches that rely on evidence to achieve success. We wanted SUNY to compete and hold its own in the world—to become the best at getting better—and we couldn't do it on a dime.

In 2011, after two years of heavy lobbying and winning the support of a diverse coalition of supporters, faculty, students, and finally the governor and state legislature, New York passed a groundbreaking five-year measure called NYSUNY 2020 Challenge Grant Program. The legislation secured a rational tuition plan that allowed students and their families to plan for the cost of a degree at SUNY. It shifted tuition-setting power from the legislature to SUNY's board of trustees and put a cap on how much tuition could be raised ($300) in a single year over five years. There could be no surprises, no steep hikes. SUNY and the legislature also committed to sending any of the money raised by a tuition hike right back to the campuses, enhancing programs and student services. Now we had a reliable funding stream that could support programs and new faculty hires. Also, the legislation held the promise of a maintenance-of-effort assurance from the state, as well as provisions that strengthen the academic programs of the university centers and position SUNY to be a leading catalyst for job growth throughout the state.

Though this was a fair, rational, practical approach to helping fund the university and had support from faculty, administration, and students, the legislation's sunset clause meant that it went out of effect in 2016. When the rational tuition policy was in place, SUNY's annual tuition remained the lowest among all state university systems in the Northeast and in the lowest quartile of all such public institutions of higher learning in the country. We were able to add hundreds of new faculty positions. Tuition-setting power has, for the time being, reverted to the legislature. But we at SUNY remain committed to securing it again.

Considering that SUNY has so many remarkable features—size, scope, scale, scholarship, social impact—it surprised me from my earliest days in New York, and even before I arrived, that the university didn't have a more recognizable unifying brand. Part of this has to do with the individual identities of our campuses, each with its own rich history, mascots, and school spirit. But while empowering campuses to continue to nurture their identities, we also wanted SUNY to present itself to the world as a recognizable whole and a dynamic, unified, self-aware entity. At the same time that we undertook the strategic planning process, we thus also began an overhauling branding initiative. We modernized our brand and attached it to every opportunity we had to tell our story about our approach to creating a stronger system.

In many ways, SUNY's new brand has grown alongside the social media boom. Twitter caught fire in 2009, corresponding with our own new pushes to bring SUNY to the fore. Facebook matured and expanded around us, as our initiatives did. We use social media and any public platform we can command to tout our accomplishments, not to brag but to share—to show other systems what we are doing and how we are working, in the hope that they can learn from what we have learned and in the process become better themselves.

In the past eight years we created SUNY Smart Track, the most advanced and comprehensive student financial aid programming and tools in the country. We have created the first statewide cradle-to-career network to break down the stubborn silos that exist in the education continuum. We are, as a system, making strides in making teacher education the more clinical, robust practice it must be to ensure that legions of teachers are prepared to face the needs and challenges of students in every classroom in our state. SUNY is leading the way in changing how higher education institutions deal with sexual assault, bullying, and violence on campuses and among college students, devising measures that are proactive rather than reactive, with the goal of greatly reducing these incidents. In all of these cases, other systems, states, and the federal government are looking at the way SUNY is working—as a system—to meet the world's challenges.

There is power in systems of any kind; it is why they exist—to do together what cannot be done alone. A state university system that doesn't function in a unified way, that neglects to cultivate the systemness mindset and with it heightened functionality is not only a wasted opportunity, but a waste of valuable resources, intellectual, financial, and otherwise. Shifting a collective mindset and behavior from autonomy to partnership can be tricky at times. It takes patience and persistence, and compelling arguments for why leaders who may have different agendas and goals should get on board. But creating this shift is eminently doable with the right approaches.

At its heart, our work at The State University of New York over the past eight years has been to build a better system to meet the real-life needs of New Yorkers. Our goal is to become the best at getting better. We are, frankly, obsessed with making, measuring, and sharing our means of continual improvement.

What I Wish I Had Known When I Started I often compare my transition from a single campus to a comprehensive system like SUNY to the question, What does the dog do when it catches the car? I totally underestimated the size and scale of SUNY. But after 95 days on the road visiting all 64 campuses at the beginning of my tenure, I quickly began to embrace the power of such a complex opportunity. It turned out for the best, but maybe I should have paid more attention to the car before I "em-barked!"

What I Wish I Had Done When I Finished It turns out that everything I deeply stood for as SUNY's 12th chancellor is so deeply embedded in what I believe needs to be done in order to educate more people that I now know my work is not done. Leaving the chancellorship is *not* about leaving the work. So the end is really *not* the end.

What I Wish I Had Not Done While in Office My big regret will always be not having made more time to get to know people better. In each of my leadership positions I strove, and worked to inspire others to strive, to undertake some really heavy lifts to drive systemic change. We're pulled in so many directions, but I could have controlled my time better so that I could have connected in a deeper way with the people who worked hard for and with me. Still, I have wonderful memories of exceptional people. I wish people better understood how hard everyone on my teams worked to do the right thing. I am so proud of that kind of personal dedication.

What I Wish I Didn't Know When I Finished Likely every president or chancellor hopes their successor will stay the course and carry on the agenda that they and key stakeholders established during their tenure. But every new leader, myself included, wants a unique take on the institution's future, so it seems inevitable that some hard work will be undone or changed under a successor. I'd like new leaders to remember and that they stand on the shoulders of those who came before. Respect that.

How I Knew When to Stop When I was coming up the career ladder, I often looked at people of a certain age and said to myself, "Why don't they give it up so that there's more room for us juniors to move up?" So I am intentionally making room for others, stepping aside to let the next generation carry on, and I feel really good about that.

Leading a Public Flagship within a State System

R. Bowen Loftin

I defended my doctoral dissertation in the summer of 1974, and, after completing a 14-month postdoctoral fellowship, I embarked on my journey as an academic in January 1976. I have now been on the faculty of seven universities—all but one public—of which five were members of a state public system of higher education. As a three-time campus leader within two of these systems, I have seen the benefits and the challenges of managing a university that was part of a larger system. This essay, after providing necessary background, will explore the interesting position of a flagship public university sited within a system of other institutions from the flagship leader's point of view.

For the purpose of this essay, a state system of public higher education is an entity that consists of at least two universities that are independently accredited by one of the nation's regional accreditors. Moreover, the system has a single governing board. Each university within the system has a chief executive officer in addition to the system's chief executive. Some states may have a statewide "system" with a governing board, under which two or more systems exist with their own boards. These subsidiary systems meet my definition of a state system of public higher education.

Background

In the two states—Texas and Missouri—where I have spent most of my career, state systems are relatively new entities. In Texas, with an exception

I will note below, the systems date largely from the 1980s. Today all public universities in Texas, except for Midwestern State University, Stephen F. Austin State University, and Texas Woman's University, belong to one of seven systems. In Missouri, the University of Missouri System, which dates from the early 1960s and now consists of four universities, is the only one of its kind. The other nine universities in Missouri are independent and have their own boards of trustees. Texas boasts seven systems: the Lamar University System, the Texas A&M University System, the Texas State University System, the Texas Tech University System, the University of Houston System, the University of North Texas System, and the University of Texas System. I spent 23 years as a faculty member in the University of Houston System, where my administrative roles were limited to serving as department chair and directing a research institute. For a decade I was within the Texas A&M University System, spending a year strictly as a faculty member, followed by more than four years as the CEO of Texas A&M University at Galveston (one of two branch campuses of the system flagship). Then, for almost five years, I was interim president and president of Texas A&M University.

The campus in College Station (from which I graduated with a bachelor's degree in 1970) is the oldest public university (opening in 1876) in Texas but began as a "branch" of the University of Texas, which opened later in 1881. Texas's first public historically black college or university, Prairie View A&M University, admitted its first students in 1878 and was effectively a member of the first Texas higher education system. Tarleton State University joined the Texas A&M System in 1917. For all practical purposes the Texas A&M System was the oldest system in Texas until the consolidation of higher education institutions was effected in the 1980s. The University of Texas System began with the campus in Austin (1881) and added the Medical Branch in Galveston (1891). Later the Texas School of Mines and Metallurgy (1917) joined the system, to be followed by a number of health-related campuses.*

Missouri's one system, where I served as chancellor,† emerged from two campuses of the University of Missouri, the oldest campus in Columbia and

*The origins of the first three public higher education institutions in Texas are highly complex and not, in their entirety, relevant to this chapter. What is contained here is a very simplified version of what happened over a number of years and legislative sessions. I apologize to anyone who is unhappy that the full story is not here and to whose alma mater I may have given short shrift.

†Title usages vary among state systems. In Texas the president is the campus CEO while the chancellor is the system CEO. These usages are reversed in the University of Missouri System.

the Missouri School of Mines and Metallurgy in Rolla, along with the inclusion of a formerly private university in Kansas City (now University of Missouri-Kansas City) and the founding of the University of Missouri-St. Louis. Interestingly, Missouri chose to go no further in the consolidation process, leaving the other four-year institutions in Missouri independent.*

A System Makes Sense . . . Some of the Time

A historical (and often anecdotal) investigation of the rationales for a system will uncover a small number of common themes: efficiency of operation, efficiency of governance, harmonization of the many into the collective, a reduction in the number of appointed boards of governance, and ease of student movement between campuses, among others.

The first item on this list is almost always cited and is worthy of some attention. Clearly, there are many "backroom" operations in higher education that can benefit from economies of scale. Chief among these is procurement. Size confers buying power and in most cases can drive down the cost of procuring widely used items and services. Such procurement approaches may even transcend a university system and reside at the state level as a resource for all state agencies. While this operational efficiency may seem self-evident, I have rarely heard positive comments about it. Independence and perceived autonomy lead many, especially at the truly operational level of running an academic department, to rail against being forced to buy goods and services in this way. This is human nature, but I, and most campus leaders, see the financial benefits in such an approach and typically support it so long as exceptional paths are available when truly unique (or at least rare) equipment or services are needed. Fortunately, "sole sourcing" is usually an available recourse, albeit accompanied by the need to justify the procurement.

Among the many services used at a university, information technology has become a routine system "commodity." Here, however, we will find truly organized resistance from many academics. Those who use computing as a focus of or a means of conducting research will almost always object that the equipment and services provided to the campus or system as a whole cannot possibly meet their needs. Again, for the rare cases where this is likely true, alternative pathways usually are in place.

And the list goes on to include human resources, dining services, custodial services and groundskeeping, maintenance, financial services, and

*Again, there is more to the story than can be told here. The apology given in the preceding footnote applies again.

many more. One interesting variant, especially when the flagship is large relative to the other system members, is having the flagship provide the relevant services. The Texas A&M University System is one where the flagship has been tasked with providing a number of services to the system office and to other parts of the system. For example, when I was the chief executive at Galveston, the 10 or so members of our financial services team were simply too few to provide adequate depth of knowledge across the entire domain and to allow for necessary separation of duties to ensure proper accountability. To remedy this problem, I negotiated an arrangement with the flagship to take on 8 to 9 of the staff (leaving me with the leader and her assistant as my primary budget overseers and advisors). The flagship campus augmented these staff members with small amounts of time from several specialists at that campus. Many were concerned about the loss of the personal touch from our former employees and neglect by the "big" campus, but after a six-month breaking-in period, the arrangement was accepted. Through this intrasystem outsourcing we ultimately achieved a lower level of financial risk and a higher level of service quality. Similarly, the University of Missouri System is well down the pathway of providing some backroom services—procurement, information technology, some human resources (namely benefits), and some financial services—to its four member institutions.

So what are some of the challenges in being part of a system? One that must be mentioned is enrollment management. This is a sensitive subject, especially in places like Missouri, where a declining high school population and intensive competition for out-of-state students are the norm. Take, for example, the idea of a common application for first-time-in-college students. Texas adopted a common application years ago, not simply within one of its systems, but statewide. This arrangement has been in place so long, it is never mentioned. Here in Missouri, all four campus leaders agreed three years ago that we should move toward a common application for all four system universities and maintain a common database of applicants. In spite of solid leadership support, the common application and database have not been achieved. The resistance of those at the operational level has been and continues to be intense.

The Big Kahuna

Now we turn to a major challenge that I experienced in both of my flagship leadership roles and one that is common in similar systems across the country—the relationship between the flagship and the other members of the system. Over the years, I worked diligently to cultivate effective and respectful working relationships with the campus leaders across the system. My first leadership role was at a branch of the flagship. Owing to the structure of the system, I was accorded virtually the same operational visibility and respect that those from the other system campuses enjoyed, even though I reported to the leader of the flagship campus and not to the system chief executive. But I was not a threat to my fellow university leaders. We were able to interact socially and professionally within what they viewed as the same stratum of the system hierarchy. At Texas A&M, this situation allowed me to continue to enjoy their trust when I became the flagship leader. History, however, was rife with anecdotes of conflict both overt and covert between the flagship and the other system members. This became most evident when the leader of one of the "other" campuses became the system leader and worked hard to take out years of frustration he had accumulated while suffering (his word) under the boot (again, his word) of the flagship.

How real was the flagship's supposed disdain for the other system campuses? It is difficult to distinguish perception from reality. In my own experience, I would from time to time hear slights and snide references directed at our sister campuses. Most often I would hear administrators, faculty, and even students disparage the other campuses in terms of admissions standards, quality of faculty members, and difference in research volumes. Often these comments were matter-of-fact and seemed almost unconscious. The word "condescension" comes to mind when I recall these statements.

Who's in Charge Here?

The complex dynamics of the relationship between the flagship campus executive and the system executive have a number of touch points that can generate conflict. Take, for example, interactions between members of the system's governing board and these two executives. I have seen such interactions occur freely, and I have seen them be quite limited. Richard Legon of the Association of Governing Boards has argued that the system executive must control access to members of the board in order to better manage the flow of information and to avoid surprises.* This sounds good in

*R. Keller, "University of Missouri Curators Hear Advice on Presidential Search, Board Conduct," *Columbia Daily Tribune,* May 12, 2016.

principle, but what happens when a system leader fails to fully inform the board about campus issues, especially relationship issues with the flagship leader? I would suggest that campus leaders be encouraged to interact with board members but to do so in open ways, so that all are on the same page.

Another realm of potential difficulty for public institution leaders can arise in the context of relationships with elected officials. Most systems with which I am familiar vest the system leader with the responsibility for communicating with the legislative and executive branches of state governments. Again, this seems reasonable in theory; the reality, however, is that many elected officials may be graduates of the flagship campus and have a special affinity for it. I have seen the arrangement happen both ways—full engagement by the campus leader with the legislature (with the caveat that relevant details of interactions are shared with system leadership) and controlled engagement where the system leadership actively modulates the who, when, and how of such interactions. This approach can frustrate both the campus leader and those who support the flagship within the legislature.

The relationship between the campus leader and the system leader can also pose challenges. It is the rare system leader who does not also, even unconsciously, want to be the leader of the flagship campus. In some cases, such as the University of Houston System and the University of Minnesota System, the same person leads both the flagship and the system. While this may seem a reasonable solution at first thought, consider the preceding section. How would the other campus leaders see themselves in such an arrangement? While I had no direct authority over the leaders of the other campuses where I led the flagship, other campus leaders might read my words and actions through a different lens. Such a circumstance is even more likely when the same individual leads both the system and the flagship.

More typically, two different individuals lead the system and the flagship campus. That was the case in both of my flagship campus leadership roles. To fully understand the potential for difficulty in the relationship between these two leaders, one must also consider their antecedents. Today, it is rare, but not unheard of, for a nonacademic to assume the leadership of a major public university (consider the recent selection of a businessman as president of the University of Iowa and the selection of a former state elected official as president of Florida State University). It is becoming more common, however, for a nonacademic to assume the leadership of a state public higher education system. These nonacademics typically come from business or state government. Herein lies the potential for a difficult relationship, even conflict, between the campus leader and her or his nominal superior. The most challenging issues tend to emerge when the system leader consciously or unconsciously wants to also be the leader of the flagship campus. Ideally, the system leader is invisible at the campus level, working instead with the senior campus executives. It is often the case, however, that ego and the desire for attention can motivate system leaders to involve themselves in campus activities to garner the visibility and media coverage they may desire. After all, both senior business executives and elected officials are often type A personalities, accustomed to deference from those within their organizations and with a predilection for taking action. Such personalities may not fit well within a university but may resonate with board members who are usually politically appointed, have little or no experience in academic administration, and are action oriented. One can anticipate the meeting of two distinct cultures when the flagship campus leader has come up through the ranks while the system leader has had virtually no experience inside the university except as an undergraduate student and as a guest speaker.

Jack Be Nimble . . .

Given the very real challenges noted (and many more that limited space precludes me from discussing), one could ask, why have a system at all? I have heard colleagues state vehemently that a system can only detract and not add to the flagship's fortunes. I do not share that opinion. First of all, from a political point of view systems are here to stay. Resistance is futile! Second, systems add value in terms of efficiencies and economies of scale. The most important issue is the relationship between the system leader and the flagship campus leader. If this relationship is based on trust—derived, in part, from each individual's unique set of experiences and skills—and mutual respect, the flagship campus and the system can both be well served. If the relationship breaks down or if one seeks to undermine the other with the governing boards and the state's elected and appointed leaders, conflict will arise that can damage both the campus and the system.

So where does the responsibility lie? Governing boards, even more than search committees and search consultants, must take the time to dig deep and gauge the potential for both complementarity and discord between the two leaders that they must ultimately confirm. This is difficult because most boards are filled with members who have little or no direct experience (other than as a student) with higher education, who are volunteers with limited time to devote to the selection processes, and who—since they are usually politically appointed—may have to answer to a governor or to powerful legislators for their actions. Once the selections are made, the responsibility then falls to the two executives, especially the flagship campus leader, to make it work.

This effort may require significant time, exceptional diplomacy, compromise, patience, and subrogation of one's ego. The inherent difficulty in making it work is evidenced by the sometimes all too short tenure of either of the two leaders.

What I Wish I Had Known When I Started At Texas A&M University, I had served for more than four years as a branch campus CEO as well as a flagship vice president. So when I became the flagship president I already knew all the major players, had significant experience with the state legislature, and had met a large number of the major alumni donors. The transition was one of scale, not of substance, for me. At the University of Missouri, in spite of reviewing a great deal of material furnished by the campus and system before my arrival, I underestimated the inertia of the campus and the ingrained decentralization of financial authority. This came back to bite me in many ways.

What I Wish I Had Done When I Finished When I arrived at Missouri I had a sense of urgency imparted to me by the board, the system leader, and my own review of the university's financial and academic health. In spite of this sense of urgency, I should have moved more slowly to effect the major changes that I knew to be necessary for the institution's future.

What I Wish I Had Not Done While in Office By nature I say what I think—this was not a formula for success at Missouri. Specific, honest statements that I made were ultimately used against me.

What I Wish I Didn't Know When I Finished How fragile a once-strong institution really was. The University of Missouri has been great and can be again.

How I Knew When to Stop When they changed the locks! In all seriousness, based on my conversations with the system leader over a period of a few weeks at Missouri, it became clear that my departure was inevitable. Many interpreted the national media attention to campus protests as the reason for my departure. It was not, although it did lead to the system leader's resignation.

19 When to Take a Stand on National Policy

Perspectives from a Supreme Court Case

Mary Sue Coleman

Universities, as well as their presidents, are often at the center of attention on issues that are deeply consequential for all of higher education. When I was announced as president of the University of Michigan in 2002, I already had almost seven years of tenure as the president of the University of Iowa, and those experiences were invaluable. However, I had never before faced a spotlight like the one that shines regularly on Michigan. That spotlight is intense, perpetual, and national.

When I arrived in Ann Arbor, the most pressing issues were two lawsuits (then headed straight to the US Supreme Court) brought against the University for its use of affirmative action when admitting undergraduate and law students.

I believe fervently in the positive power of affirmative action for US higher education. Affirmative action, when applied in concert with many other individual applicant attributes, gives universities flexibility in making entering classes diverse. By considering gender, race, geography, ethnicity, life experiences, and performing and inherent talents in constructing a class, the university creates a diverse environment—one that we know from our extensive research makes a better learning context for all students.

Confronting and embracing the lawsuits is a good example of my admonition to "own what you inherit." These cases were extremely high profile with legal implications for every single higher educational institution in America. While I had followed the cases when I was at Iowa, I had no concept how much preparation would be required to move the cases forward. The quantity of background material, the legal expertise required, and the work that went into becoming a national spokesperson for the value of affirmative action was enormous almost to the point of paralysis.

As a scientist, I appreciate data. Here is a snapshot of the data that I had to master within a matter of months:

- 103 binders of trial exhibits and court documents;
- expandable folders of amicus briefs reaching a length of four feet;
- 12 lateral file drawers of printed material; and
- an additional six boxes of paperwork weighing a total of 300 pounds.

Added to this mass of materials was a century of federal civil rights legislation and another 25 years of legal interpretation of the high court's 1978 Bakke decision! I could easily have become overwhelmed.

I constantly reminded myself that even though we were aggressively defending ourselves as defendants in two lawsuits, we had other issues to address as I welcomed new and returning students as well as new faculty to the university in the fall of 2002. Concurrently, the state of Michigan was entering what would turn out to be one of the worst decades economically in its history, and universities were in no way immune to the fiscal turmoil in the state.

At this juncture, I grew to appreciate the power of having a highly accomplished and effective university communications and legal teams. They (and specifically Vice President Lisa Rudgers and General Counsel Marvin Krislov) guided me expertly through the months-long process. Thus, early on in my Michigan tenure, I grew to understand that the media matter. Our team had excellent national media contacts, media experience, and a deep knowledge of the requirements of reporters from various media outlets. They were relentless in thinking in advance about our reactions to various possible outcomes from the court. We considered and practiced responses to every conceivable scenario, which allowed me to learn how to shape our public presence on the substance of the cases. Critically, they also counseled me, in this day of 10-second sound bites, on the best way to communicate extremely complex ideas as crisply as possible. At the same time, I worked on how best to discuss all the issues in depth when the opportunity was presented.

Arguing before the Supreme Court entails many legal steps and maneuvers. There were three critical moments that centered around me over a period of four years. The first was when President George W. Bush announced that he was directing the Justice Department to file a brief on behalf of the plaintiffs in the case, effectively placing the executive branch in opposition to the University of Michigan. This declaration came as a bit of a surprise to us because of a furor that had erupted several months earlier, at a celebration of Senator Strom Thurmond's 100th birthday. At that event, Senate Republican majority leader Trent Lott enthusiastically praised Thurmond's 1948 presidential platform that opposed "social intermingling of the races." We were inclined to believe that the uproar (Lott stepped down as majority leader) would prompt the executive to shy away from any statement in opposition to affirmative action in college admissions.

In January 2003, however, President Bush directed the Justice Department to file the brief. While saying that he supported diversity, the president asserted that the University of Michigan had been using clearly illegal quotas in its admissions processes. In fact, he used the word "quota" four times in a five-minute statement. He went on to assert that we considered only two factors in admissions—race and test scores—and that race carried the heavier weight.

As an institution, we simply had to respond to these inaccuracies, and it was my job to articulate that response. We agreed that I would appear on live television (ABC's *Good Morning America*) by satellite the next day.

I remember that day so well and how nervous I was! How often does a university leader have to confront our nation's president and tell him and the country that he is simply wrong?

Here again, the communications staff was invaluable to me. They suggested, and I quickly agreed, that I should first, and rightly, praise President Bush for his support of diversity in the classroom, but then immediately express concern that he misunderstood our admissions procedures. I quickly explained that we had *no* quotas, that we considered many factors in our admissions, and that academic achievement was the most important attribute for each applicant.

The decision to take the high road in our response was well received. We used this event to educate the public that the university had never used quotas, that we valued academic achievement above all else, and that we agreed with the president that diversity was critically important in higher education classrooms.

The second critical communications moment came in the waiting period between the oral arguments at the court and decision day in late June. The conservative newspaper columnist George Will characterized this period as "High Noon for 'Diversity.'"* It was a high noon that lasted three long months for us at Michigan.

*George Will, "High Noon for 'Diversity,'" *Newsweek*, May 25, 2003.

As we waited and waited, we practiced questions and answers based on every conceivable outcome: we won both cases, we lost both, or we had a mixed decision. All the while, I focused on improving my skills as the face of the university, as the tension mounted and relentless publicity around the cases continued apace.

As is customary in waiting for Supreme Court decisions, we had no idea when the announcement would be made. Since this was a consequential ruling that would set legal precedent on the issue of affirmative action, we wanted to be present for the announcement. We made a calculated guess that it would come in the last week of June (the end of the court term), so the team and I were in Washington, DC, at the court then and ready to respond. The plaintiffs were not. This outcome was clearly good fortune but not entirely good luck.

On that morning, June 23, 2003, when the court issued its ruling and upheld the use of race in college and university admissions, we owned the day. We stood in the sunshine on the steps of the Supreme Court and faced every major news outlet in the country; the next day we appeared on the front page, above the fold, of all major US newspapers. With the help and support of so many—most notably our legal and communications teams—I led the university over the finish line. This was a historic day at the beginning of an amazing chapter in my life—and in the life of the University of Michigan—that I will never forget.

However, in our complicated world, there is an important and sobering coda to the wonderful 2003 Supreme Court ruling. And it presented a third critical communications moment for me as president. Three years later, in November 2006, voters in Michigan faced a referendum to amend our state's constitution to prohibit any consideration of race, gender, or national origin in state university admissions. Proposal 2, as it was known, would negatively affect admissions programs at all of the state's 15 public universities and 27 public community colleges. But the University of Michigan was clearly singled out by the amendment's proponents for our very public defense of affirmative action before the Supreme Court.

As a public university, we were not permitted by law to take a stand on a ballot issue. But we could work—as we had been for many years—to educate the public about the benefits for all students of diversity in the classroom. We shared this research again and again, before church groups, business leaders, and newspaper editors. I gave countless interviews and wrote many op-eds, both alone and with my university colleagues in Michigan. All the while, I worked constantly with the communications and legal teams to prepare for every conceivable voter outcome. We knew that a constitutional change prohibiting affirmative action would be a devastating outcome for many on our own campus and beyond.

By early morning after Election Day, we knew that our worst fears had been realized. Michigan voters had decided to change the state's constitution. As someone who had stood on the steps of the Supreme Court cheering a ruling that made the classroom experience better for all of our students, this voter backlash was extremely disheartening. At the same time, I knew I could not be silent. Our students would expect me to speak directly to them.

We chose an outdoor location in the heart of campus (the Diag, as it is known), and hundreds of students gathered there. I was clear with them about my profound sadness and disappointment at the vote. But I also firmly reiterated our strong and shared commitment to the principle of diversity on campus. We made it clear that before and after the vote, we had followed and would follow the law. My priority then was to assure our campus that we would hold firm to our values. We did encounter considerable criticism for my speech from those outside the university. But we persisted in holding true to our values.

As I had feared, it has been challenging not having affirmative action as a tool for helping to achieve diversity in admissions. Since the change in the Michigan constitution, our numbers of underrepresented students have fallen by about half. This is precisely the outcome encountered at selective public universities in other states that have banned the use of affirmative action, and I believe that such restrictions on university admissions are harmful for our nation in the long run.

I do remain optimistic about the importance of diversity in US higher education and know that my former colleagues from around the country will continue to work on this critical issue. It was extremely heartening for us to hear the Supreme Court decision in Fisher II (University of Texas) during the summer of 2016 upholding a narrowly tailored use of affirmative action along with the "top 10 percent" plan. Most important in that ruling was Justice Anthony Kennedy's reassertion that university officials, and not the courts, are best positioned to make decisions about admittance to our great selective universities in this country.

From these experiences, I learned a great deal about the importance of having the president of the university take and advocate a position that directly affects the university and perhaps all of higher education.

However, as nonprofit and nonpartisan institution leaders, university presidents must be careful about expressing views on specific issues and about external advocacy. In that vein, as president, I did not endorse any political candidates or give opinions about policies or societal issues that were outside the realm of higher education. This is certainly not because I and others at the university were not asked or that we did not have deeply held views about national or local issues. We did. What I always reminded myself before speaking publicly was that the voice of the president carries great weight and that when speaking I was representing the position of the university, not simply my own view.

As president, I face a constant barrage of demands to support or reject this or that cause. The imprimatur of the university is extraordinarily valuable and thus arouses the interest of many in dragging the institution into various debates. Wise presidents resist these entreaties and develop strategies to make internal decisions about when and how to use the president's voice.

My experiences with affirmative action as well as many other national policy issues and episodes of economic turmoil (not the least of which was the Great Recession) that covered almost 20 years of my tenures at the University of Iowa and the University of Michigan taught me a number of lessons about moving an institution forward in a positive way. First and foremost, I learned that it is reckless to arrive in the position of president with a fully articulated agenda. At every institution, issues, concerns, and initiatives transcend individual presidential terms. In my experience, there is plenty of time to develop your own ideas, plans, and strategies as you embrace and help the leaders and faculty work on resolving challenges from the past.

During the initial months of a new presidency, it is enormously helpful to explicitly explore, affirm, or generate a list of principles that guide all institutional policies and actions. In my view, these should be written down, shared with your inner circle, and turned into actions to which you and your team commit. It was always pleasantly surprising to me how often I examined the list of principles and the "walking the principles" document that sat close by on my desk.

The next important step for a new president is to build the right supporting team. Sometimes those individuals are already in place, and the group chemistry works. But often in presidential transitions there exist a number of vacancies. The responsibility of the new president is to fill those position with people who are individually distinguished in their field, loyal, but willing to challenge the status quo and to be enthusiastic about working within the team to keep moving the institution forward.

With the right leadership team in place, the president can assemble a robust sounding board for making decisions about when and how to take a stand on a national policy issue. Often, it will be important to bring faculty leaders or faculty experts into the discussion to help inform an appropriate institutional response or approach.

With the affirmative action debate, which stretched over two presidencies and seven years, the most important initiative that the university undertook was to mount several rigorous and thorough research projects to evaluate the educational outcomes of diverse classroom settings. The results from these research projects formed much of the legal argument for the educational value of diversity at colleges and universities.

After a clear collective decision has been made on when and how to use the presidential voice, another important step is to find venues with very different constituencies to deliver the same concise institutional message over and over again. Tracking media response (both positive and negative) over time can be a valuable tool to discern whether the president's message is resonating with those who care about the institution. Of course, as with almost any topic, conflicting opinions will emerge. However, I always found that even with those audiences that were opposed to affirmative action, my straightforward explanation and approach to the subject brought mutual respect and understanding.

Finally, in these turbulent times, being a university president can be taxing and exhausting. There were certainly moments when I found it to be so. But almost every day, I found something to smile about or to celebrate or simply to enjoy. It is an enormous privilege to be a university president and to "touch the future" in the company of bright, engaging, and creative young people. In the tough times, remember to rejoice in your good fortune to have been chosen to lead your institution.

What I Wish I Had Known When I Started You do not have the luxury to pick your issues. Own what you inherit!

What I Wish I Had Done When I Finished Created a rapid-transit connector between the University of Michigan Main and North Campuses.

What I Wish I Had Not Done While in Office Suggested that the university hold its large commencement ceremony at the football stadium of a sister university when Michigan Stadium was unavailable during a massive renovation.

What I Wish I Didn't Know When I Finished The number of times individuals and groups want the university to promote their pet cause.

How I Knew When to Stop After two wonderful presidencies over 19 years, I knew it was time for fresh ideas and renewed energy both for me and for the university.

Response to the 2017 Executive Order on Refugee and Immigration Policy

Lee C. Bollinger

On January 27, 2017, President Donald Trump signed an executive order banning people from seven Muslim-majority countries from travelling to the United States. What follows is the text of the email sent by Columbia University president Lee Bollinger to the university's students, faculty, and staff on January 29.

Dear fellow members of the Columbia community:

With the executive order issued by President Trump barring admission to the United States of Syrian refugees and imposing a 90-day ban on all immigrant and nonimmigrant entry from seven Muslim-majority nations, the fear so many have had about federal policies being changed in ways that could affect our community has become disturbingly real.

The public controversy and legal debate over the President's order is intense. Among the many strong petitions and compelling statements that have been issued is one from the Association of American Universities (AAU), of which Columbia is a member. We join with many peers in decrying this action as discriminatory, damaging to America's leadership in higher education, and contrary to our nation's core values and founding principles.

At a practical level, we are advising community members and visiting scholars from the designated countries to suspend plans for international travel. At the moment, we do not know of any Columbia students, faculty, or staff from the seven designated countries who are currently abroad. In the meantime, we urge anyone seeking further guidance to contact our International Students and Scholars Office (ISSO).

At a more fundamental level, this order undermines the nation's continuing commitment to remain open to the exchange of people and ideas. We must not underestimate the scale of its impact. An estimated 17,000 international students in the U.S. are from the seven nations covered by the entry ban. Scholars planning to travel to the United States for meetings and conferences at our colleges and universities will effectively be barred from attending. If this order stands, there is the certainty of a profound impact on our University community, which is committed to welcoming students, faculty, and staff from around the world, as well as across the nation.

As I have said on many occasions, it is critically important that the University, as such, not take stands on ideological or political issues. Yet it is also true that the University, as an institution in the society, must step forward to object when policies and state action conflict with its fundamental values, and especially when they bespeak purposes and a mentality that are at odds with our basic mission. This is such a case.

It is important to remind ourselves that the United States has not, except in episodes of national shame, excluded individuals from elsewhere in the world because of their religious or political beliefs. We have learned that generalized fears of threats to our security do not justify exceptions to our founding ideals. There are many powerful and self-evident reasons not to abandon these core values, but among them is the fact that invidious discrimination often adds fuel to deeply harmful stereotypes and hostility affecting our own citizens.

It is with regret that I have to send this communication.

Sincerely,
Lee C. Bollinger

IV PERSONAL CHALLENGES

20 Presidents and General Counsels: A Unique Relationship

Eduardo Padrón

Running a college or university is complex, and at an institution of the size and scope of Miami Dade College, that task can be quite daunting. The role of the general counsel, while often removed from the public spotlight, is indispensable. As the headlights and airbags of the college, the legal team helps illuminate the path and protect the institution from legal exposure. Most important, however, the general counsel minimizes the involvement of leadership in smaller, everyday affairs to make way for a college's most important task—focusing on providing high-quality and accessible teaching and learning experiences for students. In today's paradigm, our lawyers are busier than ever.

At MDC, as with many colleges and universities, legal counsel is an essential and crucial division of the institution, offering college leadership invaluable guidance and knowledge about the unique practice of higher education law. Regardless of the structure and size of a college's legal department, the legal team is involved in practically every aspect of the institution, and its mission remains the same—shielding the college from any legal wrongdoing and helping to foster a working and learning environment that is transparent and ethical. The former president of George Washington University, Stephen Joel Trachtenberg, who happens to be a coeditor of this book, best described the unique bond between a general counsel and a college president when he said to "keep it as well tuned as possible."

In general, college attorneys handle all public records requests, protect the brand, address free speech issues and employee grievances, assist in the property acquisitions process, and many other issues. Depending on the size of the college and the community it serves, general counsels may face other unique challenges.

At MDC, for example, we have become a steward of historic preservation in our community, and our attorneys have been key in aiding the college in the acquisition of properties such as the National Historic Landmark Freedom Tower and the David W. Dyer Federal Building, both in downtown

Miami. When it comes to the college's compliance with the Americans with Disabilities Act, our college attorney is at the forefront of our efforts to ensure that we abide by new and changing laws. Specifically, as more academic programs have transitioned to online platforms, our legal team ensures that the college complies with laws related to accessibility and records-management issues related to the Family Educational Rights and Privacy Act. Simply stated, college and university attorneys must be willing and able to address an expansive list of issues, ranging from a records request to a lawsuit from a disgruntled faculty member to a bid protest and more extreme situations such as a law enforcement situation on campus. Even when dealing with these scenarios, effective top college attorneys cannot get in the habit of always saying "no" to minimize potential exposure. They must be willing to take measured risks based on the law to truly allow institutions to thrive.

As the higher education institution with the largest and most diverse campus-based undergraduate enrollment in the country,* with more than 165,000 students and over 8,000 employees, Miami Dade College is a complex organization where attorneys naturally face wide-ranging demands and challenges. As a result, our institution employs in-house counsel and also hires expert outside legal teams when needed. This ensures that the college and its leadership abide by the rules of law and protects the integrity and reputation of the college in the community and around the world. Regardless of who provides the legal advice, the college's responsibility is to retain legal representation that is ethical and that strongly advocates for the law. A lean, in-house approach has worked well at MDC, mitigating costs and streamlining communications.

Out of the extensive list of administrators, staff members, and advisers the president consults on a daily basis, the general counsel is likely the one person he or she relies on the most. Indeed, the relationship between these two individuals is unique and constantly developing. Interactions can be discreet and confidential, and there is a great deal of deference. A president must fully trust the attorney's judgment, operating under the assumption that all legal advice or decisions have the college's best interests as a priority. Using the legal advice provided, the president is and always must be the ultimate decision maker.

Because of the general counsel's position as essentially a watchdog for the college, the person in this role must possess a singular set of skills to

*This characterization excludes community colleges that report to the Integrated Postsecondary Education Data System (IPEDS) as systems.

ensure that all legal matters at the institution are handled diligently and effectively. College attorney positions are never awarded to "yes" people, but rather to those with principles, integrity, vision, and discipline. Attorneys in higher education, as in any other field, must possess excellent critical thinking and communication skills, and use analytical thinking to decipher sensitive issues with professionalism and objectivity. Listening is key, as is an ability to interpret differing opinions without judgment and offer solutions that will move the college in a positive direction. A general counsel must also be a problem solver for the college president and his key administrators, with the ability to understand the ethical implications of a decision and advise leaders on the most appropriate path to take to ensure the institution is in compliance and acts in an ethical manner.

In addition, the general counsel must develop an open and honest relationship with the president, understanding the priorities of the president and knowing when it is best to approach the college's top administrators with a sensitive legal issue. Finally, a general counsel's priorities must align with those of the college president, and his or her decisions and legal advice must be delivered with the college's best interests at heart.

In some ways, the general counsel aids the president in setting the tone of an institution by the way he or she handles conflict and works to avoid disputes and controversy. When a situation arises, and those in a position to make decisions present differing opinions or perspectives, the general counsel can and should be the impartial party that is able to bring consensus and ultimately facilitate a decision-making process that is smooth and free of negativity. Attorneys can keep the conversation going, offering an unbiased perspective when needed, and bringing to the table the pros and cons of each situation as solutions are discussed.

In their 1989 memorandum "The College and University Legal Department," Martin Michaelson and Paul Shapiro said that while some college presidents and senior administrators view the legal office as a "fire department," others consider the general counsel a counselor of the institution:

> Their office is viewed as the institutional conscience, and the lawyers are respected advisors to the college on a broad range of initiatives as well as problems (some of which are not primarily legal initiatives or problems) covering all legal questions.*

*Martin Michaelson and Paul M. Shapiro, "The College and University Legal Department," memorandum for the National Association of College and University Attorneys (NACUA) Ad Hoc Committee on Professional Relations (Washington, DC: NACUA, 1989).

College attorneys also should embrace the concept of preventive counseling, a term coined by William Kaplin and Barbara Lee in their book *The Law of Higher Education*. They say preventive law focuses on taking steps before legal issues surface, which includes setting parameters to avoid legal disputes:

> Counsel identifies the legal consequences of proposed actions; pinpoints the range of alternatives for avoiding problems and the legal risks of each alternative; sensitizes administrators to legal issues and the importance of recognizing them early; and determines the impact of new or proposed laws and regulations, and new court decisions, on institutional operations.*

Beyond the daily tasks of the legal office of a college, the general counsel must continually assess risk and foresee potential legal challenges. The legal team should also be watchful of federal and state legislation that may affect the operations or decision making of the president and key leaders. His or her main responsibility is to ensure that the institution is always in compliance with legal mandates and obligations, but sometimes these parameters change at a moment's notice. Effective legal counsels keep tabs on the changing world of higher education law and keep the president and his immediate administrators informed of these changes and the possible implications for the college. This is partly accomplished through fostering and nurturing working relationships with fellow college general counsels, who likely face similar challenges and may have creative and cost-effective solutions to routine legal issues faced by colleges and universities around the country. It also allows attorneys to determine best practices and to keep up with trends occurring at other schools from a legal perspective.

At MDC, our in-house legal team consists of a college attorney, a paralegal, an assistant, and support staff. Together, they constitute the Office of Legal Affairs, housed within the Office of the President. This structure facilitates daily interactions among the legal team, the college president, and senior staff, and gives the college attorney maximum exposure to many of the college's affairs and transactions requiring legal guidance or intervention. The members of the legal team also serve as the liaisons between the college and outside counsel, entities brought in to handle the specific or narrow-scope requests and assignments that often come our way. Especially

*William A. Kaplin and Barbara A. Lee, *The Law of Higher Education*, 4th ed. (San Francisco: Jossey-Bass, 2006), Section 2.4.2., p. 14.

important, the college attorney at MDC regularly reviews our policies and procedures for consistency, clarity, and legal sufficiency.

Our in-house college attorney model facilitates the availability of lawyers at a moment's notice, a key factor in a successful president-general counsel relationship. Our institution has eight campuses, several outreach centers, and several dozen departments, and each of our divisions uses the services or guidance of our attorneys. Our human resources division, for example, seeks legal advice to handle employment-related lawsuits, benefits issues, and discrimination allegations. Academic and student affairs also use the expertise of our lawyers for matters related to faculty grievances, program compliance, student disciplinary actions, and copyright and intellectual property issues. The college attorney is also a key figure in any contract negotiations, lease agreements, and investment matters.

While having a legal team on campus is a great asset for smooth and effective operations, it has many other advantages both for the attorneys and for administrators and staff. There is no better way to understand and interpret the decisions made by a college president and his administration than by actually collaborating with these leaders every day and experiencing the impact of their decisions on students, faculty, and staff. The college attorney's availability on campus allows for the development of strong relationships between the legal office and key administrators, which leads to a more effective and productive decision-making process when legal matters are brought to the table. As an in-house attorney, the individual can attend college board meetings, share lunch with a dean or program administrator, and have easy access to the president when necessary. This creates a productive work culture and helps the legal team gain a deeper understanding of the goals and priorities of the college administration.

For administrators, the continuous presence of the college attorney creates an additional awareness of the legal implications of almost every decision made at the administrative level. Knowing that the legal team is simply a phone call away streamlines the legal consultation process. It also helps the college stay ahead of the game, allowing attorneys to anticipate any potential legal implications of a situation and take steps to reduce or eliminate disputes. In the end, this approach likely saves the college time and money.

In addition, having in-house counsel allows the attorneys to acquire greater familiarity with legal issues related to education, which can sometimes be unique. Attorneys also have the opportunity to understand and interpret the internal organizational idiosyncrasies of the college and its many departments, which will ultimately become useful when dispensing legal advice.

Similarly, hiring outside counsel has its advantages. It is common for colleges and universities to face legal inquiries about specific or technical issues that are best handled by an expert in the field. Bringing in a contracted legal expert who specializes in a specific subject area can give the institution an added advantage when it comes to narrow issues such as patent registrations or property acquisitions. In addition, hiring outside counsel lessens the workload for the in-house counsel's office, allowing the in-house attorneys more time to dedicate to more pressing matters.

One of the most serious issues that colleges and universities currently face is reduced funding, and legal teams are not exempt from feeling the impact of budget cuts. Kaplin and Lee, in *The Law of Higher Education*, point out that the practice of preventive law is crucial to the saving costs at a college or university.

Regardless of whether a college or university houses counsel internally or hires outside firms, costs are involved and can be astronomical. When attorneys are in house and on the college's payroll, the costs associated with their salaries and the operations of the legal office are budgeted in advance. This allows the college to foresee legal expenses and plan accordingly. It also helps keep costs low in comparison with an outside counsel, who generally charges hourly fees.

However, colleges around the country are dealing with budget cuts that affect the size of the legal team, often reducing personnel and hindering access to key resources. University leaders cannot ignore this unfortunate reality and will often require the aid of outside counsel to fill the gaps left by eliminated positions. With the use of outside counsel, costs can increase exponentially, and sometimes unexpectedly. Outside attorneys usually bill by the hour, and each firm has a different cost structure. Therefore, the legal fees can be unpredictable, and college leaders should carefully consider the parameters that trigger a phone call to an outside attorney.

It is undeniable that the legal teams of our colleges and universities are a crucial component of the daily operations of our institutions. We, as presidents, must always ensure that our relationships with our college attorneys come from a place of trust and responsibility and that we work together to ensure that our work is guided by the best interests of our students and faculty.

What I Wish I Had Known When I Started I never planned to be an educator and higher education leader. It happened by chance. Training in higher education delivery, processes, and methodologies would have helped me. Fortunately, I had great mentors.

What I Wish I Had Done When I Finished Thankfully, I am still leading our nation's largest institution of higher education, and I hope to remain involved in higher education for years to come. However, it will make me very happy as an educator and an American to see free tuition implemented for our community college students. I will work hard every day to see this dream become a reality.

What I Wish I Had Not Done While in Office Looking back at my early years as an academic leader, I probably should have paced myself a little more effectively, to ensure that my time was spent wisely pushing forward initiatives that truly advanced our mission of high-quality, accessible, and affordable educational opportunities. Anything I have ever done has had my undivided attention and passion, and sometimes my plate simply gets a little full.

What I Wish I Didn't Know When I Finished Well, I am not done yet. However, the magnitude of the effects of high tuition costs on students is something I'd rather not see nor deal with. This issue is keeping so many amazing potential students from setting foot onto college campuses. This harsh reality keeps me up at night. I wish our country would come together to find a solution to the rising costs of a college education, because only through higher education are we guaranteed a path to success and can our nation be competitive in the global knowledge economy.

21 Exiting with Grace and ahead of the Sheriff

Knowing When to Fold 'Em

Richard C. Levin

So he knew how to do even that, the hardest thing. Quit.

—John Updike, "Hub Fans Bid Kid Adieu," *New Yorker*, October 22, 1960

I was 13 years old when John Updike published his classic account of Ted Williams's last game at Fenway Park. I didn't know much about good writing then, and I didn't know much about life. But I knew about baseball. In fact, I knew just about every fact and statistic that one could know about baseball. I could recite the winner of every World Series game ever played, and I knew Ted Williams's batting average from his rookie year onward. Ditto for Babe Ruth, Stan Musial, Mickey Mantle, and Willie Mays. I also knew that there was something deeply true about what Updike was saying about Williams, the consummate perfectionist, the student of the game, later the author of a book only he could have written: *The Science of Hitting*. The Kid chose his moment, his last home field at bat of a summer in which he produced the best numbers ever achieved by a 42-year-old. He hit a towering home run and retired.

Quit at the top of one's game. For a university president, this lesson leaves more questions open than answered. How does one know one is at the top of one's game? If peak performance and reputation are knowable, and one has achieved them, does one leave immediately? Surely not, because leaving too soon might damage one's institution, and one's reputation, even more than staying too long.

Long before I started to think about when to leave, I looked at the matter from the opposite perspective: how long could I stay and remain effective? In my early years at Yale, I recognized that after two relatively short-term presidents, the institution wanted and expected a long tenure from me. I was 46 when appointed, so I had a long runway. And I had an ambitious agenda. But I wondered: How does one continue to inspire and lead a community for a long time? How does one remain an effective leader? Fortunately, a trustee provided me with the answer.

Henry Schacht was a fellow of the Yale Corporation, our governing body, and chairman of its finance committee when I assumed the presidency in 1993. A man of complete integrity and a servant-leader of the highest order, he quickly became a trusted source of advice and a true friend. Two or three years into my job, I asked him, "You were the CEO of Cummins Engine for 21 years, and when you left everyone was sad to see you go. How many years should I stay?"

Without hesitation, Henry provided the solution to the puzzle: "Don't think in terms of years; think in terms of agendas. When your initial agenda is compete, or well under way, you need to define a new agenda—a new set of goals that will motivate the organization. If, after one or two or three rounds, you run out of fresh ideas, it's time to leave."

This advice rang true and put everything in perspective. At year five, the Yale Corporation undertook, at my request, its first of what is now an institutionalized five-year review—discreetly soliciting the views of faculty, staff, students, and alumni to determine the condition of the university and the hopes and expectations of constituents concerning its future course.

The outcome materialized as if Henry Schacht had written the script. Everyone recognized that the first five years had focused relentlessly on two objectives: (1) the planning and initiation of a multiyear, comprehensive program to restore, renovate, and expand the campus, and (2) constructive engagement in civic initiatives designed to strengthen the city of New Haven and Yale's relationship with it. Efforts in both areas were judged to be successful and expected to continue, but the main message, coming from faculty in particular, was this: "You've done the hard and obviously important work of remediation in areas of weakness (campus infrastructure and our urban environment). Now define some academic priorities and lead us to achieve them!"

I had anticipated two such priorities in my inaugural address but had neither the resources nor the capacity to undertake them while focusing on infrastructure planning and investment, launching our New Haven homebuyer program, and initiating the redevelopment of downtown New Haven. Phase two would continue these efforts at infrastructure investment and civic improvement, but we would also broaden the agenda to include internationalizing the university and strengthening science and engineering.

We made dramatic advances toward internationalization in a very short time: offering for the first time full need-based financial aid to international students admitted to Yale College; awarding full scholarships to all admitted PhD students foreign and domestic; establishing the World Fellows Program for emerging global leaders; launching numerous programs in China; establishing a presumption that all undergraduates would spend a summer in a study, research, or work experience abroad; and providing the resources to fund this commitment. Progress in science and engineering was slower and remains ongoing. But we consolidated nearly a dozen PhD programs into one unified program in biological and biomedical sciences; we created two new engineering departments in fields synergistic with Yale strengths—biomedical and environmental engineering; and we began a comprehensive facilities program involving both new construction and renovation.

All the efforts in phases one and two continued into my second decade, when, at year 11, we refreshed the agenda again. Two of our new goals echoed my inaugural address: advancing the arts through comprehensive investment in our professional schools and museums, and committing the university to environmental leadership both in its teaching programs and in its own sustainability practices on campus. And we added two new ideas. First, we would raise the funds and then design and build a spectacular new home for our youngest school, the School of Management, as a means of making it more competitive with top business schools.

And second, as we were then halfway through the renovation of our 12 residential colleges, we were ready to initiate planning for the construction of 2 new ones, allowing a 15 percent expansion of our undergraduate population, with attendant requirements for additional faculty and student services resources.

Phase four was defined opportunistically, given that much of phase three was still under way as year 15 approached. At that point, unexpectedly, two astonishing opportunities became available, and we seized them both. In 2007, Bayer Pharmaceuticals decide to consolidate its global R&D operations and close its 136-acre campus in West Haven, Connecticut, just seven miles away. No other bidder had any interest in 500,000 square feet of state-of-the-art biology and chemistry labs, and we ended up purchasing the entire property, a campus nearly half the size of Yale's home base in New Haven, at about one-quarter the cost of building that amount of lab space. Developing the new campus immediately became a major priority.

Then, in 2009, we were approached by the National University of Singapore, which proposed jointly establishing an American-style liberal arts college, fully funded by Singapore, with a unique focus on comparing Asian and Western civilizations and institutions. Yale graduates had been instrumental in founding a disproportionate number of liberal arts colleges in the nineteenth century throughout the United States. Leading the globalization of America's distinctive approach to undergraduate education was an irresistible temptation and moved quickly to the top of the agenda at precisely the moment, in the depth of the financial crisis, that many projects in New Haven had been placed on hold.

By the end of my nineteenth year, in the summer of 2012, we had completed a major fundraising campaign and recovered from the financial crisis. The new School of Management campus was well under way, the newly renovated and expanded Art Gallery was about to open, the West Campus was thriving, the Singapore campus—having weathered some faculty opposition—was preparing to open the following year, and the new residential colleges—fully designed but postponed by the financial crisis—were one major gift away from moving forward to construction.

There was plenty left to do. Seeing the Singapore campus and the new residential colleges through to successful openings was a strong motivator to stay. Our fine arts plan was incomplete—the extraordinary Yale School of Drama still lacked the funds for a new theater and teaching facilities. And I had some new ideas for invigorating certain areas of historic strength and investing heavily in some critical area of relative weakness.

I was still at the top of my game. With the exception of a small group of faculty exercised about launching a campus in Singapore, I had broad and deep support from all constituencies. I had a superb leadership team—the best in higher education. I still had energy, and I still enjoyed the job.

As I contemplated the future in the summer of 2012, I wondered: perhaps Henry Schacht's rule only worked one way. If you run out of fresh ideas, you should quit. But having new ideas is only a necessary condition for staying, not a sufficient one. There are other considerations. Twenty years is a long time in the life of a university; it's a full generation. To serve beyond 20 years, and to keep one's veteran team intact, would likely diminish the institutional commitment of those 10, 15, or 20 years younger looking for their opportunity to lead. A generation of potential leaders might move elsewhere. By that calculus, it was time to leave.

Yet, in truth, it was not this rational calculation that led me to step down. As always with difficult decisions, the final arbiter is one's gut. In early August, I was hiking in the Alps, as Jane and I did nearly every summer, when I began to think about the upcoming twentieth anniversary of my appointment. Ten years before, the Corporation had celebrated my tenth anniversary with a dinner for all fellows, officers, and deans—past and present. One speaker after another expressed the hope that I would stay another 10 years.

In the clear mountain air I tried to imagine the twentieth-anniversary dinner. However celebratory the rhetoric, no one would be calling for another 10 years. The question on everyone's mind would have to be "How much longer will he stay?"

The choice was clear. I informed the Corporation upon returning from the Alps in August 2012, and my decision was announced at the end of the month. The twentieth anniversary dinner already scheduled for April 6, 2013, would be the farewell dinner. Fenway Park was not available, but one week before the dinner, I hit my last home run: I secured a $250 million gift that enabled the construction of the new residential colleges to proceed. I had learned from the Kid how to do the hardest thing.

Toward a Gracious Conclusion

Richard M. Joel

Thomas Jefferson once termed the American presidency a "splendid misery." As a university president concluding his fourteenth year of service, I can attest that both words describe my tenure, and I daresay the tenure of any modern American university president. There have been times when the strains on the American economy, the relentless pressure, multiple constituencies, social media, and constant hard choices make the burdens of office seem oppressive. But the splendor of every day—of students growing, of the capacity for innovating and shaping culture, of the majesty of ideas and ideals, of the satisfaction of advancing the institution with faculty, lay, and professional leadership—is tangible and makes the experience irreplaceable.

Fourteen years ago, my wife, Esther, and I were struggling with whether to accept the invitation to assume the presidency of Yeshiva University. I was the president of Hillel International, a Jewish campus-based experiential educational program that was wonderful and exciting. We were living in suburban Washington, DC, and life was full and successful. The prospect of a university presidency was enticing, and Yeshiva University was the central educational institution of our lives as observant Jews. But it was a complex institution, at a pivot point for its future.

There was an abundance of achievement and an abundance of challenge. Yeshiva is a values-based university charged with educating thousands, including our own children, to succeed professionally and purposefully. I had served as associate dean and professor at the university's law school and was familiar with the promise and the problems. We loved Washington and were ambivalent about New York.

Truly uncertain, we attended a performance of *Man of La Mancha* at the National Theatre. During the performance, Don Quixote opined, "Madness is seeing the world as it is and not as it ought to be." As we left the theatre, Esther said to me, "Richard, maybe we're supposed to do this." We anticipated as much as a 10-year tenure. After 12 years, I asked the trustees to begin the search for my successor, and after a year and a half, my successor was named. We are now in the midst of a seven-month transition.

It's been an eventful journey. We articulated a notion that the purpose of education is to "ennoble and enable" young people to live productive and fulfilling lives of consequence. During this tenure, enrollment increased by 15 percent, tumbled by 12 percent after 2008, and climbed once again. The faculty size and strength have improved, more are tenured, and research productivity has increased. The quality of the student body has increased significantly as has their postcollege achievement.

Like many universities, Yeshiva found that this period called for the professionalization of administration, in which we would need more complex and complete fiscal tools and face growing technological needs. Marketing and communications have grown exponentially, as the social media revolution has transformed how we communicate and even how we learn. The cultural coarseness of some blogs and the harsher-than-ever spotlight of social media have made the campus a highly visible and politicized place.

Campus challenges become fodder for sensationalism. The Great Recession accelerated the phenomenon of greater service demands coupled with greater calls for affordability, as higher education has become, all too often, an endangered business enterprise.

I was blessed to be able to develop a wonderful cadre of administrative and academic leadership, to model a truly noble experience for thousands of young people in quest of meaning. We fully replaced the university's business systems, professionalized an investment office, reimagined information technology (IT), and streamlined university services without affecting the quality of the education or the student experience.

A culture of warmth and worth developed in the institution, some of the separate silos that populate universities began to cross-pollinate, and we lowered our walls and expanded our reach to the broader Jewish communities of the world that we serve. Continuing education blossomed, service learning flourished, student services were added, and an undergraduate core curriculum developed. Our graduate and professional schools largely have new leadership, and all are of high quality and advancing with purposeful agendas. New facilities have been built, others modernized, and there is a much greater sense of campus. Student satisfaction and success levels are high. Acceptance rates to graduate and professional schools are remarkably high, our transfer rate is low, and our completion percentage rates are in the high 80s. Our training of rabbis and Jewish educators has profoundly improved; we've ordained 600 rabbis, awarded 700 graduate Jewish education degrees, and maintained relationships with the synagogue and day school communities. Perhaps most personally satisfying, Esther and I have hosted more than 1,400 students to celebrate the Sabbath together in our home.

The economic downturn produced strains. Except for promotion and tenure, salaries have remained static for several years; benefits have declined. While the university has built a sustainable strategic plan, there remains the challenge of implementing a new business model that emphasizes new revenue programs and higher levels of fundraising. We have revised our bylaws, actively involved lay leadership, and raised hundreds of millions of dollars, including one $100 million gift. We are poised to take the university forward through its next steps. In recounting the fullness of achievement and challenge of Yeshiva University, in its peculiar circumstances, I'm reminded of the statement, "Always remember you are unique, just like everyone else."

And then, it ends. The time comes to hand the baton to the next runner.

The Bible relates that Moses led the Children of Israel for 40 years, from the bondage of Egypt, through the desert, to the Promised Land. At the shore of the Jordan River, The Lord instructed Moses—his task completed—to transfer his leadership to Joshua. However, the Lord doesn't tell us when our time comes. It's up to us to know when we've completed our part of the journey. How important it is to exit with grace. I firmly believe if you lead with grace, you'll leave with grace.

Transitions have a life of their own. There is a radical downshifting in gears one must be prepared for. Perhaps the first issue you are not involved with is the selection of your successor. Your leadership might or might not ask for your input, but it is their responsibility to search and select. It requires discipline to remain an observer, yet I do feel you should share you views with your chairman, and try your best not to broaden that circle.

In truth, from the moment your successor is elected, you are in a new position. You still have the responsibility and the authority, but the line of sight has changed. Ultimately, it's not about you—nor was it ever. You must deliver not what you think your successor needs, but what he wants. While having assumed initiative and action during your tenure, you must transition to doing what's asked of you. While you may think you'd be great in running a training school for the next president, he or she must want it and ask for it. If not, that's a choice—one that's as good as any other. The best advice I received is to relax, do what is asked of you, and start smelling the flowers you've caused to blossom.

I believe it's critical to show unabashed support for your successor and, as much as possible, get out of his way. The next president is going to inherit a full plate, the great tastes you have prepared, some unfinished creations, and, yes, some of your dirty dishes. He or she does not need to worry about your position, except to be cordial. Many of your colleagues will take the lead from your behavior. This is the last gift you can give.

One area where you should be active, however, is to help ensure the board to know that it too must be invested in your successor's success. You probably enjoy good relations with trustees, so you can urge them to give the new president support, a financial cushion, and a chance to lead, and you can say some things to them that your successor cannot.

It is also critical for the departing president to prepare himself and his family for transition. There is an inevitable invisibilization that takes hold, and it is a source of relief and discomfort. No matter how you are ready to leave, it's important to know that you will have to adapt to a new life. As much as one savors a sabbatical, or a return to teaching, the pace and the world you occupy radically changes. The day after you shut that office door for the last time, a new occupant appears; hopefully, everything continues to progress. But you won't be there.

Presidents have told me there are two conflicting feelings: the train has left without you, and no matter how you have been looking forward to stepping down, there is a necessary adjustment. And yet I've been told repeatedly there is also an unbelievable lifting of weight from your shoulders. I've also been advised not to make too many plans right away. Perspectives change after a time, and you'll have an array of choices.

For me, the presidency was a family business. My wife was my partner, my psychologist (which, thank G-d, she is), my most trusted adviser, my entertainer-in-chief. She shared the public and the private life. The sensitivity we brought to each other's needs on this part of the journey will sustain us both in the future, but it's best to be aware of it. For our children, it will be mostly a time of relief. They've celebrated my tenure, have been a part of it, and had their own pressures as president's kids. But it's important to be aware that they are concerned about you, and you need to reassure them. You are also leaving your work family, extraordinary partners in this great adventure. Know that this is a difficult transition for them too, so do your best to express thanks and encourage them to remain focused on the greater agenda of the university and its community.

There's another Biblical precept, "Blessed are you in your coming; blessed are you in your leaving." If you have been able to view your journey as a blessing, and have led for the right reasons and with integrity, then your departure will be gracious. And it all will have been a blessing.

What I Wish I Had Known When I Started I didn't realize the full number of constituencies and how you are responsible for them all, yet a member of none. I'm not sure it would have made a difference. I wish I had known that the economy would tank in 2008. While we looked to the future and planned from the beginning, being able to anticipate that period would have been helpful.

What I Wish I Had Done When I Finished I wish I had been able to restore benefits that had been reduced in 2008, and I wish I had been able to write more.

What I Wish I Had Not Done While in Office I think I was often too understanding. A university is a major business, and while civility and compassion matter, colleagues must produce. With key positions, the rule should be one strike and you are out. I believe there were times I should have been more insistent with my trustees.

What I Wish I Didn't Know When I Finished People. Sometimes you get to know prominent people too well, and your efforts to maintain a generous spirit get tested.

How I Knew When to Stop I always believed leadership needs to change. I wanted 10 years; circumstances prevented my leaving. I knew it was time to leave when I had reached my key goals and thought YU was positioned to move forward under new leadership, and I had helped create a values agenda that was in place.

Concluding Thoughts

Gerald B. Kauvar, Stephen Joel Trachtenberg, and E. Gordon Gee

The topics covered in the essays and sidebars in this collection are many and varied, but they do not form a comprehensive list of important issues requiring presidential knowledge and action. Other topics to which attention must be paid include, but are not limited to, what presidents should know about the budget,* what should be the appropriate relationship between the institution and its alumni individually and collectively, the loss of privacy, how to be responsive and proactive with the media, and more. Had we but world enough and time to include them, we would not be offering a book but an encyclopedia.

We trust that the work of our contributors will stimulate thought. While proposing few recipes for success, they got the ingredients right, and we believe that presidents will find those helpful in thinking about issues that are not addressed in this book.

The Nature of the Presidency

College and university presidents and chancellors, and those who head statewide systems, are the only administrators charged with enterprise-wide responsibility. Their thinking is informed by their professional experience and their understanding of the past, present, and future challenges to higher education; by the financial viability and prospects of the institution; by advice and counsel from their colleagues who have line responsibilities for particular functions; by direction and advice from their boards as well as by important stakeholders like faculty senates, student governments, standing and ad hoc committees, and alumni; by their participation in national and international conferences on challenges and opportunities in higher education; by discussions with their peers; and, when useful, by studies.

Presidential authority is delimited by boards of trustees or regents, elected officials, legislators, and in the case of public institutions by state boards.

*A budget reveals a philosophy; it is a prediction, not a doctrine conducted by external consultants. Their minds move upon this cacophony of voices like the "long legged fly upon the stream" in the poem by Yeats.

Yet presidents' varying constituents and the general public all too often deem presidential responsibility all encompassing—that is, presidents who willingly share credit for accomplishments during their tenure with their various advisors are nonetheless blamed for every actual and perceived problem that occurs on their watch. By virtue of holding office they become responsible for every swallow that flies through the campus.

To be sure there have been instances where presidents choose not to be well informed in the hope of having plausible deniability should an unfortunate act or event become public. In such cases, the attempt is to shift responsibility to other actors—frequently those who report directly to the presidents. Like King Henry II, they ask, "Who will rid me of this meddlesome priest?"—not by directing a particular action or actor but by making clear their intent.

The link between authority and responsibility is weakened by the assumption that presidents are or should be witting of all that transpires during their incumbency. Of course, once informed of actual or potential challenges, problems, issues, threats, and opportunities, the president is surely responsible for determining (with the advice of appropriate line officials and other stakeholders, which may include the board) the appropriate institutional responses and ensuring their implementation. Barring collusion by institutional actors to thwart the president, responsibility for known defects in institutional performance is inescapable.

Were There Ever the Good Old Days?

In March of 1987, William J. McGill, then emeritus president of Columbia University, wrote to the *Columbia Daily Spectator* as follows: "I find myself quite overcome with nostalgia for the times when I had to read the *Spec* early in the morning at my desk with a cup of strong coffee. It was my first duty of every working day to determine what trouble I was in, and you were my best source."

For some, the student newspaper may still be the best source, but we think it is now more likely to be the local daily paper with news of legislative initiatives, or local media outlets hyping the latest (and often hypothetical) outrage, or a Twitter blast by some single-issue group or news outlet with a political agenda, or a photo or misguided student effort at humor on Facebook. Or, or, or.

It used to be that each academic year brought familiar challenges; as one ran around the track of the year, the billboards didn't often change. Now a president may be asked to pay ransom in bitcoin to regain control of the institution's entire information technology enterprise—a situation hard to train for and so far rare enough that one might well decide not to spend money to ward off the possibility. Vexing problems about the right ways to cope with sexual violence and its consequences, how best to protect freedom of speech and association with understandable requests for safe spaces, where to find qualified diversity candidates for faculty and staff positions, how to comply with Title IX requirements—all these and more represent compelling new challenges.

Equally compelling and challenging is the perennial responsibility to raise funds to support institutional priorities and promising initiatives—those vary, though the need to work diligently and continuously to obtain financial resources remains a presidential task and time sink. Important too is the need to maintain the academic integrity of the institution and to be certain that a gift doesn't come with restrictions that would suggest otherwise. The wisdom of the late Cardinal Cushing (the only trouble with tainted money is there tain't enough, and that money is sanctified by its uses) isn't always sufficient. Years ago one of us was offered a gift of $10 million by Muammar Gaddafi and turned it down. Wouldn't you?

Not all that presidents need to know is new, even in an age with a 24-hour news cycle. When you get a call at 3:00 a.m. that there's a fire on campus, your best friend is the local fire chief, but only if you have built a relationship with the chief—like the ones you would have built with the chief of police, the mayor, the editor of the newspaper, and other local officials who are in a position to be helpful.

Where Will New Presidents Come From?

Provosts have garnered the lion's share of presidencies, but many are less and less willing to move up; they are fundamentally educators and are happiest in that role. Will college and university leaders increasingly come from outside the academic community? If so where? Business, military, government (local, state, and federal), the professions? Are we as an enterprise doing what is needed to grow members of the academy skilled in the ways of administration and leadership that go beyond the skills that got them to their doctorates and up the professorial ladder? Unlike the corporate world, institutions of higher education do not generally groom their future executives and seem particularly averse to looking for talent inside the organization (better the devil you don't know?). Although there are some university EdD and PhD programs devoted to academic administration, they are less often the source of presidents (owing perhaps to faculty perspectives or prejudices) than vice presidents for specific subordinate roles such as development or finance or student affairs.

Presidential training activities at Harvard and other universities, and programs run by the American Council on Education (ACE) and other higher education associations can teach skills, widen perspectives, and emphasize the need to understand the culture of academe and the ways the culture is expressed in individual institutions. But where do vision, courage, empathy, and values come from? It's not sufficient for a president to keep her head down, stay in her lane, and prod management along. Today's challenges and the ones we can foresee require imagination and grit. Where does one go to get a dose of those ingredients, and how are boards and search committees going to assess those qualities?

What the Sidebars Tell Us

Having read the sidebars (and the essays), you will have gleaned that a variety of personality types have been successful leading colleges and universities. Some provided more candid answers than others, some were unfailingly gracious, still others were circumspect; all were interesting.

What I Wish I Had Known When I Started

A common response in essays and sidebars stressed the unrelenting need for the care and feeding of board members. Board members are often unprepared and unwilling to prepare for their responsibilities. Some seem eager to micromanage the institution, gain admission for an applicant, or steer a contract toward themselves or a pal. Only one contributor asked that a single comment not be attributed to the author, and we have abided by that request. But the comment itself is worth highlighting. A partial response to the issue "What I wish I didn't know when I finished" serves as a reminder of why presidents are so often chary of advice, and why they persist in digging into topics by posing the same questions or challenges to more than one individual or group. The part of the response that was not for attribution is: "How insincere some of my well-wishers could be." Another contributor provided an interesting corollary by responding to the prompt "What I wish I had not done" by writing "Ignored my gut. We all need to consult and get buy-in to decisions, but there are times when we may have a perspective that others don't share."

The symbolic nature of the presidency is another common theme. One contributor wrote, "You don't just work at the burdens of the presidency, you live them." Another commented, "You don't pick your issues, you inherit them." Presidents need to recognize that every act (and every failure to act), every slip of the tongue, every witticism, and every ironic comment will be publicized and taken as doctrine if not dogma: "During my first few years as president I continued to be surprised when I realized people had initiated new projects based on a throwaway line or side comment from me." Abjure sarcasm and irony. Both are too easily misunderstood in the classrooms and in staff meetings. Audiences quickly strip away nuance in an effort to ally themselves or their group with the president or to signal disapproval. Akin to that is the more and more frequent use of the president as a legislative punching bag for perceived evils such as tenure.

Other sidebar comments reflected on the anemic pace of academic change and on the need to understand the details of faculty governance. Presidents will need to spend more time than they might anticipate on personnel decisions (and the concomitant need to change or assign duties and responsibilities).

What I Wish I Had Done When I Finished

The most frequent regret is not saying thank you often enough to people who worked hard to support the president—faculty, staff, donors, alumni, friends, family—and in one case, to the former president for a graceful transition and subsequent advice and support. There is wisdom in the folk saying that if you see a turtle on a fence post, you can be sure it did not get there by itself.

Two contributors stressed the need to take time to carefully read documents that require presidential signatures. One even insisted that at least a week's time was needed between receipt of the document and the deadline for signing it. Not surprisingly, contributors suggested moving more slowly or cautiously in implementing major and necessary changes. By way of contrast, one contributor suggested that searches for subordinate administrators take too long and that the president should weigh in sooner. In a similar vein, one writer recommended issuing letters of appointment to staff upon arrival to remind them that they work for the new president.

What I Wish I Had Not Done While in Office

Three regrets were mentioned most often: First, the demands of the position made it difficult to spend enough time with family members and left too little time to deepen relationships with staff members. Second, dysfunctional staff members had not been removed quickly enough (the rule should be "one strike and you're out," wrote one president). One contributor argued that key positions should be filled quickly without delaying team building by conducting searches. Third, the pace of change was too fast—or too slow. In one case the trustees demanded change but wanted it to be painless. One president wrote that he was too eager to reorganize and should have understood the institution in more depth before moving. Others thought it was imperative to quickly establish the institution's top priorities.

As a general warning, one president wished he had been less quick to say what he thought. In a sense, presidents give up their First Amendment rights.

What I Wish I Didn't Know When I Finished

That I would be forgotten. Several contributors commented on the fact that so little of what one has done survives or is appreciated after one's departure and that incoming presidents too often fail to recognize or honor the fact that they stand on the shoulders of others. Other important issues involved small-mindedness in one way or another—for example, how much less some external stakeholders care than one might think, and how little people who want change understand how the institution is managed. A corollary to the latter thought is a concern that the best and brightest faculty rarely participate in governance.

How I Knew When to Stop

For many, it was losing their passion for the job or finding that it ceased to be fun. For others, it was the sense that all or much of the agenda (including fund-raising campaigns) had been accomplished. "When they changed the locks"—whether the "locksmiths" were boards or system leaders—was an undertone. Several expressed the sentiment that the job requires biting your tongue more often than you'd like. Advice? Quoting William Bowen, "It's better to leave when the band is playing than when people are looking at their watch."

Summing Up

Institutions and presidents are wonderfully varied. But for all, long-standing problems persist accompanied by new worries. Many students still drink too much; many faculty members feel more loyalty to their discipline (or lifestyle) than to the institution; costs rise more rapidly than tuition, gifts, and grants; too many legislators and members of the public want us to be trainers rather than educators; donors expect more lavish treatment or more extensive influence than can reasonably be expected; too many alumni care more about the success of their athletic teams than about student success and achievement; regulations are too frequently born, and their longevity is enviable compared with presidential tenure. New worries include the pervasive influence of the 24-hour news cycle and social media; the rise of anti-intellectualism in our land; declines in state and local budgets for education; new pressure to measure institutional success by the financial success of students in the short term; attacks on freedom of speech along with perceptions that institutions are too liberal and inhospitable to conservative ideas or faculty members.

Presidents will always need thick skins, quick minds, skilled advisors, collegiality, supportive friends and families, sympathetic donors, good community relations—and to raise more and more money for the compelling needs of the institution. And while we have tried not to give prescriptions, the poet Shelley tells us that all things except eternal love are subject to "fate, time, occasion, chance, and change" and that "gentleness, virtue, wisdom, and endurance" bar the pit over destruction's strength. Those assurances are from Shelley's epic *Prometheus Unbound,* though we might do well to remember that Prometheus's liver was eaten out daily by an eagle only to be regenerated every night. Still, Prometheus gave mankind the gift of fire. Our common enterprise also has a gift to offer: engaging and igniting minds to build *mens sana in corpore sano,* to enrich the lives of all through the arts and sciences, and to create solutions to the problems facing humankind.

Contributors

Editors

Stephen Joel Trachtenberg served as the fifteenth president of George Washington University from 1988 to 2007, and is now president emeritus and University Professor of Public Service. Trachtenberg came to George Washington from the University of Hartford, where he served as president for 11 years. His views on issues pertaining to higher education are widely published internationally. He is a fellow of the American Academy of the Arts and Sciences, the American Bar Foundation, and the National Academy of Public Administration. Trachtenberg has served in several government positions, including attorney with the US Atomic Energy Commission, legislative aide to former Indiana Congressman John Brademas, and special assistant to the US education commissioner. In addition, Trachtenberg has also served on the Rhodes Scholarships Selection Committee for Maryland, Delaware, and the District of Columbia and as chair of the White House Fellows Selection Panel. Trachtenberg was awarded the Open Forum Distinguished Public Service Award by the US secretary of state and received the Department of Treasury Medal of Merit.

Gerald B. Kauvar's final academic position was as a research professor of public policy and public administration at George Washington University. He has served as a special assistant to the president at the City College of New York, Boston University, and George Washington. He spent 22 years in the Department of Defense in a variety of senior executive positions including his final assignment as special assistant to the Secretary of the Air Force. He was selected by then Vice President Al Gore to serve as the staff director for the White House Commission on Aviation Safety and Security, for which he was awarded the Presidential Rank Award of Meritorious Executive. He has published books and articles on higher education, English and American literature, defense management, and aviation safety and security. Kauvar also spent two years at the Rand Corporation as a senior military policy analyst before returning to academe. In 2014 he was a honored by selection as a fellow commoner at St. John's College, the University of Cambridge, where he conducted research for this volume.

E. Gordon Gee is currently serving for a second time as president of West Virginia University. Gee has been a leader in higher education for more than three decades. In 2009 *Time* magazine named him one of the top 10 university presidents in the United States. In addition to his service at West Virginia University, Gee served as president of the Ohio State University (twice), Vanderbilt University, Brown

University, and the University of Colorado. Before starting his career in higher education, he clerked under Chief Justice David T. Lewis of the US Tenth Circuit Court of Appeals and was a judicial fellow and staff assistant to the US Supreme Court, where he worked for Chief Justice Warren Burger. Gee's service to education-governance organizations and commissions is extensive, including the American Association of Universities and the American Council on Education's Commission on Higher Education Attainment. He also has written extensively on law and education and is the coauthor of 11 books, including *Law, Policy and Higher Education,* published in 2012.

Authors

LAWRENCE S. BACOW served as the president of Tufts University from 2001 through 2011. A nationally recognized expert on non-adjudicatory approaches to the resolution of environmental disputes, Bacow served for 24 years as a member of the faculty at the Massachusetts Institute of Technology (MIT), where he was the Lee and Geraldine Martin Professor of Environmental Studies. He also served as chairman of the MIT faculty, and chancellor, one of MIT's two most senior academic officers. Currently the Hauser Leader in Residence at Harvard University's Kennedy School, Bacow is also a member of the Harvard Corporation, where he chairs the university finance committee. Bacow is a member of the American Academy of Arts and Sciences and the 2017 Clark Kerr Lecturer at the University of California at Berkeley. He serves on the boards of TIAA-CREF, the Loews Corporation, the Henry Schein Corporation, and Liquidnet.

REBECCA BLANK became chancellor of the University of Wisconsin-Madison in July 2013. Blank served as deputy secretary and acting secretary of the US Department of Commerce under President Barack Obama. She was a member of the Council of Economic Advisers under President Bill Clinton. From 1999 to 2008 Blank was dean and professor of public policy and economics in the Gerald R. Ford School of Public Policy at the University of Michigan. She has also served on the faculty at Northwestern and Princeton Universities and was a fellow at the Brookings Institution. Blank's contributions to the academic and policy worlds have been recognized with numerous national and international awards, as well as honorary doctoral degrees. Most recently, the American Academy of Political and Social Science honored her with its Daniel Patrick Moynihan Prize.

LEE C. BOLLINGER became Columbia University's nineteenth president in 2002. He is also Columbia's first Seth Low Professor of the University, a member of the Columbia Law School faculty, and one of the country's foremost First Amendment scholars. As president of the University of Michigan, Bollinger led the school's historic litigation in Grutter v. Bollinger and Gratz v. Bollinger. These Supreme Court decisions that upheld and clarified the importance of diversity as a compelling justification for affirmative action in higher education were reaffirmed in the court's 2016 ruling in Fisher v. University of Texas. As Columbia's president, Bollinger conceived and led the university's most ambitious expansion in over a century with the creation of the Manhattanville campus in West Harlem. A historic community benefits agreement emerging from the city and state review process for the new campus provides Columbia's local neighborhoods with decades of investment in the community's health, education, and economic growth.

ÁNGEL CABRERA is the president of George Mason University, Virginia's largest public university. Before becoming Mason's president in 2012, Cabrera led IE Business School in Madrid and Thunderbird School of Global Management, now affiliated with Arizona State University. Cabrera is the first native of Spain to have served as president of an American university. As a business educator, Cabrera played a key role in advancing professional ethics, internationalization, and corporate social responsibility. As a senior advisor to the United Nations Global Compact, he was the lead author of the *Principles of Responsible Management Education*, now adopted by more than 500 business schools around the world.

JAMES P. CLEMENTS joined Clemson University as its fifteenth president in December 2013, following five years as president of West Virginia University. Prior to his presidencies at Clemson and West Virginia, Clements served as provost and vice president for academic affairs, vice president for economic development and community outreach, and the Robert W. Deutsch Distinguished Professor of Information Technology at Towson University.

MARY SUE COLEMAN is president of the Association of American Universities. Coleman was president of the University of Michigan from 2002 to July 2014 and president of the University of Iowa from 1995 to 2002. Time magazine named her one of the nation's 10 best college presidents, and the American Council on Education honored her with its Lifetime Achievement Award in 2014. Elected to the National Academy of Medicine, Coleman is also a fellow of the American Association for the Advancement of Science and the American Academy of Arts and Sciences. As a biochemistry faculty member at the University of Kentucky, Coleman built a distinguished academic career through her research and teaching. Prior to becoming a university president, Coleman was vice chancellor for research and graduate education at the University of North Carolina at Chapel Hill and provost at the University of New Mexico.

SCOTT COWEN is president emeritus and Distinguished University Chair of Tulane University. He served as Tulane's fourteenth president from July 1998 through June 2014 and was named one of the top college presidents in the nation by *Time*. *Newsweek* twice declared Tulane, under his leadership, one of the "Hottest Schools in America." Cowen is a former chair of the Association of American Universities and the recipient of several national awards, including the Carnegie Corporation Academic Leadership Award and the TIAA-CREF Theodore M. Hesburgh Award for Leadership Excellence in Higher Education. He is a member of the

American Academy of Arts and Sciences and was a member of the White House Council for Community Solutions, which advised President Barack Obama on the needs of disconnected youth.

ROBERT H. DONALDSON is Trustees Professor of Political Science, Emeritus, at the University of Tulsa, where he was president from 1990 to 1996. Previously he was president of Fairleigh Dickinson University, provost of Lehman College of the City University of New York, and a professor and associate dean at Vanderbilt University. He is a member of the Council on Foreign Relations and was a Council International Affairs Fellow in 1973–74, serving as a consultant with the Department of State; he was also a visiting research professor at the Strategic Studies Institute, US Army War College, in 1978–79. He is author or coauthor of six books and more than two dozen articles and book chapters, primarily on the politics and foreign policy of the USSR and Russia; his most recent book is fifth edition of *The Foreign Policy of Russia: Changing Systems, Enduring Interests* (with Joseph L. Nogee and Vidya Nadkarni).

ANDREW R. DUMONT serves as executive communications manager in the Executive Office of the President at the University of Arizona. In addition to his role at the UA, DuMont writes about American literature and culture, with work appearing in *The Cormac McCarthy Journal* and the *Rocky Mountain Review of Language and Literature.* Before beginning his career in higher education, DuMont worked in supportive housing programming in Houston, Texas.

JUDITH S. EATON is president of the Council for Higher Education Accreditation (CHEA), the largest institutional higher education membership organization in the United States. She has served as CHEA's president since shortly after its founding in 1996. Before her work at CHEA, Eaton served as chancellor of the Minnesota State Colleges and Universities; as president of the Council for Aid to Education, the Community College of Philadelphia, and the Community College of Southern Nevada; and as vice president of the American Council on Education. She has held teaching positions at Columbia University, the University of Michigan, and Wayne State University. Eaton has authored numerous books and articles on higher education and accreditation-related topics and addresses accreditation and quality assurance at conferences and meetings in the United States and internationally.

A. LEE FRITSCHLER is emeritus professor of the Schar School of Policy and Government, George Mason University. Before joining the school, Fritschler was vice president and director of the Center for Public Policy Education at the Brookings Institution, assistant secretary for postsecondary education at the US Department of Education (Clinton Administration), president of Dickinson College, and chairman of the US Postal Regulatory Commission (Carter Administration). Fritschler also served as dean of the College of Public and International Affairs at the American University. He was a member of the Institutional Evaluation Programme contingent of the European University Association and a member of the International Quality Group of the Council for Higher Education Accreditation (CHEA). He has written several articles and books, including *Smoking and Politics: Bureaucracy Centered Policymaking*, 6th edition (with Catherine E. Rudder), Pearson/Prentice-Hall, 1996. His most recent book, *Public Policymaking by Private Organizations: Challenges to Democratic Governance* (with Catherine E. Rudder and Yong Jun Choi), was released by the Brookings Institution Press in 2016.

MILDRED GARCÍA is president of California State University, Fullerton, the third-largest university in the state, with more than 40,000 students, most of whom are the first in their family to pursue a college degree. A recipient of myriad awards—from the American Council on Education's Reginald Wilson Diversity Leadership Award to being named a Distinguished Alumni Honoree of Columbia University—García was appointed by President Barack Obama to serve on the President's Advisory Commission on Educational Excellence for Hispanics, a position she served with distinction from 2011 to 2016. A first-generation college graduate and the first Latina president in the largest system of higher education in the country, García presently sits on a variety of local and national boards, including the Association of Public and Land-Grant Universities, the Congressional Hispanic Caucus Institute, and the American Association of State Colleges and Universities.

ANN WEAVER HART became the twenty-first president of the University of Arizona in July 2012. As of June 1, 2017, she became president emerita and University Professor of Educational Policy Studies and Practice in the UA College of Education. Previously she served as president of Temple University, president of the University of New Hampshire, and provost and vice president for academic affairs at Claremont Graduate University. At the University of Utah, she served as professor of educational leadership, dean of the Graduate School, and special assistant to the president. Hart's research focuses on leadership succession and development, work redesign and organizational behavior in educational organizations, and academic freedom and freedom of speech in higher education.

WILLIAM R. HARVEY has served as president of Hampton University for 39 years. Harvey's extraordinary leadership is reflected in the growth and quality of the university's student population, academic programs, physical facilities, and financial base. Hampton University has built the first proton therapy cancer treatment center in the Commonwealth of Virginia—an unparalleled hub for cancer treatment, research, and technology. In addition to his distinguished leadership, he is the sole owner of the Pepsi Cola Bottling Company of Houghton, Michigan. Harvey's achievements have been recognized through inclusion in *Personalities of the South, Who's Who in the South and Southeast, Who's Who in Black America, Who's Who in American Education, International Who's Who of Intellectuals, Two Thousand Notable Americans, Who's Who in Business and Finance,* and *Who's Who in America.*

CHRISTOPHER HOWARD is the eighth president of Robert Morris University and one of the youngest college presidents in the United States. Before coming to RMU, Howard was president of Hampden-Sydney College in Virginia and vice president for leadership and strategic initiatives at the University of Oklahoma. He enjoyed a successful career in the corporate world, working in General Electric's Corporate Initiatives Group and Bristol-Myers Squibb's Corporate Associates Program. Previously Howard served on the National Security Education Board, appointed by President Barack Obama, and the MyVA Advisory Committee for the US Department of Veterans Affairs. He is a member of the board of directors of the Allegheny Conference on Community Development, a former member of the American Council on Education board of directors, the founder of the Impact Young Lives Foundation, and a member of the Council on Foreign Relations and the Young Presidents Organization. He is also a Henry Crown Fellow at the Aspen Institute.

FREEMAN A. HRABOWSKI III has served since 1992 as president of University of Maryland, Baltimore County, a research university nationally recognized for innovation and for its strong focus on student success. His research and publications focus on science and math education, with special emphasis on minority participation and performance, and he serves as an advisor on science, technology, engineering, and math (STEM) education to national agencies, universities, and school systems. Hrabowski chaired the National Academies' committee that produced the 2011 report *Expanding Underrepresented Minority Participation: America's Science and Technology Talent at the Crossroads*. In 2012 he was named by President Barack Obama to chair the President's Advisory Commission on Educational Excellence for African Americans. Hrabowski's most recent book, *Holding Fast to Dreams: Empowering Youth from the Civil Rights Crusade to STEM Achievement,* traces his development as an educator from his experiences growing up in Birmingham, Alabama, and participating as a child leader in the Civil Rights Movement.

RICHARD M. JOEL serves as president emeritus and Bravmann Family University Professor at Yeshiva University. From 2003 to 2017, he was the university's fourth president. Prior to that, he was president and international director of Hillel: The Foundation for Jewish Campus Life, for 15 years. He served as assistant district attorney and deputy chief of appeals in the Bronx and was the associate dean and professor of law at the Benjamin N. Cardozo School of Law of Yeshiva University. President Joel has spent the last 30 years working for communal welfare and committed to values-driven formal and experiential education, communal leadership, and religious identity.

WILLIAM KIRWAN is chancellor emeritus of the University System of Maryland. Prior to his 13 years as chancellor of the Maryland system, Kirwan served as president of Ohio State University for 4 years and president of the University of Maryland, College Park, for 10 years. He was also a member of the University of Maryland faculty for 24 years. Kirwan is a sought-after speaker on a wide range of topics, including access and affordability, cost containment, diversity, innovation, higher education's role in economic development, and academic transformation. He has written many articles on issues in higher education and on mathematical research, and he is coeditor of the book *Advances in Complex Analysis*. Currently, Kirwan chairs the Conference Board of Mathematical Sciences and serves as executive director of Transforming Post-Secondary Education in Mathematics. He is past chair of, among other boards, the American Council for Higher Education, the Association of Public and Land-Grant Universities, and the Knight Commission on Intercollegiate Athletics. Kirwan has received the TIAA Theodore M. Hesburgh Award, the Carnegie Corporation Academic Leadership Award, and election to the American Academy of Arts and Sciences.

MARVIN KRISLOV became president of Pace University in 2017 after serving as the fourteenth president of Oberlin College. While serving as president of Oberlin, Krislov continued to be active in public service, and he taught advanced courses every semester at the college on aspects of law and public policy. In November 2009, he was appointed to the National Council on the Humanities, the 26-member advisory board of the National Endowment for the Humanities. Before entering academic life, Krislov served as acting solicitor from 1997 to 1998 in the US Department of Labor and as deputy solicitor of national operations from 1996 to 1998. He had previously served as associate counsel in the Office of Counsel to the President.

RICHARD C. LEVIN is a senior advisor at Coursera, where he served as CEO from 2014 to 2017. Coursera provides open online education from 150 top universities to tens of millions of learners worldwide. In 2013, he completed a 20-year term as president of Yale University, where he is the Frederick William Beinecke Professor of Economics, Emeritus. Levin served on President Barack Obama's Council of Advisors for Science and Technology, and he is a director of American Express, C3 IoT, and the William and Flora Hewlett Foundation. He is a fellow of the American Academy of Sciences and the American Philosophical Society.

R. BOWEN LOFTIN is currently director of national security research development and professor of physics and computer science at the University of Missouri, where he served as chancellor from February 2014 to November 2015. In February 2010 he became the twenty-fourth president of Texas A&M University, where he was also professor of industrial and systems engineering. From June 2009 to February 2010 Loftin served as the university's interim president. In May 2005 Loftin was named a vice president of Texas A&M University with the assignment to be the chief executive officer of Texas A&M University's branch campus in Galveston, Texas. From 2000 to 2005 he was at Old Dominion University, as professor of electrical and computer engineering and professor of computer science. Before coming to Old Dominion University, he was professor in and chair of the Department of Computer Science and director of the NASA Virtual Environments Research Institute at the University of Houston. Loftin's awards include the University of

Houston-Downtown Awards for Excellence in Teaching and in Service (twice), the American Association of Artificial Intelligence Award for an Innovative Application of Artificial Intelligence, NASA's Space Act Award, the NASA Public Service Medal, the 1995 NASA Invention of the Year Award, and the IEEE Virtual Reality Conference Career Award. He is the author or coauthor of more than 100 technical publications, including a personal memoir, *The 100-Year Decision: Texas A&M and the SEC.*

JANE MCAULIFFE is the inaugural director of national and international outreach at the Library of Congress, president emeritus of Bryn Mawr College, and dean of arts and sciences emeritus at Georgetown University. She has also held tenured faculty positions at Emory University and the University of Toronto. McAuliffe has written extensively on Islam and the Qur'an, as well as on Muslim-Christian relations. Her works include *Qur'anic Christians* (1991), *'Abbasid Authority Affirmed* (1995), *With Reverence for the Word* (2002), *Encyclopaedia of the Qur'an* (2006, six volumes and online), *Cambridge Companion to the Qur'an* (2006), *Norton Anthology of World Religions: Islam* (2014), and *The Qur'an: A Norton Critical Edition* (2017). McAuliffe is past president of the American Academy of Religion and an elected member of the American Philosophical Society, the Council on Foreign Relations, and the American Academy of Arts and Sciences.

JOHN M. MCCARDELL JR., currently sixteenth vice-chancellor of The University of the South and president emeritus of Middlebury College, is a distinguished historian and respected national leader in liberal arts education. He possesses a record of achievement as a scholar of the American South and is the author of *The Idea of a Southern Nation,* which won the Allan Nevins Prize. His specialty is US history in the nineteenth century with special emphasis on the South. He has served as chair of the board of directors of the National Association of Independent Colleges and Universities, as chair of the Division III Presidents' Council of the NCAA, and on the boards of the Episcopal High School and Washington and Lee University. He currently serves on the board of the Tennessee Independent Colleges and Universities Association, the Porter-Gaud School in Charleston, SC, and the Board of Managers of the South Carolina Historical Society.

CARY NELSON is Jubilee Professor of Liberal Arts and Sciences and professor of English at the University of Illinois at Urbana-Champaign. He is also an affiliated faculty member at the University of Haifa. He served as vice president of the American Association of University Professors (AAUP) from 2001 to 2006 and as president from 2006 to 2012. He is author or editor of more than 30 books, among them *Revolutionary Memory: Recovering the Poetry of the American Left, A Devil's Dictionary for Higher Education, No University Is an Island: Saving Academic Freedom,* and *Dreams Deferred: A Concise Guide to the Israeli-Palestinian Conflict and the Movement to Boycott Israel.*

S. GEORGIA NUGENT, senior fellow at the Council of Independent Colleges (CIC), is president emerita of Kenyon College and former interim president of the College of Wooster. Before assuming the presidency of Kenyon, she served as assistant to the president, associate provost, and dean of the Center for Teaching and Learning at Princeton University and as professor of classics at Princeton and Brown Universities. She has also taught on the classics faculties of Cornell University and Swarthmore and Kenyon Colleges. Nugent is currently a member of the governing boards of St. Lawrence University, the University of Richmond, and the American University of Sharjah. She is also the president of the Society for Classical Studies.

EDUARDO PADRÓN is president of Miami Dade College, a national model of student achievement and the largest institution of higher education in America. In 2016, President Barack Obama awarded him the Presidential Medal of Freedom, the highest civilian honor in the US, for being a prominent national voice for access and inclusion in higher education. In 2009, *Time* magazine included Padrón among the 10 best college presidents in the United States; in 2010, *Florida Trend* magazine named him "Floridian of the Year"; and in 2011, the *Washington Post* recognized him as one of the eight most influential college presidents nationwide. He is the recipient of the Carnegie Corporation's Centennial Academic Leadership Award, the National Citizen Service Award from Voices for National Service, and the Hesburgh Award, the highest honor in US higher education. He is also an Ascend Fellow at the Aspen Institute. He serves on the boards of the Council on Foreign Relations, the White House Fellows Selection Panel, and the International Association of University Presidents. He is the past chairman of the Business-Higher Education Forum, the American Council on Education, and the Association of American Colleges and Universities.

ROBERT A. SCOTT is president emeritus and University Professor Emeritus at Adelphi University, where he served as president from 2000 to 2015. Scott was president of Ramapo College of New Jersey from 1985 to 2000, and he has served as a leader of two state higher education coordinating agencies (Indiana and New Jersey). He is the only person to hold the three top positions in American higher education: head of a private university, a public institution, and a state coordinating board. In fall 2015, he served as senior visiting research fellow at the Rothermere American Institute and visiting fellow at Mansfield College, both at the University of Oxford. From 2015 to 2017 he served as a Frederick Lewis Allen Room Scholar at the New York Public Library. He is under contract with the Johns Hopkins University Press to write a book on university governance and leadership. Scott is author or editor of more than 200 essays and articles, as well as 9 books and monographs, and for 12 years hosted a regularly televised program entitled *Exploring Critical Issues*. Scott is a member of the board and executive committee of the Paul Taylor Dance Foundation, a member of the community advisory board for Flushing Bank, a member of the board of Notre Dame of Maryland University, and a member of the Council on Foreign Relations.

ALLEN L. SESSOMS, a physicist, diplomat, and education administrator, has served as president of Queens College (City University of New York), Delaware State

University, and the University of the District of Columbia. He is currently a senior vice president at the Hollins Group, specializing in higher education consulting. Sessoms worked as a scientific associate at the European Organization of Nuclear Research (CERN) and then moved to Harvard University. He joined the US State Department and subsequently served as director of the Office of Nuclear Technology and Safeguards, counselor for scientific and technological affairs at the US Embassy in Paris, and minister-counsel for political affairs and deputy chief of mission (deputy ambassador) at the US Embassy in Mexico. Sessoms served as the executive vice president and also the vice president for academic affairs at the University of Massachusetts System.

Charles Steger served as the fifteenth president of Virginia Tech for 14 years, stepping down in June 2014. Steger spent almost his entire career at Virginia Tech. Early in his career, he accepted the position of dean of architecture and went on to become the vice president of development before becoming president. Steger has been appointed by five governors of Virginia to various boards dealing with higher education, homeland security, information technology, and international education. He is a fellow in the American Institute of Architects. Steger also serves on the board of directors for Union Bank, is a commissioner with the Virginia Racing Commission, and is on the board of trustees of Randolph-Macon College. Steger now serves as the executive director of the Global Forum for Urban and Regional Resilience at Virginia Tech in Blacksburg.

Holden Thorp is provost and executive vice chancellor for academic affairs at Washington University in St. Louis. He is Rita Levi-Montalcini Distinguished University Professor and holds appointments in both chemistry and medicine. Thorp joined the university after spending three decades at the University of North Carolina at Chapel Hill, where he served as the tenth chancellor from 2008 through 2013. In his research career, Thorp developed technology for electronic DNA chips and methods for determining the geometry of metal-binding sites in metalloenzymes. He cofounded Viamet Pharmaceuticals and Innocrin Pharmaceuticals, which are commercializing new drugs for fungal disease and cancer. Thorp is currently a member of the boards of the College Advising Corps, the National Humanities Center, the St. Louis Symphony Orchestra, and Barnes-Jewish Hospital.

Ben Trachtenberg is an associate professor of law at the University of Missouri, and he served as chair of the campuswide MU Faculty Council on University Policy from 2015 to 2017. After graduating from law school, Trachtenberg clerked at the US Court of Appeals for the Second Circuit with Judge José A. Cabranes. He has published in the *Florida Law Review*, the *Oregon Law Review*, the *Hastings Law Journal*, the *Nebraska Law Review*, the *New York Times*, the *Chronicle of Higher Education*, and the *ABA Journal*, among other publications. At the MU School of Law, Trachtenberg, who has received multiple teaching awards, teaches criminal procedure, evidence, and professional responsibility.

SANFORD J. UNGAR served from 2001 to 2014 as president of Goucher College. He is currently director of the Free Speech Project at Georgetown University, a Lumina Foundation fellow, and a visiting lecturer in the Government Department at Harvard University. At both Georgetown and Harvard, he teaches a seminar for undergraduates on free speech. Ungar is the author or editor of six nonfiction books, including *The Papers and the Papers: An Account of the Legal and Political Battle over the Pentagon Papers,* which won the George Polk Award. He was director of the Voice of America from 1999 to 2001 and was previously dean of the School of Communication at American University. During his journalism career, he was a staff writer for the *Washington Post,* Washington editor of the *Atlantic,* managing editor of *Foreign Policy* magazine, and cohost of *All Things Considered* on National Public Radio. His chapter in this volume was produced, in part, during a residency at the Bellagio Center of the Rockefeller Foundation. It previously appeared in slightly different form in the September/October 2015 issue of *Trusteeship,* the magazine of the Association of Governing Boards.

MICHAEL K. YOUNG became the twenty-fifth president of Texas A&M University on May 1, 2015, and a professor at the Bush School of Government and Public Service. Previously, he served as president and tenured professor of law at the University of Washington and president and distinguished professor of law at the University of Utah. He served as dean and Lobingier Professor of Comparative Law and Jurisprudence at the George Washington University Law School, and he was the Fugo Professor of Japanese Law and Legal Institutions and director of the Center for Japanese Legal Studies at Columbia University for more than 20 years. He also has been a visiting professor and scholar at three universities in Japan. A graduate of Harvard Law School, Young served as a law clerk to the late Chief Justice William H. Rehnquist of the US Supreme Court and has held a number of government positions, including deputy legal advisor, deputy under secretary for economic and agricultural affairs, and ambassador for trade and environmental affairs in the Department of State during the administration of President George H. W. Bush. He also served for eight years on the US Commission on International Religious Freedom, which he chaired twice. He was recently appointed to the Homeland Security Academic Advisory Council.

MARK G. YUDOF, who served as the nineteenth president of the University of California from June 2008 through September 2013, is a professor of law at the University of California, Berkeley, and has been emeritus professor of law at Berkeley since 2015. He served as chancellor of the University of Texas System from August 2002 to May 2008 and as president of the four-campus University of Minnesota from 1997 to 2002. Before that, he served as dean of the law school at the University of Texas at Austin from 1984 to 1994 and as the university's executive vice president and provost from 1994 to 1997. Yudof is a renowned authority on constitutional law, freedom of expression, and education law.

Nancy L. Zimpher is among the most in-demand thought-leaders in higher education in the United States and around the world. From 2009 to 2017, Zimpher served as the twelfth chancellor of The State University of New York, the nation's largest comprehensive system of public higher education. Prior to SUNY, she served as president of the University of Cincinnati, chancellor of the University of Wisconsin-Milwaukee, and executive dean of the Professional Colleges and dean of the College of Education at the Ohio State University. Throughout a career that began in a one-room schoolhouse, Zimpher has formed a paradigm-shifting vision that rises to meet the expansive responsibilities of public higher education in the twenty-first century. "To educate more people and to educate them better" is the mantra at the center of her collective-impact theory of action. Zimpher is cofounder and chair of StriveTogether, a national network of innovative partnerships that holistically address challenges across the education pipeline. She has authored or coauthored numerous books, monographs, and academic journal articles on teacher education, urban education, academic leadership, and university-community engagement.

Index